Unity and Modularity in the Mind and the Self

This book explores the relationships between intellectual development, self, and personality and proposes a comprehensive theory. It addresses how humans become aware of themselves, how the various products of self-awareness interrelate to produce an integrated self-system, and how this includes the domains of cognition and personality.

The book answers these questions on the basis of four empirical studies. The first highlights the development and organisation of self-awareness in regard to cognitive abilities, personality, and thinking styles from 10 to 15 years of age. The second highlights how children's actual cognitive abilities and self-representations interact with their parents' respective representations. The third explores the relationships between general reasoning and processing abilities and the various domain-specific abilities and characteristics examined in the other studies. The final study examines the place of the Big Five factors of personality – extraversion, agreeableness, conscientiousness, neuroticism, and openness to experience – in the self-system. Finally, a general model is proposed which specifies the modular and the transmodular aspects of the mind.

Andreas Demetriou is a professor of psychology at the Department of Educational Sciences and the Vice-Rector of the University of Cyprus. He has studied the development of the mind for over two decades and his current work aims to integrate conceptions of the mind, personality and the self into a comprehensive theory.

Smaragda Kazi is a research associate at the University of Cyprus.

Routledge international library of psychology
Series editor: Peter K. Smith

Collaborators
Maria Platsidou
Kiriaki Sirmali
Ioanna Tsiouri
Grigoris Kiosseoglou

Unity and Modularity in the Mind and the Self

Studies on the relationships between self-awareness, personality, and intellectual development from childhood to adolescence

Andreas Demetriou and Smaragda Kazi

London and New York

First published 2001
by Routledge
11 New Fetter Lane, London EC4P 4EE

Simultaneously published in the USA and Canada
by Routledge
29 West 35th Street, New York, NY 10001

Routledge is an imprint of the Taylor & Francis Group

© 2001 Andreas Demetriou and Smaragda Kazi

Typeset in Garamond by
Wearset, Boldon, Tyne and Wear
Printed and bound in Great Britain by
TJ International Ltd, Padstow, Cornwall

British Library Cataloguing in Publication Data
A catalogue record for this book is available
from the British Library

Library of Congress Cataloging in Publication Data
Andreas, Demetriou, 1950–
    Unity and modularity in the mind and the self: studies on the relationships
    between self-awareness, personality, and intellectual development from
    childhood to adolescence/Andreas Demetriou and Smargada Kazi.
        p. cm.
      1. Child psychology. 2. Self-perception. 3. Personality. 4. Intellect.
    I. Kazi, Smargada.   II. Title

BF721 .A66 2000
155–dc21

                                                                00-038960

ISBN 0–415–23399–2

August 13, 2001

To Litsa Demetriou

Contents

List of tables

List of figures

Acknowledgements

This book presents a major part of a long research programme which started in 1992 and still continues. Specifically, the first three of the studies reported in this book were conducted from 1993 to 1996 at the Department of Psychology, Aristotle University of Thessaloniki, when Andreas Demetriou was a professor of developmental psychology and Smaragda Kazi a PhD student and research assistant at this Department. The fourth study was conducted at the University of Cyprus. Moreover, the book was first drafted in Thessaloniki but, in its present form, was written at the University of Cyprus in the period 1996 to 1999, after Andreas Demetriou was appointed professor of psychology at the Department of Educational Sciences and Smaragda Kazi joined as a research associate. We will always remain grateful to our Alma Mater, the Aristotle University of Thessaloniki, for providing all kinds of support and the intellectual atmosphere needed for these and all our previous studies that culminated in the theory presented here. Also, we are grateful to the University of Cyprus, our present academic home, for infusing its vigour to our 23-year-old research programme thereby causing it to thrive and move in new and then unforeseen directions.

The completion of the studies reported here would not have been possible without the collaboration of our colleagues who worked with us at various phases of the programme. We will always be grateful for their contribution. Specifically, Maria Platsidou co-ordinated the collection of data of the first study and she has tested the participants of the third study. She has also contributed to the development of the tasks and inventories used in the first three studies. Kiriaki Sirmali contributed to the collection of data of the first three studies and she has been very instrumental in the development and implementation of the electronic data files. Ioanna Tsiouri was involved in the collection, decoding and filing of the data during the last two years of the programme. Gregoris Kiosseoglou has contributed to the development of the electronic data files and he has advised us about some of the statistical analyses performed on the data of the first study. Finally, Anastasia Efklides has contributed to the development of some of the tasks addressed to social thought.

Many other persons and institutions have contributed to the completion of this programme. Special thanks are due to Robert Campbell, William Graziano, John J. McArdle, Peter Smith and Robert J. Sternberg, for the constructive criticisms and suggestions they offered at various phases of the writing of the book. Warm thanks are extended to the children and parents of many of the children who agreed to participate in our studies, many of them for two or three consecutive years.

Being involved in a long and demanding programme of research such as this, together with heavy academic governance, is very taxing for one's personal and family life. Litsa Demetriou has developed the personal and family ambience and stability that make these endeavours acceptable and pleasant components of everyday life and she has ensured that no guilt is to be paid for taking large portions of time from our enriching common life. These contributions are part of this programme and thus the senior author of this book will always be grateful. The second author is deeply grateful to her parents, Loanni and Eprosini, for providing the opportunities and support necessary for the activities and the studies which culminated in this book.

Thanks are also due to the Ministry of Education and Religion, Greece, the Experimental School of the Aristotle University of Thessaloniki, the 2nd, the 13th and the Evosmos Gymnasium and Lyceum, Thessaloniki, for granting permission to conduct these studies during school hours.

Last but not least, we are grateful to the Johann Jacobs Foundation, Zurich, Switzerland, for its generous financial support of all the studies reported in this book. Without this support these studies and the writing of the book would simply be impossible.

Correspondence: Andreas Demetriou, Department of Educational Sciences, University of Cyprus, P.O. Box 537, Nicosia 1678, Cyprus.
Phone: +357 2 892045; Fax: +357 2 339064; E-mail: ademetriou@ucy.ac.cy

Preface

This book aims to integrate research and theory about intellectual development, self, and personality into a comprehensive theory. In this sake, the book attempts to answer questions such as the following: How do humans become aware of themselves? How do the products of self-awareness interrelate to produce an integrated self-system, which includes the domains of cognition and personality? That is, how is it possible that persons have a strong sense of unity and identity while they are very differentiated and diversified in their abilities, characteristics, and tendencies? How do persons come to know and influence each other? How is the sense of unity so strongly preserved in development despite the fact that abilities, processes, and characteristics change extensively as a result of development?

These questions are discussed throughout the book. The theoretical frame of the discussion is formed in Chapter 1. This chapter draws from four different traditions in psychology, which have by and large remained separate, if not avoidant of each other. That is, the nomothetic tradition of cognitive developmental psychology, the differentially oriented psychology of intelligence and personality, the socially and clinically oriented psychology of the self, and modern cognitive science. Specifically, the theories about the organization of mind, personality, and self from the different traditions are compared with the aim to uncover their common assumptions despite differences in terminology and methods. Moreover, an outline of the development of self-understanding and self-representation regarding cognition is also given in this chapter.

A series of four studies are then presented which were designed to provide the empirical evidence necessary to build an overarching model able to answer our questions. The first study, which is presented in Chapters 2, 3, and 4, aims to highlight self-awareness in regard to cognitive abilities, personality, thinking styles and possible changes in self-awareness during growth. The method of this study is presented in Chapter 2. Specifically, 840 individuals from 10 to 15 years of age were examined by the following five types of tasks or questionnaires:

a Tasks addressed to six domains of thought (mathematical, causal, social, spatial thought, drawing, and creativity).

b Tasks requiring participants to evaluate aspects of their involvement with most of these tasks (i.e. relative difficulty and success on tasks).

c A questionnaire examining how participants represent themselves in regard to various processes involved in each of the cognitive domains represented in the task battery.

d A questionnaire addressed to various personality/social characteristics (ambition, impulsivity, systematicity, self-control, etc.) and general cognitive characteristics (e.g. learning, reasoning ability).

e Finally, a questionnaire addressed to different styles of activity and thought which are associated with different kinds of occupation (i.e. activities which require originality, or to follow rules, or to evaluate other people).

Chapter 3 deals with the nature and organization of self-awareness in regard to all of the processes examined. Specifically, a series of confirmatory factor analyses and structural equation models suggested that there are two basic knowing levels in the mind. In as far as cognition is concerned, the first level involves processes and abilities oriented to knowing the environment, such as quantitative, causal, social, and spatial thought. In as far as personality and thinking styles are concerned, this level involves dispositions and characteristics, such as ambition, systematicity, impulsivity, orientation to creative or executive types of activities, etc. The second involves processes and abilities oriented to knowing the processes and characteristics involved at the environment-oriented level. The self-oriented processes reflect accurately the organization and interrelationships of the environment-oriented processes. The interaction between the two levels occurs under the constraints of the meaning making and processing potentials available at a given age. In psychometric terms, this may be regarded as the *g* factor of intelligence. These potentials are felt and registered by the thinker as effort and efficiency independent of particular domain. Thus, they provide the basis of a sense of unity that we have despite our multi-structural construction at both knowing levels. At the level of the self-oriented processes, this sense of unity ensures a minimum degree of consistency in the individual's self-evaluations and self-representations. In fact, this sense of unity is projected at the level of the person's self-construct through self-representations of learning ability, logicality, and impulsivity. These dimensions of self-representations function as the go-between agents that connect the cognitive dimensions with the dimensions of personality and thinking style.

Chapter 4 focused on the developmental aspects of our questions. Testing for age differences in mental architecture by means of multiple groups confirmatory factor analysis indicated that the mental architecture is stable throughout adolescence. That is, both the environment-oriented and the self-oriented cognitive and personality processes, abilities, and dispositions preserve their organization despite extensive changes in their efficiency and power as a result of development. At the same time, the relationships between the environment-oriented and the self-oriented level of the mind become closer with growth. As a result, from a normative point of view, self-representation gradually becomes more accurate but also more conservative. However, there are stable individual differences in persons' attitudes to self-evaluation and self-representation. Specifically, these attitudes remain generally stable over time, despite extensive changes in the environment-oriented abilities. It is argued that this is caused by a moderation function which is personally specific. Thus, this function operates as a *personal constant* that is consistently applied across the board of cognitive and personality functions and abilities thereby ensuring stability in their intra-individual covariation. Assuming this constant explains at one and the same time both the unity and the modularity of the mind. That is, that there are accurate mental maps of cognitive and self-processes and tendencies in all normal persons together with relative differences in self-evaluation and self-representation across persons vis-à-vis each of the abilities and tendencies.

Chapter 5 presents our second study, which focused on the social aspects of self-awareness. Specifically, this study aimed to answer the following three questions:

1   How do children's actual cognitive abilities and self-representations about these abilities relate to their parents' respective representations?
2   How do these relations change over time?
3   Are children aware of their parents' representations about them and parents about their children's self-representations?

To answer these questions, a sub-sample of the participants of the first study were examined longitudinally together with their parents by the batteries and inventories described above and also by some new ones. The results indicated that the same dimensions underlie both self-representations and the representations persons hold about each other. Change in abilities and self-representations over time is determined by intra-individual dynamics much more than by inter-individual dynamics. However, parents' representations do reflect children's actual general and specialized abilities and they influence children's self-representations to degrees that vary from system to system. The type and strength of these interactions changes with growth. Thus, it seems that humans can negotiate and affect each other's self- and reflected representations because they share the same architecture and because they are aware of this.

Chapter 6 presents our third study. This study aimed to explore in detail the relationships between the dimensions of processing efficiency and the various domain-specific abilities and characteristics examined in the other studies. Therefore, a number of participants from the first study (i.e. 83 subjects aged 11, 13, and 15 years) were examined by a series of Stroop-like tasks addressed to speed of processing and processing control, and also by a series of tasks addressed to short-term memory. Also there were tasks addressed to analogical and syllogistic reasoning and to various environment-oriented domains, such as quantitative, causal, social thought. Structural modelling and parametric analysis showed clearly that self-representations of cognitive efficiency are directly connected to speed of processing and logical reasoning and from there they exert influences on the other cognitive and personality dimensions of self-representation.

Chapter 7 presents our fourth study. This study focused on the relations between cognitive self-image, personality, and thinking styles. Specifically, in this study, the participants were examined by an improved version of all of the self-representation inventories used in the other studies presented in this book. Moreover, these participants were also examined by an inventory addressed to the "Big Five" factors of personality (that is, extraversion, agreeableness, conscientiousness, neuroticism, and openness to experience). Structural modelling revealed the position of these factors of personality in the general architecture of the mind and the self as depicted in this book. Specifically, on the one hand, personality dispositions reflect actual and reflected cognitive functioning and ability; on the other hand, they influence thinking styles which direct actual choices and behaviour. For instance, persons with a strong sense of cognitive efficiency tend to be open to experience. In turn, these persons orient themselves to activities which require originality. Alternatively, conscientious persons tend to be systematic and not impulsive and to orient themselves to activities which require an executive style.

Chapter 8 provides an integrative discussion of the results of the four studies. A general model is proposed which postulates that the mind is at one and the same time modular and transmodular. The mind is modular at both the level of the environment-oriented cognitive processes and personality dispositions (these are computationally and functionally distinct) and the level of the self-representation of them (their self-representations reflect the organization of the environment-oriented level). However, it is also unified or transmodular because the very ability to oversee, record, and differentiate the modules is by definition a transmodular function. Moreover, the personal constant identified here is a transmodular mechanism because it operates on all modules causing systematic adjustments on all of them at both the level of performance and subjectivity. This constant integrates influences from both general processing efficiency and temperamental dispositions. Thus, humans have mind because there are environment-oriented systems and internal dispositions that they could become mindful of. In evolution, mindfulness emerged as a result of humans first observing and manipulating each other and then as a result of self-observation, self-evaluation, and self-mapping. The self is the personalized aspect of this system and it may refer to cognitive abilities and processes (e.g. I am good in reasoning, learning, mathematics, drawing, social interaction, etc.) or to personality traits or dispositions (e.g. I enjoy being with people; I am stable; I am irritable, etc.). These traits and dispositions set the tone of each person's idiosyncratic functioning. At the same time, everything is embedded in a social context where minds, selves, and personalities interpret and interact with each other. Development increases the interco-ordination between the levels and dimensions of mind both within and across persons.

Foreword

During the beginning of the 1970s, when I studied psychology as an undergraduate student, Piagetian theorizing was all the rage. One could not get a psychology degree without studying Piaget's theory fairly intensively. Within a few years, revisionists were challenging almost every tenet on which Piaget built his system, and within a few years more, what had seemed like an unassailable system had come to seem to be of great historical value but of lesser current interest.

The gradual recession of Piagetian theory, like a similar recession of the grand theories of learning and personality, changed not only the content of what people thought about constructs such as development, learning, and personality, but also the way people thought about them. Instead of constructing large-scale, integrated, systemic theories, psychologists and others more and more constructed theories on a small scale, or even abandoned theory altogether in favour of narrow empirical generalizations. Some psychologists, such as myself, viewed this phenomenon as a throwing out of the baby with the bath water. Research conducted on the basis of microtheories, or even of no theories, is not likely to advance far our understanding of human development or of anything else.

The result of throwing out the baby with the bath water can be observed by reading almost any of our journals. One encounters empirical studies testing small questions that often are asked out of any meaningful context. Sometimes it is not even clear what the questions are, and when it is clear what they are, it is not always apparent why the investigators, or anyone else, should care about them. Readers will encounter none of these problems in reading the current book.

In their work on *Unity and Modularity in the Mind and the Self*, Andreas Demetriou, Smaragda Kazi, and their colleagues attempt to change all that. They go beyond even Piaget in seeking to construct and empirically test a broadly based theory of the mind and its development. They describe a basic architecture of the self as a system, cognitive aspects of the self-system, a processing system, environment-oriented systems, and a hypercognitive system that helps put all of these systems together. They then relate these various systems to temperament, personality, thinking styles, and the self. The only other individual of whom I am aware who has attempted to build such a comprehensive model of the self was the late Joseph Royce. Like Royce, Demetriou, Kazi, and their colleagues introduce a large amount of challenging terminology and use multivariate techniques in their research that will be difficult for some readers to understand. But it is worth the reader's while to seek such understanding.

Some readers will argue with the approach, with the details of the systems, with the way the systems are put together, or with the level of empirical support the experiments provide. Indeed, a model this complex cannot be adequately tested by any small set of experiments, and would be difficult fully to test even with a large number of experiments. But the contribution of a theory is almost never in the theory's being "right": virtually all scientific theories are wrong. They serve only as heuristic devices for generating research and as stepping stones to the successor theories that eventually will replace them. Indeed, one can argue that a theory that lasts too long – some might see Freud's theory as a case in point – lasts as long as it does only because it is difficult to disconfirm or even to test.

Thus, the comprehensive theory presented in this book needs to be judged in terms of whether it will generate further theory and research, by Demetriou's research group, and by other groups as well. This I hope and expect the theory will do. Investigators need to view development as an integrated whole, rather than as a stream of unrelated aspects of cognitive, social, and personality development. There is a richness of theory and experimentation presented in this book that rarely is encountered in psychology, and readers in any field of psychology will profit handsomely from observing how these investigators think about the complexity of the human mind.

Some might find the theorizing too rich, attempting to do too many things too complexly, all at once. But if psychological investigators are to err, I would argue that it should be on the side of richness. For too long, the study of development has consisted of multitudinous disconnected bits. The work presented in this book undoubtedly will help put all these bits back together again, as well they need to be.

ROBERT J. STERNBERG
Yale University

1 Introduction

From cognitive structures to mind, personality and self

The construct of the self comprises all self-descriptions that individuals hold about themselves, as well as all self-prescriptions that they direct to themselves. Self-representations reflect the individuals' concept of their own personhood in its various characteristics, functions, talents, proclivities, and abilities. They also involve the individuals' representations, fantasies, and ideations of how they would like themselves to be, especially in those abilities, characteristics, functions, talents, and proclivities which are most important for them. Finally, this construct may also involve the individuals' strategies for self-modification and self-realization. As such, the construct of the self is very important because it influences the individuals' actual behaviour, their motivation to initiate or disrupt activities, and their feelings about themselves. In other words, the self-construct influences the individuals' chosen course of life, their efficiency in following this course, and the satisfaction they derive from it.

Because of its theoretical and practical importance, the study of the self has been the focus of a number of different traditions in psychology since the turn of the 20th century. The study of the self figured prominently in the early work on thought and intellectual development (Baldwin, 1894; James, 1892), in the work of the symbolic interactionists, which focused primarily on the enculturation and the socialization of the individual (Cooley, 1902; Mead, 1925), the work of the psychodynamic school which focused on the emotional and dynamic aspects of the formation of personality (Freud, 1923), and in the work of the early students of personality who explored the links among motives, personality, and the self (Allport, 1937).

The study of the self fell into disrepute during the dominance of behaviourism. The study of the self requires the investigation of internal and subjective phenomena, while behaviourism accepts only observables as legitimate objects of scientific study (see Harter, 1998, 1999). However, the fall of behaviourism, with the concomitant dominance of the cognitive revolution, has brought the self back into focus. Nowadays, cognitive

(Neisser, 1994; Sternberg, 1988), developmental (Case, 1991; Fischer and Aboud, 1993; Higgins, 1987, 1991; Moretti and Higgins, 1990; Damon and Hart, 1986), educational (Boeckaerts, 1997; Nicholls, 1990) and social and cross-cultural psychologists (Bandura, 1989, 1990; Triandis, 1989) work in close liaison with the mainstream researchers of the self (Brown, 1998; Emmons, 1995; Epstein, 1973, 1991; Harter, 1998, 1999; Markus and Wurf, 1987; Markus and Kityama, 1991; McAdams, 1995), in order to highlight the organization, dynamics, functions, functioning, and development of the self.

It is beyond the scope of this book to review all of the literature in the field. Therefore, this introduction will focus on research and theorizing which is directly relevant to the studies to be presented here. Specifically, the studies examined the following questions:

1   To what extent are developing persons able to evaluate their own performance in a number of different cognitive domains, such as mathematical, spatial, causal, or social thought?
2   How do developing persons represent themselves in regard to these domains? That is, do they posses a map of self-representations in which different cognitive functions and abilities are separately represented and which can be called upon when the individuals need to act or speak about themselves?
3   How is this map organized and how does it relate to actual cognitive performance? That is, does it reflect the organization of actual cognitive performance or is it organized in ways specific to the self-representation system?
4   How do persons' actual cognitive capabilities and self-profiles interact to influence their more dynamic characteristics, such as their ambitions and their preferred life-styles and orientations? In other words, how is mind related to personality?
5   How do developing persons' self-representations interact with the representations held about them by important others, such as their parents? That is, how are one's self-representations about a variety of domains shaped in relation to others' representations?
6   What of the self, how, and why does it change with development in each of the dimensions mentioned above?

In short, the studies to be presented in this book aimed to highlight what persons know and think about their own mind during critical years of development, and how this knowledge and these thoughts relate both to the actual organization of mind and to the knowledge and thoughts that important others hold about them. Moreover, the studies aimed to show

how these representations interact with more dynamic aspects of the self, such as personality attributes, preferred thinking or activity styles and orientations, which are, of course, factors of self-development. Therefore, this introduction will review literature related to: (i) the composition and structure of the self-concept; (ii) the development of the processes and functions involved; and (iii) the factors that contribute to the formation of the self-concept. The aim of this review is to show how the present studies build on earlier work in order to highlight phenomena that are still not fully understood.

The structure of the self

The basic architecture of the self-system

The basic postulates of James's (1890, 1892) theory about the structure of the self are still accepted by modern theories of the self, albeit using a different terminology. James (1890, 1892) was the first to describe the self as a hierarchical and multi-dimensional construct. Specifically, James proposed that the self involves two hierarchical levels, the "I-self" and the "Me-self". The I-self is the knower, and as such includes all self-observation and self-recording processes which generate the knowledge that we have about ourselves. This knowledge is the Me-self, which, according to James, involves three aspects: a material self, a social self, and a spiritual self. The material self subsumes our representations about our body and our possessions. The social self refers to all characteristics recognized by others. The spiritual self involves our thoughts and dispositions about ourselves, both descriptive and evaluative. James believed that the three aspects of the Me-self are also organized hierarchically, with the material self at the lowest level and the spiritual self at the top. It is argued below that this hierarchical conception of the self is still accepted by modern theories of the self. It may also be noted that James forecast the current view of the domain-specificity or modularity of the various aspects and components of the self with his disclaimer that various, apparently incompatible, self-descriptions or self-representations may be held simultaneously. It is not uncommon, for example, to see people with positive self-representations in the academic domain and negative self-representations in the domain of physical appearance.

James's distinction between a knowing (the I-self) and a known self (the Me-self) is present in modern cognitive, social, and neuropsychological theories of the self. Specifically, in Markus's model (see Markus and Wurf, 1987) the working self-concept is differentiated from the collection of self-representations possessed by the individual. The working self-concept is directly involved in the formation and control of behaviour at both the intra- and the inter-personal level. At the intra-personal level, the working self-concept is believed to influence the following functions:

  i   *Information processing*, that is, it enhances sensitivity to self-relevant stimuli thereby contributing to better processing of self-congruent stimuli and it shields out or twists of self-incongruent stimuli.
 ii   *Self-regulation*, that is, it causes changes in overt behaviour but also adjustments in the self-concept itself.
iii   *Motivation*, that is, it orients the system to choices conducive to self-actualisation and self-enhancement.

At the inter-personal level, the working self-concept is considered to influence the following functions:

  i   *Social perception*, that is, it is used as a filter for the interpretation and the evaluation of others' behaviour.
 ii   *Situation and partner choice*, that is, different styles of self-monitoring orient the person to different types of everyday activities.
iii   *Interaction strategies,* that is, the behaviour and the signals emitted during interpersonal interactions are intentionally formulated so as to transmit a particular identity to the partner.

With regard to its content, the working self-concept involves any presently accessible self-representations. Therefore, in this model, the working self-concept is the active part of the self. As such, it assumes the functions of the Jamesian I-self, which generates self-descriptions which belong to the Jamesian Me-self.

The cognitive aspects of the self-system

What cognitive processes are involved in the self-as-knower of itself? And how exactly are the various functions, processes, and abilities, which comprise the self-as-known, represented and organized? Our model provides an answer to these questions. This model, which is illustrated in Figure 1.1, depicts the mind as a hierarchical edifice comprising three main levels. First, there is a very basic level of processing potentials related to information-processing as such. Second, there is an environment-oriented level, which involves cognitive systems that represent and process information from different domains in the environment. Third, there is a self-oriented level, which involves processes and knowledge guiding self-understanding, understanding of other minds, and self-regulation. The term "hypercognitive system" has been coined to refer to this level. The adverb "hyper" in Greek means "higher than" or "on top of" or "going beyond", and when added to the word "cognitive" indicates the supervising and co-ordinating functions of the hypercognitive system (Demetriou, 1998a, 1998b, 2000; Demetriou and Efklides, 1994; Demetriou, Efklides, and Platsidou, 1993a).

The processing system

This system is defined in terms of three parameters: "speed of processing", "control of processing", and "working memory" (see panel B of Figure 1.1). Speed of processing basically refers to the maximum speed at which a given mental act may be efficiently executed. Usually, in tests of speed of processing (Jensen, 1998), the individual is asked to recognize a simple stimulus as quickly as possible, for example, to name a letter or read single words in one's nature language. Under these conditions, speed of processing indicates the time needed by the system to record and give meaning to information. Traditionally, the faster an individual can recognize the stimulus, the more efficient his processing system is thought to be.

The information that is of value or interest at one particular moment seldom appears alone – it usually coexists alongside other information which must be distinguished and ignored. The control function refers to the processes that identify and register goal-relevant information and block out dominant or appealing but actually irrelevant information. Control of processing determines the system's efficiency in selecting the appropriate mental act. This function is usually tested under conditions that can generate conflicting interpretations, such as the well-known Stroop phenomenon (Stroop, 1935). In this test, words denoting colour are written with a different ink colour (i.e. the word "red" written with blue ink), and the individual is asked to name the ink colour as quickly as possible. These conditions accurately test control of processing, because the subject is required to inhibit a dominant but irrelevant response (to read the word) in order to select and emit a weaker but relevant response (name the ink colour) (Demetriou *et al.*, 1993; Dempster and Brainerd, 1995; Houghton and Tipper, 1994).

Finally, once information is selected and encoded, it must be actively represented in relation to the present problem. Storage refers to the processes which enable a person to hold information in an active state while integrating it with other information until the current problem is solved. A common measure of the storage function is the maximum amount of information *and* mental acts that the mind can efficiently activate simultaneously. Our conception of the processing system builds on and integrates the work of a number of other scholars in the neo-Piagetian and the information processing tradition (Baddeley, 1991; Case, 1985; Case, Okamoto, Griffin, McKeough, Bleiker, Henderson, and Stephenson, 1996; Halford, 1993; Kail, 1988; Pascual-Leone, 1970).

The reader may wonder how these low-level processes relate to the high-level construct of personality and the self, which are the focus of the present book. It suffices to say here that the studies to be presented in this book aim to test the assumption that the condition of these processes contributes directly and indirectly to the formation of both one's own self-representations of intellectual efficiency and the representations of important others. In turn, these effects are transferred to many other domains of cognitive and social functioning because they direct the individual to choose activities which appear to them suitable for their perceived level of efficiency.

The environment-oriented systems

In as far as the environment-oriented level is concerned, empirical research in our laboratory has initially identified and delineated five environment-oriented systems (see panel A of Figure 1.1) (Demetriou and Efklides, 1985, 1989; Demetriou, Efklides, Papadaki, Papantoniou, and Economou, 1993b; Demetriou, Pachaury, Metallidou, and Kazi, 1996; Demetriou, Platsidou, Efklides, Metallidou, and Shayer, 1991; Demetriou *et al.*, 1993a; Demetriou and Kargopoulos, 1998a, 1998b; in preparation; Shayer, Demetriou, and Prevez, 1988).

  1 The *categorical-analytic* system deals with similarity-difference relations. It involves processes that enable the thinker to compare stimuli and specify their similarities and differences, and build concepts able to represent them. Thus, this system underlies abilities such as classification and analogical reasoning.

  2 The *quantitative-relational* system deals with quantitative variations and relations. Numerical operations are the primary operations involved in this system. Other, more complex processes, such as proportional or algebraic reasoning, are used to process more complex quantitative aspects of the environment, experienced or represented. Thus, this system constitutes the ground for mathematical thinking.

  3 The *causal-experimental* system deals with cause-effect relations. It involves processes such as hypothesis formation, hypothesis testing by experimentation, and construction of models able to express the causal structure of the phenomenon of interest. Thus, this system underlies scientific thinking.

  4 The *spatial-imaginal* system deals with orientation in space and the imaginal representation of the environment. This system involves processes such as mental rotation, scanning, and transformation of mental images. Thus, this system underlies the ability to build mental models of the environment and of one's own actions and characteristics.

  5 The *verbal-propositional* system deals with the truth and falsity and the validity and invalidity in the flow of information in verbal statements or in systems that represent the environment. This system involves operations underlying deductive reasoning, such as implication, transitivity, incompat-

ibility, etc. Thus, this system underlies the ability to transmit information systematically but also to check if the information transmitted by others is systematic and consistent.

Recent research in our laboratory, following the work of other scholars (e.g. Case, 1992; Case *et al.*, 1996) has identified two other systems:

6 The *social-interpersonal* system deals with the relations between individuals. This system involves operations and processes that enable understanding and manipulation of the forces underlying social interactions, such as motives and intentions (Demetriou, Kazi, and Georgiou, 1999).

7 The *drawing-pictographic.* This system involves multiple skills and operations which integrate many of the systems above into an idiosyncratic whole which is particular to humans. That is, this system makes use of imaginal and kinetic processes and abilities for the sake of the pictorial representation of the relations associated with any of the systems summarized above. Through this system humans can represent their environment or their thoughts themselves by the production of drawings or any other kind of signs (Bonoti, 1998; Loizos, 1992).

The organization of these systems obeys the following principles. First, these systems are considered to be *domain-specific.* That is, each specializes in the representation and processing of different types of relationships in the environment. Second, the systems are *procedurally specific.* That is, each system involves different types of mental operations and processes. These reflect the peculiarities of the relations which characterize the system's domain of reality. Contrast, for instance, arithmetic operations with mental rotation. Third, the systems are *symbolically biased.* That is, each system makes use of symbols, such as mental images, numbers, or language that are also domain-appropriate; information related to space, for example, is best represented through mental images, whereas information on quantitative relations is best represented through mathematical notation. Finally, the systems are *functionally and developmentally autonomous*, at least to a certain extent. That is, each system can function without the support of the others systems to process its own domain and it may follow partially independent or idiosyncratic developmental course in relation to pace and forms of change. Because of these characteristics, the systems are called *specialized capacity systems* (SCSs).

According to the theory, these systems are themselves hierarchically organized. Specifically, each of them is considered to include the following components:

1 Core or kernel elements that are more or less innately determined. Subitization or the recognition of small numbers, the perception of causality, the perception of depth, or the early preference for the human face, may be taken as examples of core elements of the quantitative, the causal, the

spatial, and the social SCSs, respectively. Core elements remain relatively unchanged during development, although they improve to a certain extent, especially at the early phases of development. Thus, they form the background for the development of operating rules and knowledge to be described next.

2 Operating rules and computational processes. Arithmetic operations, hypothesis testing, mental rotation, and communication skills are examples of operations in the quantitative, the causal, the spatial, and the social SCSs, respectively. These rules and processes undergo extensive changes during development. In fact, stage theories of cognitive development, such as the Piagetian theory or the neo-Piagetian theories (e.g. Case, 1985, 1992; Fischer, 1980; Halford, 1993; Pascual-Leone, 1970, 1988) were mostly concerned with their development.

3 Knowledge and beliefs. These describe the various aspects of the domains of the world associated with each of the SCSs and also the relationships of the person with each of the domains. They accrue as a function of the functioning of core processes and operating rules. Thus, this part of the SCSs changes continuously as a result of ongoing functioning (Demetriou and Valanides, 1998). Theories of conceptual change (e.g. Carey, 1985; Vosniadou, 1994) are mainly concerned with part of the organization of the SCSs.

Moreover, these systems are organized into the higher-order realms shown in Figure 1.1, that is visual thought and creativity, analytical-inferential thought, and inter-personal thought. The seven systems themselves do not fully coincide with systems and abilities discovered by other scholars. However, the three higher-order constellations correspond, by and large, to the three realms of abilities described by Sternberg's (1985) triarchic theory, that is, creative, analytical, and real world abilities, respectively. The interested reader is referred to other sources for a discussion of the relations between our theory and other theories in as far as these systems are concerned (Demetriou *et al.*, 1993a; Demetriou, Pachaury, Metallidou, and Kazi, 1996; Demetriou and Raftopoulos, 1999).

The hypercognitive system

It was argued previously that the environment-oriented systems are domain-specific, computationally specific, and symbolically biased. Obviously, problem-solving creatures other than humans (such as animals and computers) may also possess thinking or action systems governed by these three principles. We know, for instance, that many animals possess elaborate spatial abilities and that they can grasp the causal or the quantitative structure of the world (Gallistel, 1993). Moreover, specialized programmes can enable computers to be extremely efficient causal modellers, elegant graphical

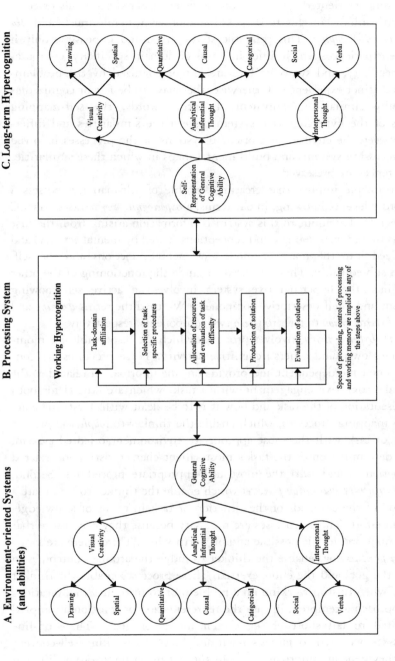

A. Environment-oriented Systems (and abilities)

B. Processing System

C. Long-term Hypercognition

Working Hypercognition

Task-domain affiliation

Selection of task-specific procedures

Allocation of resources and evaluation of task difficulty

Production of solution

Evaluation of solution

Speed of processing, control of processing and working memory are implied in any of the steps above

General Cognitive Ability

Visual Creativity

Analytical Inferential Thought

Interpersonal Thought

Drawing

Spatial

Quantitative

Causal

Categorical

Social

Verbal

Self-Representation of General Cognitive Ability

Visual Creativity

Analytical Inferential Thought

Interpersonal Thought

Drawing

Spatial

Quantitative

Causal

Categorical

Social

Verbal

Figure 1.1 The three levels of mind and their internal structure

Note

Attention is drawn to the equivalence between the structure of abilities in the environment-oriented level and their representation in the hypercognitive system. Attention is also drawn to the assumption that the processing system is occupied by the self-monitoring and self-regulation processes involved in working hypercognition.

designers, or unparalleled quantitative processors. However, mere possession of environment-oriented systems is not sufficient to credit animals or computers with mind. For this to be possible another principle must hold: *the principle of self-mapping*. This principle states that mind is possible only if cognitive experiences which differ in terms of domain-specificity, computational specificity, and symbolic bias are felt or cognized by the problem-solver as distinct experiences. Otherwise, they have to be felt or cognized as functionally similar or equivalent. In other words, the self-mapping processes of the hypercognitive system discern the similarities and differences between the environment-oriented systems or the processes involved in the processing systems and build mental maps in which these similarities and differences are preserved.

This principle implies that creatures capable of self-mapping possess a second-order level of knowing, in our terms, a *hypercognitive system* (see panel C of Figure 1.1). The input to this system is information arising from the first two levels (sensations, feelings, and conceptions caused by mental activity) and is organized into the maps or models of mental functions and the self, described subsequently. These are used to guide the functioning of the other levels. Thus, the hypercognitive system involves an active self-knowing component and a self-descriptive component. We used the terms *working* and *long-term hypercognition* to refer to these two components, respectively.

Working hypercognition involves processes which are responsible for monitoring one's own (and others') cognitive activity. These processes are considered to be time-dependent and provide on-line information related to the individual's cognitive engagement with a task, which are crucial for both the representation of the task and how it is to be dealt with. First, there are task-SCS mapping processes, which enable the thinker to *couple* the present situation or task with the most appropriate environment oriented system, through determination of the task's most salient characteristics and related past experiences and *select* the most task-appropriate procedures. Second, there are *difficulty evaluation processes* which enable the thinker to formulate a conception of the demands of the situation or task in terms of knowledge, skills, and effort. These processes are necessary because they can ensure that working on a problem is possible and/or worth while. Third there are *success evaluation processes* that enable the thinker to judge the attained outcomes in terms of the goal and the effort exerted. These processes enable the thinker to decide when to stop working on a problem or to introduce modifications in the approach attempted, in case the representation or solution attempted is evaluated to fall short of the current needs or goals. These on-line processes seem related to James's I-self and Markus's working self-concept because they generate information about the self in action vis-à-vis different types of tasks (see panel B of Figure 1.1).

Long-term hypercognition. On-line self monitoring processes draw and feed-back on long-term hypercognition, so that long-term hypercognition includes the products of prior functioning of working hypercognition and it serves as a guide to its current functioning. These products are organized in mental "maps" able to direct understanding and decision making in regard to future person-environment encounters which are of some value to the individual. We have (Demetriou *et al.*, 1993a) proposed three kinds of maps; specifically, two general maps comprising what is involved in the mind, and how the mind can be used to meet the demands of the world, and a self-centred map which contains the individual's representations of his own mind and his preferred ways of using it. In other words, long-term hyper-cognition involves a theory of mind, a theory of intelligence, and a theory of the cognitive self. The basic attributes of these theories are summarized below:

The model of the mind

This theory contains rules, knowledge, and beliefs related to the structure and functioning of the cognitive system. The model defines the specific cognitive functions, for example, that memory is distinct from thought, or that there are different types of mental operations, such as those performed by each of the environment-oriented systems described above. This part of the model is related to earlier work on metacognition, carried out in the 1970s and 1980s (Adekoya, 1994; Brown, 1987; Demetriou and Efklides, 1989; Demetriou *et al.*, 1993a; Flavell, 1979; Fabricius and Schwanenflugel, 1994; Makris, 1995).

The personal theory of mind also involves the realization that the mind is capable of influencing behaviour and human interaction, that beliefs, opin-ions, desires, and wills – the mental states that individuals have at a given moment – may be the source of their behaviour and thus moderate their interactions with others. For instance, people act aggressively when they feel threatened or when they want to undermine others' interests in favour of their own. This part of the theory of cognition is related to what has come to be known in recent years as the theory of mind (Perner, 1991; Wellman, 1990).

The general model of intelligence

This theory involves an individual's knowledge and beliefs in relation to two important issues. First, it comprises his conception of how the various cog-nitive functions can be most efficiently and productively utilized. For example, it contains rules suggesting the best ways that memory can store or recall different types of information. For instance, a rule may specify that rehearsal is a more efficient strategy for memorising a short list of digits, but organization according to meaning is preferable for remembering a long shopping list involving many categories of products. Second, it involves the individual's knowledge about what constitutes intelligent behaviour in a given environment and time. For example, we must learn quickly, speak fluently and accurately, be socially flexible and considerate, must control our behaviour, etc. This theory specifies how we must regulate our behaviour to achieve personal goals and avoid unnecessary conflicts within our particular social or cultural group. Thus, the theory of intelligence held by an individual may be viewed as a value-guided system, in which the individual's knowledge and expertise is emphasized to maximize the gains of action based on his interpretation of the specific situation (Demetriou *et al.*, 1993a; Sternberg, Conway, Ketron, and Bernstein, 1981).

The cognitive self-image

This theory resides at the intersection of one's theory of mind and model of intelligence. It involves how individuals view themselves as intelligent thinking beings and answers questions such as: How flexible or intelligent or wise am I? Which kinds of problems am I, or am I not, good at solving? How efficient am I in using different cognitive functions like memory, imagery, problem solving, etc? The cognitive self-image involves all the implicit and explicit attributes that individuals ascribe to themselves in regard to different mental functions, abilities, strategies, and skills (Demetriou *et al.*, 1993, Demetriou, Kazi, and Georgiou, 1999).

Our description of long-term hypercognition suggests that it overlaps considerably with James's Me-self. In fact, the theory of cognitive self presents a high-resolution picture of what James might have included in the cognitive parts of his Me-self, had he been alive to witness the explosion of knowledge in cognitive psychology and the psychology of intelligence that came after his death. However, our long-term hypercognition also involves more general experiences, knowledge, and skills regarding intellectual functioning. This obviously grows out of one's own functioning which is very personal and self-centred but, at any time, it sets the frame in which this functioning takes place. Thus, placing these three dimensions of the persons' knowledge about the mind under the same theoretical umbrella opens the way for the integration of self-psychology with modern cognitive and developmental science.

What is then observed by and reflected in the hypercognitive system? Ideally, the whole set of systems and subsystems involved in the other two levels of the architecture of the mind, that is the level of the processing system and the level of the environment-oriented systems described above.

In conclusion, this model portrays the mind as a hierarchical and multi-system universe, involving both domain-general cognitive processes which constrain the kind and complexity of the aspects of the environment that can be understood and processed, and domain-specific cognitive processes which are tuned to different aspects of the environment. It also involves a higher-order hypercognitive level which monitors, records, and guides the other two levels. Thus, the input to this level is information from the other two levels (sensations, feelings of power and general efficiency that reflect the activity of the processing system, and also specialized sensations and feelings that reflect the activity of the domain-specific systems) and its output are feelings, tendencies, intentions, representations, thoughts, skills, and strategies which aim to represent and control the functioning of these levels (for example, selective attention strategies for the control of the processing system as contrasted to strategies which are useful only for particular domains, such as mathematics or drawing).

Temperament, personality, thinking styles, and the self

The discussion so far was concerned with the cognitive rather than with the dynamic aspects of the human understanding, experience, and behaviour. However, cognition in general and self-regulation in particular are never entirely cool. Striving to attain a goal generates emotions, which colour and influence understanding and action. Moreover, it is a truism that there are alternative ways to understand and experience the same situation and deal with it. Traditionally, these differences are ascribed to differences in personality and style, which frame emotions and the mind. Personality refers to more or less stable and decontextualized tendencies and dispositions in the individual to interpret the world and interact with it in idiosyncratic ways (Caspi, 1998). Thinking styles involve ways of organizing and controlling behaviour which orient the individuals to particular kinds of information processing and action which thus tend to dominate over other kinds of information processing or action. These mechanisms originate from both personality dispositions, such as extraversion or openness to experience, and preferred ways of approaching and processing information, such as abstract conceptualization and reflection as contrasted to doing and experimentation (Sternberg, 1988, 1990; Ferrari and Sternberg, 1998). Moreover, there is the self-system itself. That is, "the phenomenological agency that coordinates the demands of the immediate situation with constraints imposed on the individual by dispositions and residues of life experiences" (Graziano, Jensen-Campbell, and Finch, 1997, p. 393).

How do these systems and functions relate with each other and with the systems and functions of the cognitive aspects of the mind discussed in the

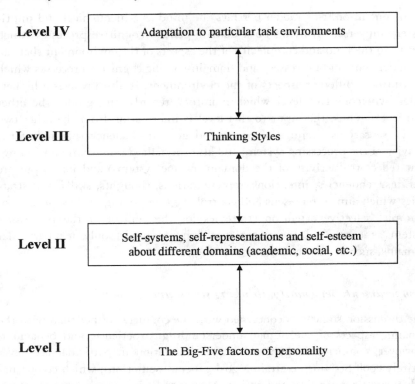

Level IV — Adaptation to particular task environments

Level III — Thinking Styles

Level II — Self-systems, self-representations and self-esteem about different domains (academic, social, etc.)

Level I — The Big-Five factors of personality

Figure 1.2 The general model of the organization of personality, the self-esteem, actual behaviour and thinking styles

section above? There is no generally accepted answer to this question. It is highly interesting, however, that integrating hitherto unco-ordinated work from research on personality and the self suggests that these dimensions of the human personality and the self are organized in a way which is very similar to the organization of the mind. We will try to substantiate this claim by comparing models about personality, thinking styles, and the self. Figure 1.2 summarizes these models and demonstrates their complementarity and overall similarity with the organization of the mind.

Temperament is considered as the substrate upon which personality, thinking styles, and the self are constructed. According to Kagan:

"the word *temperament* is used by some, but not all, scientists to refer to psychological qualities that display considerable variation among infants and young children and, in addition, have a relatively, but not indefinitely, stable physiological basis that derives from the individual's genetic constitution. It is also understood that the inherited physiological processes can mediate different phenotypic displays as the child grows and that experience always influences the form of the behavioral display. The temperamental qualities investigated most often by psychologists, pediatricians, and psychiatrists, which are obvious to parents, include irritability, a happy mood, ease of being soothed, motor activity, sociability, attentiveness, adaptability, approach to or avoidance of novelty, ease as well as intensity of arousal in reaction to stimulation, and regulation of arousal states."

Kagan (1994) p. 16

Therefore, temperament involves the early tendencies and dispositions which are gradually shaped into the dimensions of personality and style to be discussed below. How are these dimensions actualized into patterns of adaptation in the real environment?

Graziano and colleagues (Graziano, Jensen-Campbell, and Finch, 1997; Graziano, Jensen-Campbell, and Sullivan, in press), building on the work of McAdams (1995), have recently proposed that social adaptation is grounded on a three-level hierarchical structure (see Figure 1.2). Level I involves the so called "Big Five" factors of personality, that is, *extraversion, agreeableness, conscientiousness, neuroticism, and openness to experience*. Individuals high in extraversion are sociable, active, talkative, optimistic, pleasure-seeking, self-confident, warm, and not inhibited. Individuals low in extraversion are aloof, withdrawn, shy, and self-inhibited. Individuals high in agreeableness are soft-hearted, generous, kind, forgiving, sympathetic, warm, and trusting. Individuals low in agreeableness are suspicious, headstrong, shrewd, impatient, argumentative, and aggressive. Individuals high in conscientiousness are organized, ambitious, energetic, efficient, determined, precise, industrious, persistent, reliable, and responsible. Individuals low in conscientiousness are distractible, lazy, careless, impulsive, hasty, immature, defensive. Individuals high in neuroticism are worrying, nervous, anxious, moody, tense, self-centred, and self-pitying. Individuals low in neuroticism are self-confident, clear-thinking, alert, and contented. Finally, individuals who are open to experience are curious and with wide interests, inventive, original, imaginative, non-traditional, and artistic. Individuals who are not open to experience are conservative, cautious, mild.

Level II, involves the self-systems, such as global self-esteem, social self-esteem, and academic self-esteem. That is, it involves the person's self-representations, value-systems, and general action strategies, which translate the Level I dispositions into particular modes of understanding and action. Finally, Level III (which corresponds to Level IV in Figure 1.2) involves perceived adaptations to particular task environments, such as academic adjustment, peer relations, classroom behaviour, etc. According to the model and the evidence presented in support of it by Graziano and colleagues, the Level

II self-systems both are differentially related to the Level I personality dispositions and function as mediators between these dispositions and domain-specific perceived adjustments and related self-narratives. As a result, different types of situation-specific adaptations may originate from the same personality disposition if this is coupled with different kinds of self-representations.

Sternberg's (1988, 1990; Ferrari and Sternberg, 1998) conception of thinking styles and their relationships to personality and cognitive abilities seems complementary to the models outlined above. Ferrari and Sternberg posit that "styles may represent an important missing link integrating intelligence, personality, and real-world performance" (1998, p. 933), perhaps because cognitive styles involve organizing and control mechanisms which orient individuals to particular forms of information processing which are most comfortable and therefore preferable. These mechanisms originate from both personality dispositions, such as extraversion or openness to experience, and preferred ways of approaching and processing information, such as abstract conceptualization and reflection as contrasted to doing and experimentation (Kolb, 1977). Thus, these styles are illustrated to interfere between the self-systems and actual performance in Figure 1.2.

Sternberg (1988) called his theory of thinking styles "the theory of mental self-government" to stress his view that styles govern the functioning of thinking and self-actualization much as governments govern countries. This theory defines the styles of self-government in terms of five dimensions: function, form, level, scope, and leaning. Only the first two of these dimensions were involved in our research, and these will be discussed below.

Function refers to what the mind does to cope with the world. Like governments, the mind legislates and plans, implements and executes, and judges and evaluates. Thus, there are three styles in the functioning of the mind: The *legislative,* the *executive,* and the *judicial style.* "The legislative style characterises individuals who enjoy creating, formulating, and planning for problem solutions" (Sternberg, 1990, p. 140). Thus, this style requires high levels of self-awareness and reflectivity and it predisposes for autonomous, creative, planning, and system-creation activities. Individuals characterized by this legislative orientation may be directed to occupations which require this style, such as those of the artist, the scientist, the policymaker, etc. Clearly, this style is close to openness to experience of the Big Five factors of personality. The executive "style implements rather than plans for execution" (Sternberg, 1988, p. 203). Thus, this style predisposes for rule-following activities which evolve in well-defined contexts. Executive individuals may be directed to rule-abiding occupations, such as those of the lawyer, the police officer, the constructor, and the doctor. If a parallel is to be drawn here with personality factors, executive individuals seem to have many of the properties characterising conscientiousness. Finally, the judicial style involves judgmental activities, such as evaluation of people, systems, ideas, and rules and it directs to occupations such as those of the judge, the admissions officer, etc. The relationships between this style and the Big Five factors of personality do not seem obvious. Sternberg claims that "although any complex task typically involves all three functions of self-government, in most individuals, one of the functions tends to be dominant" (Ferrari and Sternberg, 1998, p. 927).

Form refers to the preferred ways of approaching and dealing with problems. Sternberg proposes that there are four forms of self-government. The *monarchic*, the *hierarchic*, the *oligarchic*, and the *anarchic*. "In the monarchic form a single goal or way of doing things predominates. People with a monarchic style tend to focus single-mindedly on one goal or need at a time" (Ferrari and Sternberg, 1998, p. 928). The hierarchic form allows for many goals, each with its own priority. Thus, people with a hierarchic style tend to have multiple goals, whose attainment is organized hierarchically according to their interrelationships and importance. The oligarchic form also allows for multiple goals, but in this form all goals are considered equally important. Thus, people with an oligarchic style may focus on many goals simultaneously; however, if these goals compete or conflict with each other, they may not attain any goal. Finally, those with an anarchic style are intolerant of rules and so avoid organizing and planning goals and activities; they may shift from one goal or task to the other without fully realizing any one. Clearly, form is related to conscientiousness. One could assume that persons with a hierarchic style would be high on this dimension. In contrast, anarchic persons would normally be low in conscientiousness.

According to Sternberg, these dimensions are related. Thus, they may interact to produce various combinations of "real world characters", although it is conceivable that certain combinations are more probable than others. For instance, it seems plausible that a legislative style goes better with a hierarchic rather than an oligarchic style, whereas an executive style goes better with an oligarchic rather than a hierarchic style. In a similar vein, one might predict that different styles or different style combinations might lead to different life orientations, such as those concerned with the selection of an occupation. For example, it might be assumed that legislators would direct themselves to creative occupations, such as artist or researcher, whereas executives might direct themselves to rule-abiding professions, such as public servant or policeman. These questions are both interesting and potentially important from a practical point of view. However, to our knowledge, neither Sternberg nor any other scholar has yet provided evidence or theoretical guidelines on the possible combinations or on their potential effects on life-orientations.

This portrait of mind bears an important implication in regard to the more evaluative and dynamic aspects of the self, namely self-worth, self-esteem, and self-efficacy. Specifically, there has been considerable debate in the literature over the question of whether individuals possess a general or global representation of their worth or value as persons or whether there are differentiated representations which reflect the individuals' evaluations of how good or efficient they are in each of different domains. The classic figures in the field espoused the first of these views. James (1890, 1892) believed that there is global self-esteem, which is produced by a kind of averaging process which takes into account the persons' successes and failures in different domains. Cooley's views were very close as he also believed that there is an overall concept of self-respect. More recently, Coopersmith (1967) endorsed this view and he presented empirical evidence in line with it.

At present, however, the field has swung towards the multidimensional view. Specifically, using more differentiated probing and analytical methods, a number of researchers have recently shown that self-esteem and self-evaluation are multifaceted and domain specific (see Bracken, 1996; Byrne, 1995; Harter, 1990, 1998, 1999; Hattie, 1992; Marsh, Byrne, and Shavelson, 1992; Marsh and Hattie, 1995, 1996; Oosterwegel and Oppenheimer, 1993; Shavelson and Marsh, 1986). In fact, the currently prevailing view is that self-esteem is a hierarchical construct, with the general self-concept at the apex, a number of major domains at a middle level, such as the self-concept about the academic, the social, the emotional, and the physical domain, and a number of more specific domains within each of these main domains, such as maths and science in the academic domain or physical ability and physical appearance in the physical domain. The direction of causality in these models runs from lower to higher level constructs. Thus, it is assumed, for instance, that self-perceptions of competence in a particular domain (such as maths) contributes to the formation of the next level construct (such as academic achievement) which in turn influences the general self-concept (Byrne, 1995; Marsh, Byrne, and Shavelson, 1992; Marsh and Hattie, 1995). It must be noted, however, that there are scholars who argue that different qualities of the self may not be integrated under an overarching self-concept, either descriptive or evaluative (Costanzo, 1991; Graziano and Waschhull, 1995; Kagan, 1991).

It is interesting to note that our model of the mind outlined in the previous section is consistent with the model of personality and the self outlined in this section. Specifically, it is reminded that, according to that model, the mind is organized as a three-level universe, involving a level which includes environment-oriented systems, a level which includes general processing functions and capacities, and a level which includes self-oriented processes enabling self-awareness and self-regulation. The model of the self and personality discussed in this section also seems to involve these three hierarchical levels. Specifically, it seems that the Big Five factors of personality correspond to the domain-specific systems that reside at the environment-oriented level of knowing. In a similar vein, temperament might be considered as the equivalent of processing potentials in the domain of self and personality. That is, one might assume that processing potentials constrain the complexity and type of information that can be understood at a given age, and temperament constrains how information is to initially be received and reacted to. Finally, at a third level we have the self-systems, both general, such as global self-worth, and localized or specialized, such as academic or physical self-esteem. These seem to correspond to the various self-representations which reside in the long-term hypercognitive maps of the organization of the mind. Thinking styles may build on these three levels thereby functioning as the interface between mind, self, and personality, on the one hand, and actual life choices and behaviour, on the other. Obviously, testing and validating these relationships would be an important step in the direction of integrating research and theory on the mind, self, and personality. The studies to be presented below aim to contribute to this integration.

The development of self-understanding and personality

In recent years, there has been a proliferation of research and theorizing on the development of various aspects of the self. Reviewing this work is beyond the scope of this book, but the interested reader is referred to Harter (1998, 1999), who has recently provided an excellent review and evaluation of this work. Our synthesis will focus only on those phenomena which are relevant to the studies to be presented in the following chapters. Specifically, we will attempt to highlight and clarify the development of self-evaluation and self-representation in regard to the cognitive dimensions of the self from childhood to adolescence. To the extent this is possible, we will also try to review research on how development in these dimensions is related to development of thinking styles and socially relevant dimensions of the self-system. To facilitate understanding, we will first review research that examines the developmental course of these dimensions and then we will focus on research investigating the causation of development.

Levels in the development of the self-representation

The development of self-representations is modelled according to three dimensions: their structure and organization, their content, and their accuracy (see Harter, 1998, 1999). With regard to structure, neo-Piagetian conceptions seem to dominate. Specifically, based on the reformulation of the stages of cognitive development proposed by Case (1985, 1992) and Fischer (Fischer, 1980; Fischer and Pipp, 1984), both Case (1991) and Fischer (Fischer and Aboud, 1993) themselves, as well as other researchers (Harter, 1998, 1999; Higgins, 1987, 1991), have advanced models of the development of the self-system which claim that, with development, self-representations: (i) involve more dimensions which are better integrated into increasingly more complex structures; (ii) move along a concrete to abstract continuum so that they become increasingly more abstract and flexible; and (iii) become more accurate in regard to the actual characteristics and abilities to which they refer.

Thus, according to these models, self-representations in early childhood involve observable characteristics which are seen in isolation from each other and which are unrealistically positive (I have blue eyes, I can run fast). In early to middle childhood representations start to be interconnected, especially if they refer to very obvious or strong characteristics or experiences. This gives rise to taxonomic self-descriptions (I am good, fast, clever, etc.) which indicate a continuity of self-representation over time. Due to the fact that thought is still unidimensional (Case, 1991), opposites such as good and bad, happy and sad, etc., can not yet be truly integrated. Thus, self-representations at this phase are still generally positive and therefore frequently inaccurate, because the negative side of a dimension is avoided. At this phase the child shows awareness that others evaluate him (Stipek, Recchia, and McClintic, 1992). At this early phase, self-evaluations and others' evaluations are not yet integrated. However, this awareness provides the basis for the formation of a more objective and accurate self-system (Higgins, 1987).

Interestingly enough, research on awareness about the nature of thought and intelligence suggests a similar picture. That is, pre-schoolers may be able to differentiate between thought and other cognitive functions (such as perception) or non-cognitive functions (such as movement). However, they do not clearly understand that thought involves many different functions (such as inference, attention, etc.) nor do they understand how it works (for instance that is only partially controllable). Likewise, pre-schoolers do not conceive of intellectual ability as an internal quality of the mind; rather, they consider it as directly related to various characteristics, such as work habits and conduct, and therefore believe that it may be increased by practice and hard work (Nicholls, 1990).

In middle to late childhood, higher-order generalizations can be formed, as the child is now capable of building bi-dimensional concepts (Case, 1985) or representational systems (Fischer, 1980). These give rise to trait labels which integrate self-evaluations and self-representations referring to different domains (e.g. "I am smart because I do well in different areas, such as English and Social Studies"). Moreover, the integration of opposites is possible at this phase (e.g. although generally smart, I am not very good at maths). As a result, self-evaluations become more differentiated and accurate because they can sustain both positive and negative self-descriptions. The global concept of self-worth also appears at this phase (Harter, 1990) indicating that the I-self starts to function as a general self-monitoring and self-evaluation agent which can integrate the various aspects of the Me-self.

In agreement with this interpretation, children at this phase begin to understand the constructive nature of thought. For instance, they realize that it is by means of thought that ambivalent expressions can be understood (Carpendale and Chandler, 1996). Also, in the period from age 8 to 10, children begin to differentiate between various cognitive functions, such as memory and inference or attention and thought. However, they cannot differentiate between different aspects of the same cognitive function, for instance, that there are different kinds of memory (Fabricius and Schwanenflugel, 1994). As early as the first grade, children can clearly distinguish between different domains of activity, such as maths, reading, music, and sports. In fact, first-grade children understand that each domain involves both a competence component, which refers to the general demands of the domain, and a subjective component which refers to how they personally value activities within each of the domains. However, children at this phase do not make finer distinctions between various aspects of competence or subjective value, such as task difficulty, expectations for success, and learning ability within a domain (Eccles, Wigfield, Harold, and Blumenfeld, 1993). In line with these findings, Nicholls (1990) showed that children begin to differentiate the various dimensions of ability and intelligence during this period. They begin to recognize, for instance, that skill is required for some tasks and that different tasks may require different abilities. However, children still believe that effort is the primary source of success, not yet realizing that ability may be an underlying system of processes which can be translated into different kinds of performance in relation to specific tasks.

In early adolescence thought becomes able to deal with the possible (Inhelder and Piaget, 1958), the suppositional (Demetriou *et al.*, 1993b), and the abstract (Case, 1985; Fischer, 1980), because representations can now be viewed from the perspective of other representations (Demetriou, 1998a, 1998b; Demetriou, Efklides *et al.*, 1993a). Thus, the traits of the previous phase can now be integrated into higher-order abstractions about the self (for instance, I am intelligent because I am smart and creative or I am extravert because I am sociable and talkative). However, several authors maintain that abstractions about the self are not yet well integrated at this phase (Case, 1991; Fischer and Aboud, 1993; Higgins, 1991). Therefore, although both positive and negative abstractions may coexist within the self-system, they are not subsumed under a common self-concept which bears at one and the same time an overarching identity and characteristics differentiated according to different domains.

In middle adolescence, abstractions begin to be linked with each other. Consequently, at this phase, a more accurate and modularized representation of the self becomes possible. For instance, adolescents can represent themselves both as intelligent and unintelligent, extravert and introvert, etc. This enables adolescents to pair their various qualities with different types of activities, preferences, and orientations. As a result, there may be both a generalized self-definition in answer to the question "who am I?" and "what do I want to become in life?" as well as a more specific self-definition in response to the question "What is more suitable for me given that I am good here and not so good there?" Therefore, a self-system which is simultaneously integrated and differentiated begins to be established at this phase. However, the command on this system is not fully developed at the beginning. As a result, adolescents may vacillate between extremes, be inaccurate, and feel distressed when the pendulum swings toward the negative side of dimensions and characteristics.

These difficulties are removed in late adolescence. By this phase the individual becomes able to co-ordinate abstractions into higher order abstractions and thus impose coherence on his conception of himself, which was lacking in middle adolescence. For instance, the seemingly incompatible poles of a dimension (e.g. extravert vs. introvert) can now be integrated into a higher order dimension (e.g. "flexible", i.e. one can behave as an extravert in some situations and as an introvert in others, depending on particular characteristics and demands). Self-evaluation can now be more accurate, because each of the various dimensions and modules of the self can be approached and evaluated in relation to a specific context.

Awareness of particular cognitive processes and operations develops gradually in close liaison with the functional state of the processes concerned. Specifically, Flavell, Green, Flavell, and Grossman (1997) have shown that mental operations related to imagery can be differentiated from operations underlying other processes, such as verbal reasoning, from about the age of six years. However, our studies (Demetriou and Efklides, 1989; Demetriou et al., 1993a) suggested that no differentiation between different problem-solving or reasoning strategies, such as mathematical and spatial problems, is possible before approximately age 13. At age 14, adolescents begin to differentiate between spatial thought and experimental or mathematical thought, although they cannot differentiate between experimental and mathematical thought. Some differentiation between these two types of thought appears initially at about age 16 culminating during the college years. The disparity between the findings of Flavell and colleagues and our own results is only apparent. We take it to indicate that at each phase of development individuals can become aware of any cognitive process or function under the condition that it is activated in a form which falls within the capabilities of this phase. In other words, awareness of cognitive functions recycles to follow the developmental changes in form and complexity of cognitive functions. These results also suggest that some processes are more transparent to awareness than others. For instance, imagery is more amenable to awareness than verbal or causal reasoning.

The differences and interrelationships between the various dimensions of intellectual competence are also elaborated during adolescence. For example, it is understood that difficulty involves a normative component. That is, that the more often persons succeed on a task, the easier that task is. At the same time, it is gradually understood that difficult tasks require more effort. Adolescents now begin to understand that effort can compensate for low ability only to a certain degree, and that while high ability is an advantage in general, it may not always suffice. Therefore, in adolescence, self-evaluations of intellectual competence and academic achievement become more accurate and more modest. A standard finding in this regard is a decline in self-evaluation scores and academic self-esteem from late childhood to early adolescence. Beginning in middle adolescence self-evaluations of performance become more domain-specific, more accurate, and generally more positive than at the beginning of adolescence (Eccles *et al.*, 1993; Nicholls, 1990; Phillips and Zimmerman, 1990; Stipek and MacIver, 1989).

The outline of development of the various aspects of self-evaluation and self-representation attempted above suggests a clear conclusion: although the same dimensions are always involved, self-evaluation and self-representation in regard to each other undergo extensive changes from infancy to adulthood.

The development of personality and thinking styles

Evidence related to the development of personality and thinking styles is less clear than that regarding the development of self-understanding about the various cognitive aspects of mind and the self. Specifically, there is evidence suggesting that the basic structure of personality remains invariant from early childhood. Costa and McCrae (1997), after reviewing a large body of research, concluded that "the five factor model of personality appears to apply equally well to school children, college students, and adults from the full age range" (p. 280).

It must be noted, however, that there is evidence to suggest that there are some developmental changes in the structure of personality. The studies reviewed by Kohnstamm and Mervielde (1998) suggest that three of the Big Five factors (i.e. agreeableness, extraversion, and conscientiousness) are more commonly found in childhood than are the other two (i.e. neuroticism and openness to experience). Moreover, these studies suggest that even when all Big Five factors are found in childhood they cannot account for young children's behaviour: two additional factors are needed which capture the particularities of children's behaviour and experience, namely, motor activity and dependency. These factors disappear in adolescence.

In addition to these structural changes, there seem to be developmental changes in the relative strength of each of the Big Five factors. There is evidence to suggest that, from adolescence to adulthood, individuals tend to become more conscientious, more emotionally stable, and more agreeable, but less extraverted and less open to experience (Costa and McCrae, 1997). Interestingly, the individual's position on the various scales seems to stabilize at about the age of 30 years, indicating that the variety of social roles we assume throughout our adult life, our experiences, and the many cultural changes we face and have to cope with "have little or no impact on basic personality traits. This fact should be the basis for a new perspective: Personality is not a product of the life course, an outcome or dependent variable, but a robust and resilient set of dispositions within the individual that themselves help shape the life course. People are not mere pawns of the environment, but active agents who steadfastly pursue their own style of being throughout life" (Costa and McCrae, 1997, p. 283).

Evidence related to the development of cognitive style is very similar, and suggests that the basic dimensions of cognitive style, such as reflection-impulsivity or field dependence-independence, are in place very early in life. Moreover, research indicates that an individual's position on these dimensions becomes stabilized rather early in development (Kagan, 1965; Witkin, Goodenough, and Karp, 1967), thereafter functioning as a factor of individual differences on measures of intellectual abilities (Zelniker, 1989), cognitive development (Pascual-Leone, 1989; Pascual-Leone and Goodman, 1979), and social skills. At the same time it is recognized that an individual's style is subject to change due to general intellectual growth, learning and experience. Pascual-Leone and Goodman (1979) have shown that field dependence decreases as short-term memory increases, and Globerson's research (1985) indicates that field-dependent individuals can be trained to act in an independent-like fashion. To date, there is no research on the development of thinking styles as specified by Sternberg and as discussed here.

Factors affecting the formation of the self-system

Baldwin (1894) was probably the first to clearly speak about the "bipolar self". This term conveyed his conviction that the self is gradually formed through a process of increased awareness of one's own experiences, projection of this awareness to other persons, and internalization of others' behaviour and experience through the process of imitation. Thus, Baldwin theorized that the formation of the self is a process in which the person herself and the others merge into an inextricable whole. Variations of this position continue to permeate theorizing about the construction of self-awareness in general and the formation of the various aspects of the self in particular. For instance, many infant researchers and theorists believe that the infant is born with an in-built ability to differentiate the self from the non-self and in-built *intersubjectivity skills*. These skills enable the infant to actively handle interpersonal interactions and continuously strengthen both a sense of the self and of others (Kougioumoutzakis, 1985; Meltzoff and Moore, 1995; Trevarthen, 1979).

Investigators of the child's theory of mind have also invoked self-observation and observation of others as a source of representations about the mind. These investigators assume that as children mature, they engage in activities and problem-solving which require them to activate different mental functions and which initially are frequently unsuccessful. For example, if an unpleasant thought pops into their mind which they want to stop, they may realize that this is not always possible as the thought continues to recur. Or, when asked to explain something, they may realize that they do not have all the necessary information and skills (Flavell, Green, and Flavell, 1995). Later, when children begin to engage in problem-solving activities in different domains at school, they gradually realize that each domain requires different mental operations. On these occasions, children gradually come to "see", so to speak, their actual mental processes as processes, rather than simply as products of the functioning of these processes, such that they become sensitive to the presence of different functions and purposefully act to make them work efficiently. This implies that the development of theories and problem solving about domains of the world is conducive to the development of both a general theory of mind and a self-centred theory which specifies the person's strengths and weaknesses in regard to the constructs involved in this general theory of mind.

On the other hand, it is also assumed that the contribution of social interactions is equally important in the discovery of the mind. The basic hypothesis is that problem-solving in humans frequently occurs in groups, where people have the opportunity to observe others trying to solve the same problem. Of course, what is going on in another person's mind is completely private; however, especially in environments targeted to problem-solving, such as the school, people exchange experiences. Through these exchanges, one may project her own mental experiences onto another and check for accuracy directly or indirectly. For instance, in schools, students present teachers with their work for comments and evaluation. These experiences generate information, concepts, hypotheses, and models related to one's own mind which gradually become more refined, focused, differentiated, and accurate (Demetriou and Efklides, 1994; Demetriou *et al.*, 1999a, 1999b; Nicholls, 1990; Stipek and MacIver, 1989; Stipek *et al.*, 1992).

The feedback provided by others is not always received as intended; frequently, it is filtered through the receiver's own representations of the sender and also through those representations the receiver believes the sender holds about him. Of course, the sender may adjust the feedback in terms of her own representations of the receiver as well as to how she believes the receiver interprets her representations. In other words, reciprocally reflected representations may be as important as moderators of ongoing interactions and self-concept formation processes as are the actual situations in which the interaction takes place and the first-order individual representations of the situation or the interactions. In fact, the symbolic interactionists (Cooley, 1902; Mead, 1925) have gone as far as to argue that the self is by and large what the individual thinks the others think about her. Cooley's view of the other as a looking glass is probably the strongest expression of this position. According to this view, the reflected appraisals of important others (i.e. the representations that a person has about another person's representations of him), are incorporated in one's own representations of the self and become part of one's self-concept.

Recent research suggests that these relationships are very complex. It was found, for instance, that the relation between reflected appraisals (i.e. what one believes that others think of one) and self-appraisals (i.e. what one thinks of oneself) is stronger than the relation between actual appraisals of important others and self-appraisals (Berndt, in press; Felson, 1993). This fact concurs with our earlier-stated assumption that there is global self-worth or a general feeling of self-efficacy, which is used to calibrate particular appraisals, either ascribed to the self or to others. In other words, persons tend to project to others their own self-representations. At the same time it raises a number of interesting questions about the source of the others' appraisals for the individual. For instance, to what extent do others' appraisals reflect the individual's actual ability and to what extent do they reflect the individual's self-appraisals? And if others' appraisals reflect both an individual's actual ability and this individual's self-appraisal, to what extent are they influenced by general dimensions of ability and self-representation, such as processing efficiency and global self-worth, as contrasted to domain-specific ability and corresponding self-appraisal?

It seems plausible that no generalized answer can be given to these questions, because the exact nature of relationships may vary from domain to domain. For instance, there may be functions, cognitive or others, which are more transparent to self-monitoring. We already reported that persons become aware of operations pertaining to spatial/imaginal thought earlier than they become aware of mathematical or causal reasoning. It is justifiable to assume that the relationships between the various types of appraisals would vary as a function of the differential amenability of different functions to monitoring by the self or the others. Moreover, the intersubjective space underlying reciprocal evaluations represents a very dynamic field, which may vary with time. This is particularly true for interpersonal relationships, which depend on development, such as the parent-child relationships. In this kind of relationships development can alter dramatically the condition of both actual abilities and processes and self-evaluation and self-representation, especially at certain critical periods. For example it was found that children as young as 2–3 years old are sensitive to the expectations of their parents and evaluations in regard to a variety of tasks (Stipek *et al.*, 1992). However, it is only during adolescence that self-evaluations tend parallel to the corresponding evaluations of parents (Oosterwegel and Oppenheimer, 1993). One of the studies to be presented in this book was designed to provide evidence that would highlight the dynamic interaction between cognitive abilities, self-evaluations, parents' evaluations, and reflected appraisals from childhood to adolescence.

Finally, it is important to understand the development of thinking styles in its various dimensions. Indeed Sternberg (1988; Ferrari and Sternberg, 1998) has theorized that thinking styles are modifiable during development. However, to our knowledge neither he nor anyone else has attempted to trace how they change with development or if changes occur in their relationships with various dimensions of cognitive abilities or of the self-system (Sternberg, personal communication, 21 October, 1997). Ferrari and Sternberg (1998) have recently pointed out that to understand how children develop requires new theories of intelligence that would integrate the development of mental abilities with the development of personality and thinking styles into a unified framework. They suggest that thinking styles are affected by parenting style (e.g. some parents encourage independence and originality more than others), schooling (e.g. some schools or teachers orient students to legislative occupations while others promote executive style activities; see Grigorenko and Sternberg, 1995), and culture (for instance, some cultures value self-autonomy and independence and others emphasize conformity and reciprocal support, see Triandis; 1989). To develop these theories requires evidence on the developmental interpatterning of changes in cognitive processes and abilities, the various aspects of self-evaluation and self-representation sketched above, and thinking styles. The studies to be presented in this book were designed to provide this evidence.

Questions to be investigated

The studies to be presented in this book aimed to highlight the structural, functional, and developmental interrelationships between various aspects of self-evaluation and self-representation, cognitive abilities and processes as such, and personality dispositions and thinking styles. Specifically, these studies were designed to answer the questions following:

1 The first question is related to the internal architecture of the hyper-cognitive system itself. The reader is reminded that our theory assumes that this system includes both working hypercognition, which refers to a cybernetic cycle of on-line self-monitoring and self-regulation vis-à-vis the goal requirements of the moment, and long-term hypercognition, which refers to the person's knowledge and beliefs, self-monitoring and self-regulatory skills, and strategies in regard to intelligence, cognition, and the self. Specifically, one of the primary objectives of this book is: (i) to map the dimensions and functions involved in these two types of hypercognition; and (ii) to specify their interrelationships.

2 A second issue refers to the interrelationships between the hypercognitive system and the systems involved in the other two levels of the mind. That is, how are domain-specific cognitive abilities, such as those involved in the SCSs, and more general cognitive functions, such as processing efficiency, memory and reasoning, represented in the hypercognitive system? In other words, does the hypercognitive system involve a kind of mental map in which both SCSs and general cognitive functions are distinctly represented? Our answer – which is stated as a prediction to be tested by the studies to be presented here – must by now be clear to the reader. That is, the existence of this map is a necessary derivation of the principle of self-mapping, which states that cognitive experiences which differ in their domain affiliation, computational identity, and symbolic bias are felt or cognized by the individual as distinct. In fact, without such a map, the hypercognitive system would be unable to exert its directive and interfacing functions at nodal points in the decision-making processes underlying problem solving. Moreover, our earlier discussion on the role of the processing system in the formation of global self-worth suggests that a direct link must exist between self-representations resulting from experiences of mental efficiency in general and the status of self-worth. However, the sparsity of related research does not allow accurate predictions about specific contributions of various cognitive abilities and processes to the formation of the various dimensions of self-representation.

3 How do an individual's profile of cognitive capabilities and personality dispositions and his self-profile in this regard interact to influence his ambitions and preferred lifestyle and orientations? For our research on these issues, we take two theories as a basis. Specifically, to specify the role of personality, we use the theory of the Big Five factors of personality. To specify the role of thinking styles, we use Sternberg's theory of self-government. Specifying the interrelationships between an individual's cognitive and personality profile to one of Sternberg's styles might allow us to predict, with relative accuracy, that individual's likely life orientation. For instance, those who regard themselves as strong on reasoning and reflection and they are open to experience would be directed more to activities which require originality and autonomy; individuals who are conscientious and see themselves to be systematic would be directed to executive-type activities; those who consider themselves as critical and evaluative are more likely to choose judicial-type activities.

4 All of the questions above focus on the individual. However, individuals do not develop or function alone. We have seen above that many scholars believe that the influence of others, parents in particular, are very important in the formation of both an individual's self-monitoring and self-management skills and of the individual's self-concept itself. Thus, another aim of the studies to be presented here is to highlight how children's abilities and self-representations contribute to the formation of their parents' representations and how the parents' representations feedback and influence children's abilities and self-representations. Based on earlier research, it can be predicted that parents do have views about the various cognitive and social/personality attributes and characteristics of their children (Miller, 1988, 1995), which change with development (van Aken, van Lieshout, and Haselager, in press). If the architecture proposed above is a strong characteristic of the human mind, we would have to expect that it would also structure the intersubjective space of mutual representations. That is, the systems and dimensions above must be present in both the self-representations and the representations that different persons hold about each other. If this is to be found true, it would imply that the architecture of mind proposed by our theory is a common language that can be used by individuals to negotiate their views and beliefs about each other.

5 Finally, the studies to be presented in this book aim to provide information on the development of the various aspects of the hypercognitive system, particularly possible changes in their interrelations with the SCSs and the processing system. Two major predictions can be stated in this regard. First, our theory posits that the hypercognitive system is a constructional hierarchical level of the human mind. This assumption suggests that a minimum degree of accuracy in self-representation and self-evaluation will always be discernible, if highlighted with means appropriate for each age.

Therefore, the mental maps of an individual's cognitive abilities, for example, should generally reflect the organization of his cognitive abilities, at any and all stages of life. Abilities applied to the environment always generate differential experiences which, once somehow recorded, constitute the raw material for the mental maps. Second, development in general is a powerful experience in and of itself. When we speak of cognitive development we are referring to a process which, by its very nature, enhances knowledge and awareness of both the environment and the subject of development, the developing individual herself. Therefore, at periods of major developmental change, we expect the accuracy of self-evaluations to be perturbed until the system enters a phase of relative stability. The eventual outcome will be that general self-evaluation and self-representation becomes more accurate and realistic. At the same time, it is reasonable to expect that there are systematic differences between persons in their ability to evaluate themselves, despite overall changes in this ability as a result of development.

2   Study 1

Structure and development of cognitive abilities, self-evaluation and self-representation

The first study to be presented in this book aims to provide evidence related to all but the fourth of the questions stated in "Questions to be investigated" in Chapter 1. That is, this study focused on the nature, interrelationships, and development of the following:

i   Certain self-evaluation processes involved in working hypercognition.
ii The various dimensions in the individual's self-representation and self-attribution of ability in relation to several thought systems.
iii Some of the thinking styles specified by Sternberg's theory of self-government.
iv Several general social/personality characteristics.

To examine these functions a rather complex research design was employed. According to this design participants solved problems addressed to different domains, evaluated their involvement in relation to these problems, and answered several inventories probing how they represent themselves in regard to the cognitive, social, and thinking style dimensions that are of interest to the study (see Table 2.1).

To investigate cognitive performance, the tasks targeted the following five of the seven specialized thought systems described in the introduction: the quantitative, the causal and the spatial SCS, and also social thought and drawing. In addition, the cognitive batteries included several tasks addressed to specific aspects of creativity. Therefore, the study addressed thinking processes traditionally associated with scientific reasoning and academic achievement (quantitative and causal thought), artistic thinking and skill (imaginal thought, drawing, and creativity), and social understanding and interaction (social thought). Analysis of the task batteries will provide the basis for specifying how different types of thought processes are represented at the level of the self-system and how they correlate with the various dimensions of personality and thinking styles.

Table 2.1 Experimental design and flow of testing events

Pre-performance evaluation	Solution of cognitive tasks	Post-performance evaluation	Self-representation
Tasks	*Tasks*	*Tasks*	A COGNITIVE SELF-IMAGE INVENTORIES
Quantitative	Quantitative ($\alpha = .623$)	Quantitative	1 Cognitive abilities
• Proportions	• Proportions	• Proportions	• Quantitative
• Algebra	• Algebra	• Algebra	• Causal
Causal	Causal ($\alpha = .606$)	Causal	• Imaginal
• Experimentation	• Experimentation	• Experimentation	• Social
Imaginal	• Hypothesis formation	Imaginal	• Drawing
• Mental Rotation	Imaginal ($\alpha = .500$)	• Mental rotation	2 General personal characteristics and strategies
Social	• Visual memory	Social	• General personal characteristics
• Understanding social relationships	• Mental rotation	• Understanding social relationships	• General cognitive strategies and characteristics
Drawing	Social ($\alpha = .583$)	Drawing	B THE THINKING STYLES INVENTORY
• Drawing of landscapes of varying complexity	• Understanding social relationships	• Drawing of landscapes of varying complexity	• Goal setting, planning, and problem solving strategies
	• Dialectical thought		• Occupational preferences and activity styles
	Drawing ($\alpha = .704$)		
	• Drawing of landscapes of varying complexity		
	Creativity ($\alpha = .704$)		
	• Ideational fluency		

Note

Participants were asked to evaluate the difficulty and the success of their performance on the tasks. Two tasks were always evaluated, an easy and a difficult task (see "Method" below).

For the purposes of the present study, self-evaluation refers to participants' evaluation of the difficulty of the various tasks and the adequacy or success of the solutions they gave to the tasks. That is, it refers to judgements about some aspects of the subjective experience generated at particular person-task encounters. Difficulty and success evaluation were probed separately in order to test our model's assumption (Demetriou, 1993, 1998a; Demetriou and Efklides, 1989; Demetriou *et al.*, 1993a) that these two aspects of the self-evaluation process are distinct from each other. For practical reasons, certain tasks (to be mentioned later) were excluded from this part of the study.

Moreover, each type of self-evaluation was twice assessed, i.e. before and after working on the tasks, in order to highlight the relationship between on-line and long-term hypercognition. Specifically, any evaluations made prior to solving a task are obviously related more to past experiences with similar tasks rather than to the present tasks. Therefore, these evaluations may show how long-term hypercognition affects working hypercognition. Evaluations produced after solving the tasks are obviously affected by the recent experience of working on the tasks. Therefore, this type of evaluation may show how working hypercognition contributes to the formation of the mental maps involved in long-term hypercognition.

Self-representation refers to how the individual perceives himself in regard to a given disposition, style, type of activity, or dimension of ability. That is, it refers to judgements that an individual makes about himself in regard to a dimension or attribute of ability or behaviour. In the present study, participants were examined with several inventories (see below) to investigate self-representation with respect to the cognitive realm, the social/personality realm, and thinking styles and activity preferences. The cognitive inventory addressed both domain-specific abilities and domain-general abilities. The social/personality inventory addressed general personal characteristics, such as ambition, self-control, and social orientations (i.e. self-autonomy and self-reliance versus reciprocal support and reliance on the social group). The thinking styles inventory addressed two dimensions of Sternberg's theory, namely functions (i.e. legislative, executive, and judicial) and forms of mental self-government (i.e. monarchic, hierarchic, oligarchic, and anarchic).

This brief outline of our experimental design makes it clear that, to a large extent, this is a confirmatory study. That is, this study was designed to substantiate several assumptions of our theory regarding the organization and development of cognitive abilities and processes and the individual's self-evaluation and self-representation in regard to these abilities and processes. Moreover, the study was designed to provide evidence that could be used as a basis for integrating cognitive development theory with theories related to the development of both the self-concept and thinking styles. Following, we will first describe the participants, tasks, inventories, and procedures of the study, and then state the hypotheses that will be tested by our study.

METHOD

Participants

A total of 840 participants from 10–15 years of age were examined (see Table 2.2). The study focused on this age span because it is highly interesting from two different points of view. First, it is well known (see Introduction) that during this period the systems and processes of all three levels of the mental architecture undergo major changes. Specifically, classic Piagetian (Piaget, 1950) and current cognitive developmental theories (Case, 1992; Case *et al.*, 1996; Demetriou, 1998a, 1998b; Fischer, 1980; Van Geert, 1994) assume that this period is associated with both major representational and strategic changes which alter the nature of thought, and also with more limited changes in the organization of cognitive processes. Specifically, it is posited that change at the age of about 11–12 are representational and strategic; later, in the period 13–15 years, changes are assumed to consolidate the achievements of the previous period and expand their range of application (see Demetriou, 1998a, Demetriou and Valanides, 1998). The present study will enable us to see how the two types of change are reflected in the development of the self-system itself. Our study will also allow us to see if different types of change in the self-system (e.g. changes in the accuracy of self-evaluations versus changes in self-representations) are associated with changes in different levels or dimensions of the mind or with changes in the relationships between these levels or dimensions.

A second reason for focusing on this age span is related to the project's focus on parental influences on self-system development (see the second study presented in this book). Specifically, we aimed to study the way in which changes in the individual's self-system interact with parental representations. Thus, we opted to focus on an age span which is associated with major (and thus easily observable) changes in the self-system in order to trace how these changes influence and are influenced by parents.

Except for the last age group, participants were drawn from three SES groups: working class families whose parents had received only primary education; lower middle class families whose parents had received secondary education; and upper middle class families where at least one parent had received university education. The last age group was drawn from upper middle-class families only. Thus, the study was designed to provide

Table 2.2 Composition and age (in months) of the sample

Age group	SES	Gender	1st wave N	2nd wave N	3rd wave N	Mean Age at 1st wave	Age range at 1st wave
10.5	Low	F	35	8	8		
		M	42	11	11		
	Middle	F	20	8	8	126	122–132
		M	26	8	7		
	Upper middle	F	16	9	9		
		M	15	9	9		
11.5	Low	F	32	8	7		
		M	37	8	8		
	Middle	F	24	8	8	139	135–145
		M	23	8	7		
	Upper middle	F	13	8	8		
		M	16	11	11		
12.5	Low	F	45	8	6		
		M	47	8	5		
	Middle	F	19	8	8	150	147–153
		M	21	12	10		
	Upper middle	F	10	7	7		
		M	14	10	7		
13.5	Low	F	52	5	5		
		M	47	7	7		
	Middle	F	9	8	4	163	158–168
		M	12	10	10		
	Upper middle	F	27	8	8		
		M	25	10	9		
14.5	Low	F	44	7	7		
		M	43	6	5		
	Middle	F	14	9	9	176	170–187
		M	13	9	6		
	Upper middle	F	24	11	9		
		M	19	8	7		
15.5	Upper middle	F	30	13	–	186	180–192
		M	26	7	–		
Total			840	275	230		

Note
The second wave took place 12 months after the first, and the third 12 months after the second wave.

evidence on the effects of social factors on the various dimensions of self-representation. It must be noted here that, although developmental psychology is showing increasing interest in the effects of these factors on development, the investigation of their possible effects on the dimensions of self-evaluation and self-representation studied here has been very meagre.

Finally, the two genders were about equally represented in each of the SES groups throughout the age spectrum represented in the study.

Task batteries and questionnaires

Six domains of thought or ability were represented in this study: the quantitative-relational, the causal-experimental, and spatial-imaginal domain,
social understanding, drawing, and creativity. Apart from creativity, two
types of measures were taken for each of these five domains: cognitive
performance measures, which reflected the solutions which the participants
provided to the tasks; and self-evaluation measures, which reflected the
participants' evaluation of their own performance on the tasks. Only cognitive performance measures were taken for creativity. These batteries will be
described below.

  These scales were generally reliable as the Cronbach's α (see Table 2.1)
ranged from .6 to .7 in all but the battery addressed to the spatial-imaginal
domain ($\alpha = .5$).

Cognitive batteries and scoring

The quantitative-relational tasks

The quantitative-relational tasks addressed two types of mathematical
thought, proportional reasoning and algebraic reasoning.

Proportional reasoning tasks

Participants were given two tasks systematically varying in difficulty,
both related to the effect of watering on plant productivity. For the level 1
task, participants were asked to determine how each of the two plants
watered twice a month (plants A and B produced 2 and 3 Kg/hectare,
respectively) or four times a month (the two plants produced 6 and
6 Kg/hectare) are affected by the increase in watering.

  For the level 2 task, the two plants were watered 2 or 4 times/month in
each of two fields I and II, under the condition of using/not using pesticides.
This task was presented in a 2 (plants A and B) × 2 (the two conditions of
pesticide use) × 2 (the two fields) × 2 (the two watering frequencies) data
table and the participants were again requested to specify the overall effect
of watering on the productivity of the two plants. Our earlier research
(Demetriou, Platsidou, Efklides, Metallidou, and Shayer, 1991) suggested
that the level 1 and the level 2 tasks can be solved, on average, by seventh
and ninth grade students, respectively.

Algebraic reasoning tasks

The participants were asked to solve the following three equations:

    i specify x, given that $x = y + 3$ and $y = 1$;
    ii specify x, given that $x = y + u$ and $x + y + u = 30$;
    iii when is it true that $L + M + N = L + P + N$?

It can be seen that the three tasks, which are based on Kucheman (1981), required coordination of well-defined, reciprocally defined, and undefined symbolic structures, respectively, in order to be solved (see Demetriou *et al.*, 1996). Three instead of two problems were used here to compensate for the complexity of the proportional reasoning tasks described above. Our earlier research suggested that item 1 can be solved by grade 7 students and items 2 and 3 by grade 9 students.

Scoring

The responses to the two proportional reasoning tasks were scored as 0 (no, irrelevant, or entirely wrong responses), 1 (correct responses with no explanation or explanations indicating insufficient grasp of proportionality), or 2 (fully correct and sufficiently explained responses). The responses to the algebraic reasoning items were scored as 0 (wrong) or 1 (correct responses).

The causal-experimental tasks

Five tasks addressed the causal-experimental SCS: two tapped the ability to design an experiment in order to test a hypothesis; the other tested the ability to integrate hypothesis with data into a comprehensive model.

The experimental tasks

The level 1 task tapped the isolation-of-variables ability in its simplest form. Specifically, the participants were asked to use any of four different kinds of seed (wheat, lentils, beans, and pines) to test if growing in a shadowy place as compared to a sunny place affects the plant growth rate. To solve this problem, the participants must be able to understand that the same kind of seed has to be used across the two conditions of light intensity.

    The level 2 task examined the participants' ability to design an experiment able to test a complex hypothesis. Specifically participants were asked to design an experiment to test the following hypothesis: "The productivity of wheat is not affected by increasing watering frequency (2 or 4 times/month) in field I but it is affected in field II, whereas the productivity of beans is not affected by increasing watering frequency in field I but is affected in field II." Our earlier findings (Demetriou *et al.*, 1993b) suggested that by 7th grade the level 1 task can be solved, and the level 2 task by 9th grade.

The hypothesis-evidence integration task

In the hypothesis-evidence integration task a 3 (three experiments) × 2 (two plants) × 2 (two areas) table was presented, showing the results of three experiments that were designed to test the hypothesis that a given "pesticide affects the productivity of wheat in cloudy areas but not in sunny areas whereas another pesticide has the opposite effect on the productivity of beans". The results were shown in kg/hectare, and in only one of the experiments were the four productivity figures consistent with the hypothesis. Participants were to answer three questions in reference to the table: (1) specify the experiment that produced results consistent with the hypothesis; (2) give three reasons to account for the different results; (3) state whether a hypothesis must be rejected when some of the experiments confirm the hypothesis and others yield inconsistent results. Our earlier research (Demetriou *et al.*, 1993b) suggested that this task can be solved at grade nine.

Scoring

The two experimentation tasks were scored as 0 (no, irrelevant, or entirely wrong responses), 1 (the kind of plant is kept constant in the level 1 experiment but the explanation given indicates insufficient grasp of the isolation-of-variables scheme; in the level 2 experiment some of the plant × field × watering combinations may be right), or 2 (a fully correct experiment and adequate explanations).

Each of the three items of the hypothesis-evidence integration task was scored as 0 (no, irrelevant or entirely wrong response), 1 (partially correct response indicating a basic understanding that a given hypothesis constrains the expected pattern of data), and 2 (fully correct responses indicating that the participants were able to translate the hypothesis into a complete model of expected and not expected results, and to understand that experiments may fail to produce evidence consistent with the hypothesis if extraneous variables are not fully controlled).

The spatial-imaginal tasks

Two types of spatial-imaginal tasks were used: mental rotation and visual memory tasks.

Mental rotation

The level 1 mental rotation task required participants to specify which of six alternatives depicting the letter B in various orientations is letter B. The level 2 mental rotation task required participants to specify which of six figures matches the three-dimensional object that would result from the rotation of letter Z around its oblique axis. Prior research in our laboratory (Loizos, 1992) indicated that the two items can be solved at grade seven and nine, respectively.

Visual memory

To test imaginal memory, a visual memory task was selected from the Kit of Factor Referenced Tests (Ekstrom, French, and Harman, 1976). For this task, participants were shown a target picture with various complex patterns of figures and given four minutes to study the figures and their relative placement in the picture. Participants were then given a set of 16 test pictures which supposedly included some of the patterns in the target picture and they were to specify ("yes/no") whether the pattern shown on each of the 16 test pictures was involved in the target picture (again, within a four-minute time frame).

Scoring

The mental rotation tasks were scored as 0 (choices of figures having no resemblance to the target stimulus), 1 (choices of figures resembling the target stimulus in some respects), and 2 (choices of figures fully representing the target stimulus).

The sixteen items of the visual memory task were scored on a pass/fail basis. These sixteen items scores were pulled into two mean scores.

Social thought tasks

Two types of tasks addressed social thought: interpersonal relationships and relativistic thinking.

Interpersonal relationships tasks

To test this domain two tasks were used, each of which presented an incident involving several characters whose behaviour and intentions affected each other in various ways. The first story was about two students, Kostas and Michalis, who concealed a third student's (Demetris') maths notebook, making the maths teacher scold Demetris and lower his grade. Subsequently, Michalis laughing "confessed" to Demetris, but Kostas apologised. Demetris answered them that he could no longer be Michalis' friend. Participants were asked (1) to discuss the teacher's behaviour and (2) to express their opinion as to who was most at fault. The second story was similar in both spirit and content, but the relationships among the characters were more complex. Subjects were given two questions similar to those for story 1. A pilot study conducted for the purpose of this project indicated that level 1 and level 2 tasks clearly presented differences in degree of difficulty and that, on the average, they could be answered by grade seven (story 1) and grade nine students (story 2).

Scoring

Responses to each of the two items in the tasks were scored as 0 (responses indicating that participants understood only the surface characteristics and external behaviour of the characters), 1 (responses indicating that participants considered several aspects of behaviour, although without any general integration of behaviours, intentions, and moral principles), or 2 (responses indicating that participants attempted to form a balanced evaluation of a character's behaviour on the basis of everybody's behaviour, intentions, and moral principles).

Relativistic thinking

The task chosen to address relativistic thought was first used by Chandler, Boyes and Ball (1990). The task presented a debate over extending the right to have a driving licence at the age of 16. According to story, parents argue against the right, citing evidence that adolescents break traffic rules and drive irresponsibly, while adolescents argue for the right citing evidence of their skilful and more accurate responses compared to older persons. Participants were to answer five questions related to this story:

1   specify both sides of the argument;
2   give reasons for the difference between the two arguments;
3   explain why each group invokes different evidence in relation to the same issue;
4   consider whether the two groups would have the same view if they had the same evidence;
5   discuss whether both groups can be right and the criteria on which they would have to base their decision.

Scoring

Performance on each of the five items involved in the relativistic thought tasks was scored as 0 (no, irrelevant responses or responses indicating that neither position is satisfactorily understood), 1 (responses indicating that only one position has been considered and all evaluations derive from that position), or 2 (responses indicating relativistic thought, i.e. both positions are considered when determining the relative importance of all evidence).

Drawing

For the drawing tasks (Case, 1992), participants were asked to produce a drawing for each of the following two statements:

Level 1 task   A man and a woman are standing hand-in-hand in the park. Their child is playing in front of them and a tree can be seen behind them.

Level 2 task   Draw three or more boats on the water at sunset. Some of the boats are close to you and others are further away. Try to draw the boats three-dimensionally. According to Case's (1992) findings, these tasks represent level 1 and level 3 of his vectorial stage, which are attained at grades seven and nine, respectively.

Scoring

Using Case's criteria (1992), performance on the two drawing tasks was scored as 0 (the elements – persons and objects – specified in the instructions are missing from the drawing or the drawing is very simplistic), 1 (the elements specified in the instructions may be present in the drawing but they are simply juxtaposed so that no organization can be discerned), 2 (the elements are present although they are given in outline and organized into a foreground, such that no three-dimensional organization may be discerned), 3 (the elements are clearly organized into an ensemble and there is clear differentiation between the foreground and the background), or 4 (the drawing satisfies all of the criteria associated with a score of 3, but also signifies skill in drawing as indicated by the accurate depiction of details in both the figures themselves and the details that signify the interrelationships among the figures).

Creativity

In order to test creativity, the Ornamentation and the Symbol test were selected from the Kit of Factor Referenced Tests (Ekstrom *et al.*, 1976). The authors considered that these two tests tap ideational fluency, which is regarded as a component of creativity.

The ornamentation test included two parts: in part 1, the outline of the upper part of 24 spoons are presented and the subject is asked to draw a different decorating figure in each of them; part 2 requires the same for 24 caps.

The symbol test also included two parts: in part 1, participants were to draw up to five symbols for each of the following concepts: library, close the door, sad, rush, keep off the grass; in part 2, subjects were asked to do the same for the following concepts: post office, open the window, happy, quiet, do not pick the flowers.

Scoring

Performance on these tests was scored according to the criteria described in the Kit of Factor Referenced Tests (Ekstrom *et al.*, 1976). Thus, each of these two tests was given two scores corresponding to the two parts involved in each of them. The two scores of the ornamentation test varied from 0 to 24 and the two scores of the symbol test varied from 0 to 25.

Tests addressed to self-evaluation and self-representation

Two types of self-awareness measures were taken: specifically, self-evaluation of the performance attained on many of the tasks described above; and self-ratings in regard to a number of cognitive, social, and personality characteristics. These are described below.

Self-evaluation tests

Participants were asked to evaluate two aspects of their experience of being engaged with most of the tasks described above: adequacy or success of solution and task difficulty. They were requested to give these evaluations twice, first before actually working on the tasks and then after having solved the tasks. Thus, four self-evaluation measures were taken: success and difficulty evaluation before (pre-performance evaluation) and after working on the tasks (post-performance evaluation).

Of the tasks described above only the following were targeted for self-evaluation: the two proportional thought tasks and the first and the third of the algebra reasoning tasks, the two experimentation tasks, the two mental rotation tasks, the two understanding social relationships tasks and the two drawing tasks. All self-evaluations were made in reference to a 7-point scale.

Pre-performance self-evaluation measures

A task battery was prepared for the pre-performance self-evaluation measures, in which the tasks were similar both in structure and in content with the actual to-be-solved tasks described above; only names and numbers were different. Participants were instructed "not to solve these tasks, but only to read each of them carefully and state whether [they] can solve it and how difficult it appears to [them]". There were two self-evaluation questions for each task:

1   Can you solve this problem? The 7-point scale varied from 1 (I can do nothing) to 7 (I can solve it very well).
2   How difficult does this problem seem to you? Answer this question irrespective of how you answered the question above. The 7-point scale related to these questions varied from 1 (it is very easy; I would have no difficulty) to 7 (it is very difficult; I find it difficult even to understand what I would have to do).

Post-performance self-evaluation measures

After solving the tasks that were involved in the batteries described above, participants had to answer the two self-evaluation questions following:

1   How happy are you with the solution you gave? That is, how correct do you think your answer is? The 7-point scale in regard to this question varied from 1 (it was completely wrong) to 7 (it was absolutely correct).
2   How difficult was this problem for you? That is, irrespective of how happy you are with your solution, try to express how difficult you found the problem and how difficult it was to solve it. The 7-point scale in regard to this question varied from 1 (it was very easy; I had no difficulty whatsoever) to 7 (it was very difficult; I found it difficult even to understand what I had to do).

Self-representation inventories

Three inventories were devised to obtain information on participants' representations of themselves as cognitive and social beings. The first inventory focused on the domains of thought represented by the cognitive and self-evaluation task batteries described above. The second addressed more general cognitive strategies and abilities, such as learning and reasoning, and also characteristics of the subjects' approach to everyday problems. The third addressed thinking styles. All three questionnaires included statements describing an ability, process, characteristic, disposition, or preference, and participants were to specify to what degree these were personally applicable. All statements were specified in reference to a 7-point scale (1 = "It does not apply at all" to 7 = "It applies very much").

Cronbach's α for the various scales is shown in Tables 2.3, 2.4, and 2.5

where it can be seen that these scales proved to be reliable as α ranged between .6–.7 for the most part, and sometimes was higher than .8.

The inventory on cognitive abilities

The statements in this inventory addressed five of the domains targeted by the task batteries, that is, quantitative, causal, spatial, social thought, and drawing (see Table 2.3). Creativity was not addressed in this inventory because there were items addressed to originality in the other inventories. All statements related to a domain were designed to tap several aspects or components of the domain.

Statements addressed to *quantitative thought* referred to the subject's facility in solving mathematical problems or applying mathematical knowledge to everyday problems (e.g. "I immediately solve everyday problems involving numbers"); the ability to induce or use mathematical rules (e.g. "I can easily derive the mathematical rules behind many specific examples"); and the facility to think in abstract symbols (e.g. "I prefer to think in terms of abstract mathematical symbols rather than specific notions"). Statements addressed to *causal thought* referred to hypothesis formation (e.g. "When something I use spoils, I usually make various guesses as to what might have caused it. I try to think of all the possible reasons that might have caused it"); experimentation (e.g. "To find out which of my guesses is correct, I proceed to methodically consider each time only the things my guess proposes"); and model construction ability (e.g. "From individual instances, I like deriving a general explanation for everything"). Statements addressed to *spatial thought* referred to visual memory (e.g. "I retain a very clear picture of things"); facility in thinking in images (e.g. "When I have to arrange things in a certain space, I first visualize what it will be like if I place them in certain way and then I arrange them in fact"); spatial orientation (e.g. "I orient myself easily in a strange place if I am given instructions"). The statements addressed to drawing referred to ability to draw a man, a landscape, and a map (e.g. "I can draw a person very accurately"; "I can paint a building as if it were a photograph"). Finally, the statements addressed to social thought referred to the facility in understanding other's thoughts and feelings (e.g. "I understand easily the intentions of others before they express them"; "I am interested in understanding others' problems").

Inventory on general personal characteristics and strategies

The questionnaire included two sections, one addressed to personal and the other to cognitive strategies and characteristics (see Table 2.4).

General personal characteristics

The questionnaire included 35 statements directed to participants' self-perception in regard to a number of general cognitive, emotional, and social dimensions. Specifically, there were items representing social status or position (e.g. "I like being the centre of attention"), self-control (e.g. "I know to control my feelings", "I control myself and I don't shout when I am arguing with someone"), preferred strategy in dealing with problems (e.g. "I prefer to face situations rationally rather than emotionally"; "I frequently ask others for help in the problems that are worrying me"), ambition (e.g. "I am an ambitious person"; "If I succeed in my ambitions, it will be good for others too"), social orientation (e.g. "I like doing things for the good of others, even if it is not in my own interest").

General cognitive strategies and characteristics

This section contained 35 statements to ascertain participants' self-representations as cognitive and thinking beings. Questions were directed specifically to self-assessment of one's feeling of one's own cognitive power or efficiency (e.g. "I feel I can sort everything out"; "I understand immediately when someone explains something to me"); learning ability (e.g. "I never forget what I learn"; "I retain a lot of elements of what I hear"), and the ability to process information logically and exhaustively (e.g. "I like going behind the surface of things and finding relations that others do not see"; "I like drawing logical conclusions, which can be justified by the data I have"), the ability to communicate conclusions to others in a coherent and convincing way (e.g. "I can explain what I mean clearly to others, even when it is about difficult issues"), logical argument (e.g. "I like drawing logical conclusions, which can be justified by the data I have"; "In discussions with others, I often examine whether what they are saying fits the reality"). This section also included a number of statements that aimed to reveal whether the subjects regarded themselves as primarily self-sufficient (e.g. "One gets good ideas by oneself"), or socially dependent cognitive beings (e.g. "When people discuss their ideas, they end up with better ideas").

The thinking styles inventory

This inventory included two sections, one addressed to Sternberg's forms of self-government and another addressed to functions of self-government.

Items	Factors	
	Drawing	Maths

Quantitative-relational thought

1 I like defining relations between things with mathematical accuracy.		.604
2 I prefer to think in terms of abstract mathematical symbols rather than specific notions.		
3 I can easily derive the mathematical rules behind many specific examples.		.685
4 I like converting rules into mathematical formulae.		.728
5 I like solving mathematical problems.		.764
6 I remember the mathematical formulae I have been taught.		.723
7 I can easily apply the mathematical rules I have been taught to new problems.		.714
8 I immediately solve everyday problems involving numbers.		.529

Causal-experimental thought

1 I always think that things may not be as they seem.
2 When I hear one interpretation of an event, I always think that it may not be the real one.
3 When something I use spoils, I usually make various guesses as to what might have caused it. I try to think of all the possible reasons that might have caused it.
4 To find out which of my guesses is correct, I proceed to methodically consider each time only the things my guess proposes.
5 And when I find that one guess is correct, I always remember that one of the others may also be correct.
6 From individual instances (e.g. I hear about different accidents occurring on different days in different parts of the country) I like deriving a general explanation for everything (e.g. that the Greeks are not good drivers or that the Greek roads are slippery).
7 I am ready to alter my explanation when I have evidence that contradict it.
8 When there are many ways to deal with a problem (e.g. there are three different medicines which can be used to treat an illness) it is preferable to choose the best way after the appropriate experiments.

Spatial-imaginal thought and drawing

1 When I bring to mind something I have read, I have a picture of the page in my mind.
2 Even if I meet someone once, I never forget the face.
3 I retain a very clear picture of things.
4 To understand a text, I convert the lexical description into pictures.
5 I orient myself easily in a strange place if I am given instructions.
6 In an unknown town, I understand very easily from a map where I have to go.
7 I like bringing to life in pictures in my mind those things or events which I have enjoyed.

Suppositional thought	Understanding others	Empathy	Visual memory	Experimentation	Spatial orientation	Mathematical symbolism
						.711
.498						
.659			.300			
.376						
				.492		
				.529		
				.670		
				.631		
.393						
			.589			
			.752			
			.724			
			.433		.395	
					.784	
					.766	
		.489				.387

Table 2.3 (continued)

Items	Factors	
	Drawing	Maths

8 When I have to arrange things in a certain space, I first visualise what it will be like if I place them in certain way and then I arrange them in fact.

9 I like drawing. .675

10 I like looking at paintings. .514

11 I can draw a person very accurately. .774

12 I can paint a building as if it were a photograph. .751

13 I can paint a landscape very well. .788

14 I can easily make a map of an area. .620

15 I can imagine new things and paint them so that everyone understands how I imagined it to be. .676

16 I can draw an animal running so that it seems lifelike. .682

Social thought

1 I understand easily what others are thinking before they express their thoughts.

2 I understand easily the feelings of others before they express them.

3 I understand easily the intentions of others before they express them.

4 I am interested in understanding others' problems.

5 I judge people's actions on the basis of their intentions, and not only on the basis of what they do.

6 To judge people's behaviour, you must take into account the context in which it takes place.

7 When someone says something, I frequently wonder what else he means.

8 When someone says something, I frequently wonder what motive he has.

Note
The Cronbach's α was tested separately for each set of items loading on a factor. The α for each of these factors was as follows: Drawing: $\alpha = .840$; Math: $\alpha = .829$; Suppositional thought: $\alpha = .628$; Understanding others: $\alpha = .777$; Empathy: $\alpha = .633$; Visual memory: $\alpha = .660$; Experimentation: $\alpha = .593$; Spatial orientation: $\alpha = .635$; Mathematical symbolism: $\alpha = .-111$.

Suppositional thought	Understanding others	Empathy	Visual memory	Experimentation	Spatial orientation	Mathematical symbolism
		.525				
	.719					
	.813					
	.741					
		.711				
		.613				
.407		.371				
.705						
.735						

Table 2.4 Items and varimax factor structure of the inventory on general personal characteristics and strategies and on goal setting, planning, and problem solving strategies.

Items	Factors				
	Ambition to excel	Impulsivity	Learning ability	System-aticity	Logical reasoning
General personal characteristics					
1 I know to control my feelings.					
2 When I work, I can conceal my feelings from others.					
3 I prefer not to do something if there is the slightest possibility of failing.					
4 First I decide to do something and later I consider the consequences.					
5 I frequently start something, even if I know that I might not accomplish it.					
6 One minute I am happy and the next minute I am sad without wishing to be.					
7 When someone makes a bad comment on my behaviour, I try to think if I was right or wrong.					
8 I am lost for words and I can not think when someone shouts at me.					
9 I control myself and I don't shout when I am arguing with someone.					
10 Instead of arguing with someone, I prefer to get up and leave.					
11 I consider how I should speak to someone so that I don't make him/her angry.					
12 In general, I am cool in the face of difficulty.					
13 If I insult someone and hurt him/her when I am angry, afterwards I think about it and apologise.					
14 When I am sad, nothing can put me in a good mood.					
15 I prefer to face situations rationally rather than emotionally.					
16 Without meaning to, I shout when I get angry.					
17 Even when I am afraid, I do not show my fear.	.704				
18 I do not let my fear overwhelmed me.					
19 I am an ambitious person.					
20 I like being the centre of attention.					

.533

.639

21 I want everyone to ask my opinion.
22 When I like something, I do it whatever others think.
23 I enjoy being admired by others.
24 I like doing things for the good of others, even if it is not in my own interest.
25 I like doing things to make others happy, even if it is not in my own interest.
26 For me, the most important thing is to achieve my goals, even if it upsets others.
27 If I succeed in my ambitions, it will be good for others too.
28 I set myself very distant targets and I try to achieve them however tired I may get.
29 I frequently ask others to do things for me.
30 I am an independent person.
31 I take care of my own needs by myself.
32 I frequently ask others to help me with my lessons.
33 I frequently ask others for help in the problems that are worrying me.
34 I manage well in my relations with other people.
35 I always succeed in solving my problems in the best way.

General cognitive strategies and characteristics

1 I think a lot about something I do not understand.
2 I try to make sense of complex situations.
3 I feel I can sort everything out.
4 I like thinking about complex things.
5 There are some things I will never understand whatever I do.
6 I like thinking about serious issues.
7 I like thinking of lots of different ways I can solve the same problem.
8 When I decide to think about something, I get lots of ideas.
9 When I decide to think about something, I put my thoughts in order, as I want, depending on the problem.
10 I like considering what the consequences of my actions will be.

Table 2.4 (continued)

Items	Factors				
	Ambition to excel	Impulsivity	Learning ability	System- aticity	Logical reasoning
11 When I have to do something, I think what the results of my action will be.					
12 When I am having difficulty understanding something, I prefer to think about it by myself rather than discuss it with someone.					
13 It is useful to have someone's help with something you are having difficulty understanding.					
14 I discuss with my parents about issues which can be discussed (e.g. social issues, scientific issues, etc.).					
15 I ask my teachers about issues which can be discussed (e.g. social issues, scientific issues, etc.).					
16 There are some things which you can understand only with the help of others.					
17 I like being the one with the best ideas about something.	.698				
18 I like being the one with the most original ideas about something.	.690				
19 I like it when everybody agrees with my ideas.	.474				
20 I like hearing other people's ideas.					
21 One gets good ideas by oneself.					
22 When people discuss their ideas, they end up with better ideas.					
23 When I try to understand an issue, I realise that more ideas come to me now than a year ago.					
24 As every week passes, I feel I can get more and more ideas about something.					
25 In the past, it was as if I didn't have a clue, now I know how to put my thoughts in order.					
26 I learn easily.			.585		

Item	Loading
27 I never forget what I learn.	.692
28 I understand immediately when someone explains something to me.	.590
29 When need be, I can immediately remember things I learnt a long time ago.	.696
30 I retain a lot of elements of what I hear.	.704
31 I like going behind the surface of things and finding relations that others do not see.	
32 I can explain what I mean clearly to others, even when it is about difficult issues.	
33 When I present arguments about some subject, I use all the information I have on the subject.	.553
34 I like drawing logical conclusions, which can be justified by the data I have.	.644
35 In discussions with others, I often examine whether what they are saying fits the reality.	.563

Goal setting, planning, and problem solving strategies

Item	Loading
1 I prefer to deal with one thing at a time.	
2 I am persistent: I don't rest until what I want is done.	
3 I like everything to be settled properly.	.491
4 I am single-minded: I only know what my mind tells me.	.542
5 When I set myself a target, all other targets are set aside.	.500
6 I frequently get absorbed in what I am doing and forget the other things I should be doing.	
7 I like having a lot of targets simultaneously.	
8 I set the order in which I will deal with various things depending on their importance.	.524
9 I deal with each matter as much as necessary when necessary.	.533
10 I enjoy complexity but also order.	
11 I do what is most important first and then the things that are less important.	.499
12 I organise my actions and I proceed systematically in order to achieve what I want.	

Table 2.4 (continued)

Items	Factors				
	Ambition to excel	Impulsivity	Learning ability	System- aticity	Logical reasoning
13 I know the jobs I have to do and I do them one by one.					
14 I have many, frequently conflicting, targets.					
15 I frequently examine an issue from many different angles.					
16 I like doing lots of things together.					
17 I have many ambitions in my life and I organise my actions to achieve them.					
18 Others think I don't have anything in order, but I know where everything can be found.					
19 I frequently find it hard to decide what I should do first and what second.					
20 I frequently have many things in my mind and I can't concentrate on my work.					
21 I always do what others tell me.		.426			
22 I do not sit and think what I have to do.		.682			
23 I frequently get confused when I try to do something.					
24 I can easily change the way I do something.					
25 When I have something I must do, I do the first thing that comes into my head.		.519			
26 When I have many things I must do, I do not stop to think which is the most important.		.634			

Note

The Cronbach's α was tested separately for each set of items loading on a factor. The α for each of these factors was as follows: Ambition to excel: α = .763; Impulsivity: α = .678; Learning ability: α = .757; Systematicity: α = .596; Logical reasoning: α = .679.

Table 2.5 Items and varimax factor structure of the inventory on occupational preferences and activity styles

Items	Factors			
	Professional responsibility	*Executive style*	*Legislative style*	*Evaluative style*
How I like to work				
1 I like working on problems for which there are no pre-prepared solutions.	.493			
2 I often look to see how things could be done better.			.625	
3 I often find problems where everybody thinks things are going well.			.608	
4 When I think about a problem, I often try to find solutions others have not thought of.			.595	
5 I like doing original things.			.482	
6 Quite often I get involved with problems which do not interest others.				
7 I like thinking of many ways I can solve a problem.				
8 I like choosing the best of various solutions.	.640			
9 When solving a problem, I prefer to follow existing rules.				
10 I prefer someone to tell me what exactly I should do, when I see a problem.				
11 When there is some problem, I try to think how others solve it.				
12 I like working where there are pre-defined rules of operation.		.584		
13 I get confused when there are no clear instructions as to how one should do something.				
14 If I find a solution to a problem, I do not look for others.				
15 I like deciding what is right and what isn't.	.627			
16 I frequently analyse why something is happening.	.658			
17 I often evaluate others on whether they are doing their work well.				.672
18 When I examine an issue, I try to understand what else happens at the same time.				.558
19 I like to judge others' choices.				.754
20 I frequently want to know whether people follow the rules by which they should do something.		.768		
21 I believe people should go by the rules.		.701		
22 I think that those who break a rule should be penalised.				.458

Note

The Cronbach's α was tested separately for each set of items loading on a factor. The α for each of these factors was as follows: Professional responsibility: α = .624; Executive style: α = .562; Legislative style: α = .514; Evaluative style: α = .592.

Goal setting, planning, and problem solving strategies

This section included 26 statements which addressed participants' self-perceptions regarding certain characteristics, strategies, and dispositions related to goal setting, planning, and acting. Specifically, this section targeted characteristics of general cognitive style, such as the tendency to be organized and systematic or impulsive. By and large, this section of the inventory examined the styles associated by Sternberg with the forms of self-government. That is, there were items which addressed the monarchic style (e.g. "When I set myself a target, all other targets are set aside"), the hierarchic style (e.g. "I set the order in which I will deal with various things depending on their importance"), the anarchic style (e.g. "I frequently find it hard to decide what I should do first and what second"), the oligarchic style ("I have many, frequently conflicting, targets"); finally, several items addressed dominant ways of behaviour (e.g. "I always do what others tell me", "When I have something I must do, I do the first thing that comes into my head").

Occupational preferences and activity styles

This section comprised 22 items, addressed to Sternberg's styles in terms of functions of self-government (see Table 2.5). Thus, the items probed participants' self-representations in relation to activities and occupations requiring a legislative style (e.g. "I like working on problems for which there are no pre-prepared solutions"; "I like thinking of many ways I can solve a problem"), an executive style (e.g. "When solving a problem, I prefer to follow existing rules"; "I prefer someone to tell me what exactly I should do, when I see a problem"), or a judicial or evaluative style (e.g. "I often evaluate others on whether they are doing their work well"; "I like to judge others' choices").

Procedure

The participants were tested in groups during school hours. They were given three booklets, the first containing the pre-performance evaluation tasks, the second the actual tasks to be solved and the post-performance evaluation questions, and the third the three self-representation questionnaires and the tasks from the Kit of Factor Referenced tests (i.e. the visual memory and the creativity tests). The booklets were compiled so that the presentation order of tasks and questionnaires within booklets was randomised across subjects. The testing was completed in two days separated by a period of about one week, with the first two booklets to be completed on one day and the third booklet on the next. Each testing period lasted about two hours.

HYPOTHESES TO BE TESTED

Our earlier discussion on the organization and development of abilities, self-evaluations, and self-representations (see Introduction) and the explication of the design of the study provide the background and justification for the following hypotheses.

2.1 *Performance on the tasks addressed to different systems of thought should be organized in differentiable structures.* The reader is reminded (see Table 2.1) that the following systems were involved: quantitative, causal, spatial, and social thought, drawing, and creativity. Thus, each of the sets of tasks used addresses a different domain, involves different types of mental operations and processes, and is biased toward a different symbol system. According to modern theories of cognitive development (e.g. Case, 1992; Demetriou, 1999a, 1998b), intelligence (e.g. Gardner, 1983; Gustaffson and Undheim, 1996), and personality (e.g. Graziano *et al.*, 1997), these reasons are enough to justify the expectation of modularity in the organization of intellectual processes. Moreover, a hierarchical organization is also to be expected, because some domains share common processes. For example, quantitative and causal thought share deductive and analytic reasoning, while spatial thought and drawing share visualisation and holistic and intuitive reasoning. Therefore, it is to be expected that there should be higher order organizations subsuming domains whose basic reasoning processes and strategies are similar.

2.2 *Self-evaluation measures should be organized into structures similar to the structures underlying performance.* That is, in terms of confirmatory factor analysis, the two types of self-evaluation (i.e. difficulty and success) should be distinct, and each type of self-evaluation measure should involve the same domain-specific factors as performance itself (i.e. factors representing the various domains of thought). The differentiation between difficulty and success evaluation would indicate, based on our assumptions about working hypercognition, that difficulty and success evaluation are separate functions. The differentiation between ability-specific factors in each type of self-evaluation would indicate, in accordance with the principle of self-mapping, that the self-representation maps of the hypercognitive system represent the dynamics underlying the organization of actual cognitive performance. It must also be expected that there should be different sets of domain-specific factors for each measurement occasion, i.e. factors representing success and difficulty evaluation before and after performing the tasks. This pattern would be consistent with the assumption that self-evaluations made under different circumstances reflect different degrees of involvement of working and long-term hypercognition and different states of ability.

2.3 The assumption of self-mapping suggests that *the self-representations of cognitive abilities addressed by the cognitive self-image inventory should be organized in the same structures to be abstracted from performance* (Adekoya, 1994; Demetriou and Efklides, 1989; Demetriou *et al.*, 1993a, Study 3; Efklides, Demetriou, and Metallidou, 1994; Makris, 1995). In fact, if combined with the first two hypotheses, this hypothesis states that the forces defining the organization of cognitive performance (hypothesis 2.1) first define the on-line representations involved in working hypercognition (hypothesis 2.2) and through it are eventually projected onto the level of long-term hyper-cognition (hypothesis 2.3). Thus, each individual possesses a map of his own mind which can accurately direct any necessary decision-making related to problem-solving.

2.4 The present study is also concerned with several dimensions of personality and thinking styles. Two complementary hypotheses can be stated in this regard. First, the literature on self-representation and person-ality (e.g. Costanzo, 1991; Graziano, Jensen-Campbell, and Finch, 1997; Harter, 1998) suggests that *various differing personality/social dimensions*, such as ambition, social orientation, and self-control should be abstracted from the individual's social self-representation. Second, provided that the inven-tory addressed to thinking styles was based on Sternberg's theory (1988), it is also to be expected, that *thinking styles should be abstracted as autonomous dimensions of self-representation*.

2.5 The hypotheses above convey the assumption that the human mind is a modularized edifice at both the level of cognitive abilities and functions themselves and the level of the self-representation of these abilities and func-tions. Although accurate, this assumption is incomplete as a representation of the human mind. It has already been emphasized in the introduction that all theorists of the self agree that a primary property of the self-concept is its unifying or integrative function. This is attained through such overarching constructs as the Freud's ego (Freud, 1923), Erikson's identity (Erikson, 1963), James's ideal self (James, 1892), Harter's global self-worth (Harter, 1990, 1998, 1999), and other similar constructs. It is to be expected, if these constructs are to be accorded any descriptive or interpretative value, that a minimum degree of cohesiveness should overarch domain-specific self-evaluations and self-representations. In technical terms, this implies that all kinds of self-evaluation and self-representation should covary above a certain – as yet unspecified – minimum. Where does this come from? With regard to origin, the reader is reminded that it was assumed that a general feeling of cognitive efficiency must derive directly from the functioning of the pro-cessing system. Therefore, it is to be expected that self-representations related to general cognitive efficiency must be related more to general cogni-tive processes rather than particular domain-specific modules of ability. These self-representations of general cognitive efficiency must also affect self-representations about particular domains. That is, self-representations of general cognitive efficiency are used to shape self-representations about particular domains, possibly in combination with domain-specific experiences and feelings.

2.6 Development may affect any of two very different aspects of the mind: it may affect the organization and the relationships between cognitive processes and functions, or their efficiency of application vis-à-vis the demands of the present situation or both. Our previous studies (Demetriou Gustaffson, Efklides, and Platsidou, 1992; Demetriou *et al.*, 1996) have shown that the basic structure of the environment-oriented systems is stable during development, although their relationships with the domain-general systems may vary somewhat, particularly at periods of major developmental changes. For instance, learning experiments designed to accelerate the development of causal and quantitative thought have shown that a psychometrically defined general factor is more important at puberty rather than later in life. Admittedly, these studies did not directly examine the relationships between the self-oriented level and the other two levels of the mind. However, our findings would support the assumption that the relationships between the environment-oriented systems and their respective self-representations would become stronger with increasing age, although all systems and dimensions in the cognitive architecture would be present at all age levels involved in the study. This finding would indicate that development enhances the communication between the various modules and levels of mind.

In terms of efficiency, it would be trivial to assert that cognitive abilities improve with age. However, with respect to self-representations, it is a consistent finding that self-evaluations tend to be on the positive side until late childhood, becoming more negative at the beginning of adolescence, and rising thereafter to become more differentiated and accurate. Based on this fact, it is to be expected that the various dimensions of self-representation involved in this study will follow a U-shaped developmental course, with the lower point of the curve associated with beginning adolescence. In fact, this developmental pattern is consistent with the assumptions above about the possible changes in the relationships between the levels of mind. That is, when this communication becomes better established, the accuracy of self-evaluations and self-representations improves. It is to be noted, however, that the lack of information directly concerned with the development of the dimensions of self-representation examined in this study does not allow a more specific hypothesis about possible differences in the developmental course of the various dimensions.

3   Results I

Levels, dimensions, and domains in performance, self-evaluation, and self-representation

The results of this study will be presented in the following two chapters: the first of these chapters will analyse the data on structure. That is, this chapter will explore the various dimensions involved in the various systems and levels of mind and the relations between these dimensions. Chapter four will focus on data related to development *per se*, and individual differences in development, and specifically, will first discuss the effects of various individual characteristics (i.e. age, gender, and SES) on the structure of abilities and process. Then Chapter 4 will focus on the attainment of the abilities and characteristics represented by the various dimensions of mind as specified in the chapter focusing on structure.

The reader is reminded that three different types of measures were obtained. First, a series of cognitive tasks addressed to several cognitive abilities; second, a series of inventories addressed to self-awareness about processes and experiences activated by the cognitive tasks; third, a series of inventories aimed to probe self-representations about several general and specific cognitive abilities, strategies, attitudes, and styles. Thus, analyses of structure comprised two parts. A first series of analyses aimed to identify the dimensions involved in the three types of measures obtained: that is, actual performance, self-evaluation, and self-representation. Specifically, performance on all cognitive tasks was analysed to verify that our selection of cognitive tasks was empirically valid. Another set of analyses focused on the participants' self-evaluations of performance on the various tasks, to clarify the organization of these evaluations and test whether it matched the organization of actual performance. A further set of analyses focused on the structure of the participants' responses to the various self-representation questionnaires. Finally, a series of analyses aimed to investigate the relationships between the various dimensions of cognitive abilities, self-evaluation, and self-representation.

The structure of cognitive abilities, self-evaluation, and self-representation

Cognitive abilities

The cognitive battery included tasks addressed to quantitative-relational, causal-experimental, spatial-imaginal and social thought, and drawing and ideational fluency. The reader is reminded that participants responded to five quantitative-relational items (three algebraic and two proportional reasoning tasks), five causal-experimental items (two experimentation and three hypothesis-formation items), four spatial-imaginal thought items (two mental rotation items and the two scores given to performance on the visual memory test), two drawing items, nine social thought items (two for each of the two understanding social relations tasks and five for the relativistic thinking task), and several ideational fluency items that were reduced to four scores (two for the ornamentation test and two for the symbol test).

Confirmatory factor analysis was used to explore the structure of abilities underlying performance on these tests. For the purposes of this analysis, performance in all domains was reduced to two homogeneous mean scores whenever possible (see Bentler, 1989; Demetriou *et al.*, 1993a), such that all developmental levels and subdomains were represented in each of the two mean scores representing a domain. The analysis was therefore made on the basis of 16 scores: two quantitative-relational, two causal-experimental, two social, two mental rotation, two visual memory, two drawing, two ornamentation, and two symbol creation scores. Reducing a large number of raw scores to a limited number of representative scores has been suggested by proponents of structural modelling for two reasons (Gustafsson, 1988, 1989). First, this manipulation increases the reliability of the measures fed into the analysis, thereby facilitating the identification of latent variables or factors. It is vital for the researcher to be sensitive to factor identification problems when using this approach, because these methods pose strong demands on the reliability of the measures analysed. Second, structural modelling is very demanding in computing power. Thus, reducing observed variables to a minimum enables one to explore models that might be impossible to specify.

A direct higher-order or hierarchical-factor method (see Demetriou *et al.*, 1993a, in press; Gustafsson, 1994) was employed to specify the dimensions underlying performance on the cognitive tasks. This method was selected because it is a highly restricted and hence highly accurate method for testing the model of interest; moreover, it can directly test structural relationships between factors and dimensions.

The complete model (see Figure 3.1) which is consistent with the theory involved three types of factors. That is, it involved eight first-order factors,

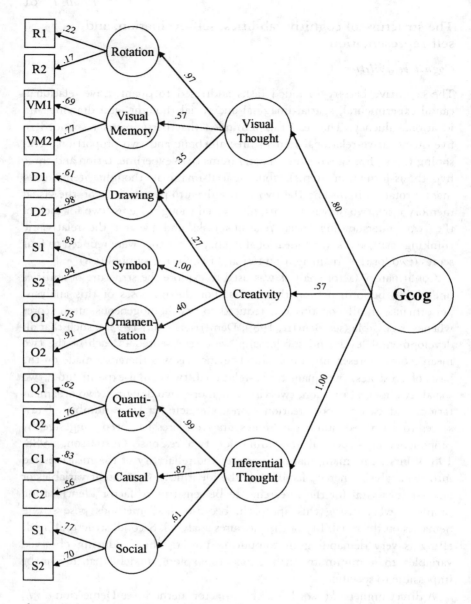

$\chi^2(80) = 98.407, p = .080, \text{CFI} = .995, \text{GFI} = .986, \text{AGFI} = .975, \text{SRMR} = .027, \text{RMSEA} = .017$

Figure 3.1 The general model of performance on the cognitive tasks

one for each of the domains or subdomains represented by the pairs of half-scores. These factors were regressed on three second-order factors. Specifically, the factors standing for quantitative, causal, and social thought were regressed on one factor. All tasks addressed to these domains involved well-defined problems primarily solved deductively. Therefore, this factor is taken to represent thought involving analytical and primarily convergent inferential thought processes. The factors representing mental rotation and visual memory were regressed on another second-order factor. Drawing was also allowed to correlate with this factor because of its strong visual component. Therefore, this factor is taken to represent visual thought, which requires primarily mental visualization and holistic thought processes. The two factors representing ideational fluency were regressed on another second-order factor. The drawing factor was also allowed to correlate with this factor, because it was assumed that drawing requires a certain degree of inventiveness, even when there are specific instructions about the object of drawing. Therefore, this factor is taken to represent creativity and divergent thought. Finally, all three second-order factors were regressed on a common third-order factor. This factor is obviously very close to the general factor of psychometric theories of intelligence. In terms of our theory, this factor may be taken to represent three types of processes which underlie performance on any task. Specifically, it represents processing constrains related to the processing system, general self-monitoring and self-regulation processes related to the hypercognitive system and general inferential processes that underlie every kind of meaning making and information integration. However, the present study does not contain measures enabling these three domain-general systems to be directly dissociated. This model was tested under the constraint that the error variances of each pair of half scores associated with the same factor would have to be equal. This constrain is based on the assumption that half scores have similar reliability. The fit of this model was good, $\chi^2(101) = 299.577$, p = .001, CFI = .956, GFI = .957, AGFI = .942, SRMR = .043, RMSEA = .048. Releasing the equality constraints resulted in a large improvement of the model fit, $\chi^2(92) = 213.641$, p = .001, CFI = .970, GFI = .968, AGFI = .954, SRMR = .035, RMSEA = .039. Finally, allowing a few of the error variances to correlate resulted to an excellent fit of the model, $\chi^2(80) = 98.407$, p = .080, CFI = .995, GFI = .986, AGFI = .975, SRMR = .027, RMSEA = .017. It needs to be noted that the introduction of these correlations between the error variances did not affect the parameter estimates of the model.

Factor loadings of this model suggest that all factors apart from the factor representing mental rotation were very powerful. Moreover, it must be noted that, not unexpectedly, the inferential thought factor correlated most closely with the quantitative thought factor and least with the social thought factor. The visual thought factor correlated most with the mental rotation factor and least with the drawing factor. The creativity factor correlated most with the symbol creation factor and least with the drawing factor. Finally, the general factor correlated most to the inferential thought factor and least with the creativity factor.

One might object here that a more parsimonious model than the three-level model presented above might fit the data equally well. In a case such as this, the more parsimonious model could of course be preferable over the more complex model. To test this possibility, four alternative models were tested. The first model involved only one factor which was related to al 16 scores. The fit of this model was very poor $\chi^2(104) = 1841.679$, p $= .001$, CFI $= .561$. The second model involved only the eight first-order factors. These factors were taken to be uncorrelated with each other. The fit of this model was also very poor, $\chi^2(112) = 1419.548$, p $= .001$, CFI $= .670$. The third model involved the eight first-order factors and the three second-order factors. The three second-order factors were taken to be uncorrelated with each other. The fit of this model, although better than the fit of the two models above, was still poor, $\chi^2(103) = 588.372$, p $= .001$, CFI $= .877$. Finally, the fourth model involved the eight first-order factors and the general third-order factor. The fit of this model was still poor, $\chi^2(104) = 393.669$, p $= .001$, CFI $= .927$, and in any case much worse than the fit of the model involving all factors, $\chi^2(101) = 299.577$, p $= .001$, CFI $= .956$. In fact, the difference between the fit of these two last models was significant, $\Delta\chi^2(3) = 94.112$, p $= .001$. Therefore, all three types of factors are needed to account for performance on the cognitive tasks used in this study.

Therefore, it can be concluded, confirming hypothesis 2.1, that the dimensions which guided the construction of the various cognitive batteries were found to be present in participant performance on these batteries. This finding is important because it sets the stage for exploring the relationships among these cognitive dimensions and the various aspects of self-evaluation and self-representation. Nevertheless, some scores proved more reliable than others. At the one extreme, the scores for the quantitative-relational SCS showed zero error variance; at the other extreme, the error variance of the two mental rotation scores was high. These two scores were therefore excluded from certain analyses to be reported below.

Self-evaluation of cognitive abilities

For two of the items addressed to each of the quantitative-relational, the causal-experimental, the spatial-imaginal, the drawing, and the social domain, the participants were asked to evaluate their success and degree of item difficulty both before and after completing the items. This allows testing whether the structure of the abilities under consideration, which is reflected in the subjective experience caused by these self-evaluations, is the same as the structure underlying performance itself. It also allows testing of the relationships between each of the two aspects of self-evaluation.

A complex structural equations model was first fit to the five pairs of preperformance success and the five pairs of pre-performance difficulty evaluation scores. The following constructs were involved in this model, which is depicted in Figure 3.2.

1 Five first-order SCS-specific factors for each of the two sets of scores. In other words, each pair of scores representing an SCS in each of the two types of evaluation was prescribed to load on a different factor. Identifying a separate factor for each SCS for each type of evaluation would support the hypothesis

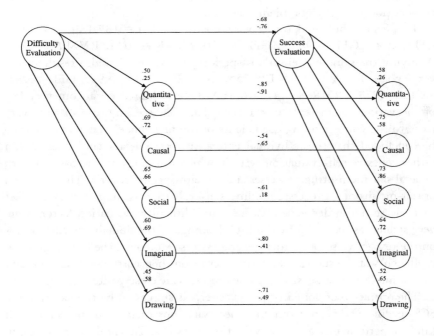

$\chi^2(113) = 137.139$, p = .061, CFI = .995, GFI = .984, AGFI = .970, SRMR = .034, RMSEA = .016 (pre-performance evaluations)
$\chi^2(116) = 128.555$, p = .201, CFI = .999, GFI = .985, AGFI = .973, SRMR = .041, RMSEA = .011 (post-performance evaluations)

Figure 3.2 The model of self-evaluation of cognitive performance

Note
The first value of each pair refers to pre-performance evaluations; the second refers to post-performance evaluations. Negative correlations indicate the reverse tradeoff between feelings of difficulty and evaluation of success.

that the forces underlying performance are registered by working hypercognition during on-line processing.

2 The five SCS-specific factors of each of the two types of evaluation were prescribed to load on a common second-order factor. This factor can be taken to represent the different processes involved in each of the two types of evaluation. This would support our assumption that difficulty and success evaluation are two distinct aspects of working hypercognition, which have their distinctive characteristics and processes that operate across different types of tasks.

3 To specify the relationships between the two types of evaluation each of the five SCS-specific factors and the general success evaluation factor were regressed on their corresponding difficulty evaluation factors. Building this relation into the model results from the assumption that feelings of difficulty generated during processing influence, at least to a certain extent, how the solution given to a problem is evaluated.

The fit of this model was very good, $\chi^2(113) = 137.139$, p = .061, CFI = .995, GFI = .984, AGFI = .970, SRMR = .034, RMSEA = .016. Applying the same model on post-performance evaluation also resulted in a very good fit, $\chi^2(116) = 128.555$, p = .20, CFI = .999, GFI = .985, AGFI = .973, SRMR = .041, RMSEA = .011. Moreover, all but very few of the various coefficients in the second model (see Figure 3.2) were very close to the corresponding coefficients of the first model. Therefore, it is to be concluded that the individual enters each person-task encounter with a rather cohesive self-evaluation system, which functions on the basis of both general self-monitoring processes and domain-specific criteria. The operation of self-monitoring processes guiding self-evaluation is suggested by the fact that the second-order general success and difficulty evaluation factors were very strong, as indicated by the high loadings of the domain-specific factors on the respective second-order general factors. Moreover, the high regression coefficients of the success evaluation factors on their corresponding difficulty evaluation factors suggest that these processes are closely interrelated.

The operation of domain-specific criteria is suggested by the fact that the SCS-specific factors are required as necessary constructs of the model over all kinds of performance and self-evaluation measures. This finding indicates, in agreement with our earlier research (Demetriou and Efklides, 1989; Demetriou *et al.*, 1993a), that the hypercognitive system involves an accurate map of the ability systems underlying cognitive performance. Self-evaluations of performance are based directly on this map.

Therefore, it can be concluded, confirming hypothesis 2.2, that the systems of ability underlying performance are preserved during on-line self-evaluation of different aspects of problem solving, such as the feelings of difficulty and the evaluation of the solution given to problems. This finding sets the stage for the exploration of the relationships between self-evaluation and actual performance or other more enduring dimensions of self-representation. In the section following we will first explore the various aspects of self-representation and then focus on these dynamic relationships among the various dimensions of ability and self-awareness.

Self-representation of cognitive abilities

The questionnaire on abilities probed the participant's self-representation in regard to various components of the cognitive abilities examined in this study. Exploratory factor analysis was first used in order to examine if the factors that guided the construction of this questionnaire (that is, our various SCSs) are present in the participants' responses. This approach was adopted because this was the initial trial of the questionnaire and therefore there was no previous information regarding the underlying dimensions involved. Specifically, all 40 items in this questionnaire were subjected to a common factor analysis, which resulted in nine factors with an eigen value greater than 1; these factors accounted for 54.8% of the total variance. These factors were then subjected to varimax rotation and the rotated factor matrix is shown in Table 2.3.

The factors abstracted confirm our prediction in terms of the dimensions underlying self-representation. Specifically, the first factor represents drawing ability as all items concerning drawing loaded on this factor. The second factor represents the quantitative SCS as all but one (item 2) item related to mathematics loaded on this factor. The third factor loaded heavily on three social thought items related to the tendency to evaluate others' behaviour on the basis of both their actions and their underlying motives and intentions (e.g. items 7 and 8). Interestingly enough, this factor also loaded on three causal thought items referring to a hypothetical attitude towards the physical world (e.g. items 1 and 2). Therefore, this factor might be seen to represent hypothetical and suppositional thought. It is reminded that this kind of thought allows the formation of alternative hypotheses about the underlying causal structure of the social or physical world. Our theory posits that this is one of the basic components of the causal-experimental SCS. The fourth factor loaded on the three social thought items related to the ability to understand others, and so represents the social understanding. Factor five seems to duplicate the two previous factors as it loaded primarily on one item related to social understanding (item 4) and one item representing the suppositional approach to other's behaviour (item 5). Factor six is clearly the visual memory factor, as it loaded on all items representing this ability. Factor seven represents experimentation (item 4) and the model construction (item 6) ability as it loaded on items representing these two components of the causal-experimental SCS. Factor eight represents spatial orientation ability, as it loaded primarily on the two items related to the ability to orient in space (items 5 and 6). Finally, factor nine proved very narrow, as it loaded primarily on only one item (item 2) of the mathematical thought section related to the use of mathematical symbols.

In conclusion, all abilities represented in the cognitive batteries were also abstracted as independent factors from participants' self-descriptions. This result confirms hypothesis 2.3, which states that the subjective structure of abilities reflects its objective structure. However the presence of the same type of factors at both performance and self-representation levels does not in itself indicate the interrelationships among the various factors. This is the question to be answered below.

To clarify these interrelationships the hierarchical-factor method was again employed. The model was fitted on a series of mean scores representing the various dimensions of self-representation; i.e. to identify the self-representation factors, two mean scores were created for most factors abstracted through exploratory factor analysis. Specifically, two mean scores were created for subjective drawing (factor 1), subjective quantitative (factor 2), subjective understanding others (factor 4), subjective visual memory (factor 6) and subjective experimentation (factor 7). The general suppositional thought factor (factor 3) was broken into two pairs of mean scores, one for suppositional thought applied to the physical world and one for the same type of thought applied to the social world. Factors 5, 8, and 9 were discarded because they either duplicated other factors or were very narrow. Therefore, this analysis was applied on 14 mean scores, in pairs taken to represent seven self-representation domains.

A model very similar to that applied on the 16 cognitive performance half scores was applied to the 14 self-representation scores. Our model comprised seven first-order factors, each representing a domain or subdomain identified by exploratory factor analysis, two second-order factors and one third-order factor. The visual memory and the drawing factors were related to a common second-order factor representing visual thought. The remaining five first-order factors were regressed on a common second-order factor. Thus, this factor may be taken to be the equivalent of the inferential thought factor of the model that was found to fit actual performance on the corresponding tasks. These two second-order factors were regressed on a general third-order factor. This factor is taken to represent that part of general self-representation related to cognitive functioning, because the present model comprised only scores reflecting self-representation in regard to the cognitive domain. This model was tested under the constraint that the error variances of each pair of half-scores related to the same factor are equal. The fit of this model was good, $\chi^2(75) = 191.903$, p = .001, CFI = .973, GFI = .969, AGFI = .956, SRMR = .041, RMSEA = .043. The fit of this model improved farther, $\chi^2(60) = 76.969$, p = .07, CFI = .996, GFI = .987, AGFI = .977, SRMR = .028, RMSEA = .018, when a few error variances were allowed to correlate (see Figure 3.3). Allowing the error variances to correlate did not affect the parameter estimates of the model.

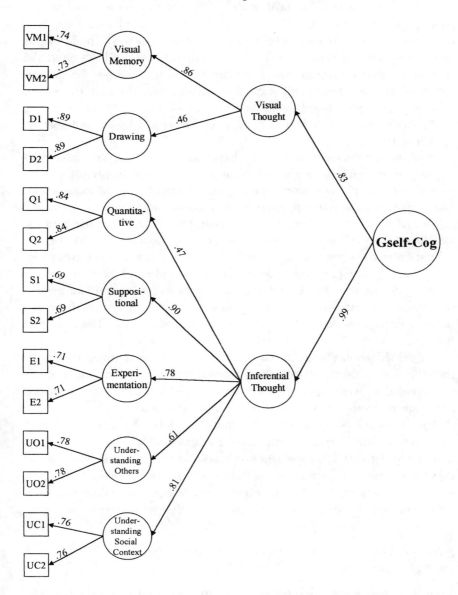

$\chi^2(60) = 76.969$, p = .067, CFI = .996, GFI = .987, AGFI = .977, SRMR = .028, RMSEA = .018

Figure 3.3 The model of self-representation of cognitive abilities

To test if a more parsimonious model would fit the data, a number of alternative models were run. A first model involved only one factor related to all 14 scores. The fit of this model was very poor, $\chi^2(77) = 1879.982$, $p = .001$, CFI $= .576$. An alternative model involved only the seven first-order factors involved in the final model. The fit of this model was also very poor, $\chi^2(84) = 1423.825$, $p = .001$, CFI $= .685$. A third model involved the seven first-order factors and the two second-order factors. The fit of this model was also not ideal, $\chi^2(77) = 464.780$, $p = .001$, CFI $= .909$. An alternative model involved the seven first-order factors and the general factor, which was related to all of the first-order factors. The fit of this model was acceptable, $\chi^2(77) = 211.765$, $p = .001$, CFI $= .968$. However, the fit of the model that involved all three types of factors was significantly better, $\Delta\chi^2(2) = 19.862$, $p = .01$.

It needs to be noted here that the hypothesis was tested that inferential thought is recognised by the person as a system that involves processes addressed to the physical world and processes addressed to the social world. This hypothesis was tested by creating two second-order factors to represent inferential thought, one related to the physical world and one related to the social world. Specifically, the quantitative, the suppositional, and the experimentation factor were related to one second-order factor and the two social understanding factors were related to another second-order factor; these two second-order factors were related to a third-order factor standing for general inferential thought processes. Finally this factor, together with the visual thought factor, were related to a general fourth-order factor. The fit of this model, $\chi^2(73) = 191.903$, $p = .001$, CFI $= .972$, was identical to the fit of the model shown in Figure 3.3 which involves only one common inferential thought factor directly related to all first-order respective factors. Thus, it was decided to retain this more restricted model which involves only one factor for inferential thought because it is more parsimonious.

The conclusion suggested by this model is clear: self-representation of cognitive abilities implicates the same domains and relationships as those underlying both actual performance on tasks addressed to these abilities and those underlying self-evaluation of this performance. In other words, the environment-oriented level of the mind, working hypercognition, and long-term hypercognition are organized according to the same domains.

Self-representation of general personal characteristics and strategies, and thinking styles

There were four inventories: the first inventory (General Personal Characteristics) comprised 35 items addressed to social and personality characteristics; the second inventory (General Cognitive Strategies and Characteristics) comprised 35 items addressed to general strategies and characteristics in terms of learning, thinking, and reasoning; the third (Goal Setting, Planning, and Problem Solving Strategies) included 26 items addressed to preferred strategies for organizing both everyday and long-term activities and is related to Sternberg's form of self-government; finally, the fourth inventory (Occupational Preferences and Activity Styles) included 22 items addressed to preferred style of thinking and activity in terms of various characteristics related to different professions and is related to Sternberg's functions of self-government.

Because these inventories were first used in the present study, exploratory factor analysis was applied to each of them to identify the dimensions underlying participants' responses. The analysis applied to the first, second, third, and fourth inventory yielded 11, 10, 7, and 6 factors with an eigen value greater than 1 which accounted for 53.6%, 55.1%, 49.7%, and 49.4% of each inventory's total variance, respectively. However, many of these factors were very narrow in terms of item composition, and in many cases they duplicated each other. Thus, in order to identify the most robust and meaningful factors, the scree test was applied on the factors abstracted from each inventory. This test indicated only three factors to be retained from each of the first three inventories and four from the fourth inventory.

General personal characteristics

The first factor loaded highly on items 20, 23, 21, 22, and 26 (items are listed according to their respective factor loadings on the factor concerned) of the inventory addressed to general personal characteristics. Obviously this factor represents one's wish to be accepted, admired, and regarded highly by others. Modern students of personality would argue that this is a *social desirability factor* (Asendorpf and van Aken, 1998). The second factor loaded highly on items 27, 13, 28, 7, and 19 of this section. Interestingly enough, items 19, 27, and 28 represent the fulfilment of personal ambitions, whereas items 7 and 13 represent a sensitivity to others. Thus, this factor may be regarded as representative of a normal tendency to *compromise one's wishes and ambitions with social obligations*. The third factor loaded primarily on items 9 and 10, and secondarily on items 11 and 12 of this section. Obviously this factor appears to represent *self-control*.

General cognitive strategies and characteristics

The first factor loaded highly on items 27, 29, 30, 28, and 26, indicating that it represents the *thinker's representation of learning*. The second factor loaded highly on items 34, 33, 22, and 35, and so it represents the *thinker's representation of logical reasoning and discourse*, because all of these items referred to the inclination to reason logically and exhaustively and embark on sound discourse with others. The third factor loaded highly on items 17, 18, 19, and 3, representing the *desire to excel in cognitive functioning and be accepted by others for this excellence*.

Goal setting, planning, and problem solving strategies

The first factor in this inventory loaded highly on items 22, 21, 26, and 25 which refer to a tendency to do the first thing that comes to mind without any planning. Therefore, it represents *impulsivity* in dealing with problems. In Sternberg's terms, this factor is close to the anarchic style. The second factor loaded highly on items 3, 13, 12, 10, and 11 and clearly represents *a tendency to be well organized and orderly*. In Sternberg's term this factor represents an oligarchic style. The third factor loaded primarily on items 8 and 9, and secondarily on items 11 and 15. These items referred to various aspects of *planning ability* such as prioritizing goals, division of labour according to the demands and priorities of a given moment, etc. Therefore, this factor is close to Sternberg's hierarchic style. It needs to be noted that these two factors seem complementary to each other. Moreover, it also needs to be noted that all three factors seem to represent different facets of the conscientiousness factor of the Big Five factors of personality.

Occupational preferences and activity styles

The first factor in this inventory loaded highly on items 16, 8, 15, and 2 (see Table 2.5 for factor loadings), all of which refer to actions aiming to ensure that the best decision will be made when dealing with a goal. Thus, this factor seems to represent general *professional responsibility*. The second factor loaded highly on items 21, 22, and 12 of the questionnaire, and all these items referred to some kind of conformity to rules. Therefore, this factor represents what one might call *rule abiding activities* or, in Sternberg's (1980) terminology, *an executive style of activity*. The third factor loaded highly on items 3, 4, 5, and 6 of the questionnaire, all items referring to different aspects of originality. Thus, this factor seems to be related to activities which require problem finding and elaboration of alternative ideas rather than the application of ready-made solutions. In other words, this is the *creative or the legislative style* factor. Finally, the fourth factor loaded highly on items 19, 17, 18, and 20 of this questionnaire, which referred to the willingness to judge or evaluate others. This factor may therefore be considered as the *judicial* or the *evaluative style* factor, which represents activities whose primary characteristic is the evaluation of others.

A second factor analysis was applied on the 96 items included in the first three of the inventories analysed above. These three inventories are concerned with general dimensions of thinking, personality, and thinking style. Thus, this analysis aimed to test for possible interpenetration of factors abstracted from the individual analyses, and to specify the most important factors underlying the self-representations evoked by these inventories. The fourth inventory addressed to activity style and professional preferences was not included in this analysis because it is concerned with more specialized dimensions of self-representation whose relationships with the more general dimensions of cognitive ability and self-representation must be specified. That is, combining these factors with those abstracted from the inventories on cognitive abilities and styles of activity and professional preferences and the cognitive battery would produce a general model specifying the universal structure of abilities and self-representation.

This analysis yielded 36 factors with an eigen value greater than 1, and accounted for 60.6% of total variance. To retain the most statistically powerful factors we used the scree test, which indicated that five factors would have to be retained. These five factors accounted for 24.5% of total variance and are the only factors that will be interpreted here and involved in the analyses to be presented below (see Table 2.4).

We emphasize that for the most part these factors replicated the factors abstracted from the individual analyses. Specifically, factor 1 integrates the first factor in General Personal Characteristics (loading on items 20, 23, and 21 of this inventory) and the third factor in General Cognitive Strategies and Characteristics (loading on items 17, 18, and 19 of this inventory). Thus, this factor represents *ambition for cognitive excellence and social desirability;* as such, it represents some of the most powerful and desirable attributes of the self. It is noteworthy that both cognitive and social attributes are integrated into this factor. The second factor in this analysis coincided with the first and the (non-discussed) fourth factor in Goal Setting, Planning, and Problem Solving Strategies, as it loaded highly on items 22, 26, 4, 25, 5, and 21 of this section. Thus, this factor seems to represent *impulsivity in acting and rigidity in setting or responding to goals*, and also some degree of perseverance in attainment of goals. The third factor coincided with the first factor abstracted from General Cognitive Strategies and Characteristics, as it loaded on items 30, 29, 27 28, and 26 of this section, clearly representing the *learning ability*. The fourth factor complemented both the second and the third factors abstracted from Goal Setting, Planning, and Problem Solving Strategies, as it loaded on items 9, 8, 11, and 3 of this section. Thus, it captured one's inclination to be well organized, foresightful, careful, and systematic. Thus, this is the *systematicity factor*. Finally, the fifth factor was defined by items 34, 35, and 33 included in the General Cognitive

Strategies and Characteristics inventory. Thus, this is the *logical reasoning and discourse factor*.

Several interesting conclusions are suggested by the data from these factor analyses. First, the social-personality and the cognitive dimensions of self-image seem to be interrelated and equally important in the individual's self-representation. The reader is reminded that the first factor of this comprehensive analysis stands for ambition, social desirability and ego asser-tion. Also, of the remaining four (of the five most powerful factors abstracted from this analysis) two represented personality characteristics (impulsivity and systematicity), and two represented cognitive characteristics (learning and logical reasoning).

Second, the differentiation between these two cognitive factors at the level of self-representation is equally interesting as it suggests that the reflecting person is able to discriminate between the information acquisition and retention functions of mind (learning and memory) and the processes enabling the thinker to go beyond the information given (reasoning and dis-course). Clearly, these findings confirm hypothesis 2.3.

Finally, the analysis applied to the Occupational Preferences and Activity Styles inventory suggests two conclusions. On one hand, professional responsibility appeared to dominate the profession-specific factors. On the other hand, it is noticeable that the different types of activities associated with different professions are clearly differentiated from the point of view of the individual thus confirming hypothesis 2.4.

The hierarchical-factor method was again employed to explore the general structure of the five factors abstracted from the comprehensive analysis of the three inventories described above and the four factors abstracted from the Occupational Preferences questionnaire. To identify these factors, two homogeneous half-scores were created for each factor, i.e. the various items addressed to a given attribute were distributed equally between each of the two half-scores representing a factor. Thus, there were two scores for each of the following factors: ambition, impulsivity, systematicity, logical reason-ing, learning, professional responsibility, and executive, legislative, and evaluative style.

In line with the method we applied when testing the models presented before, a series of models were tested with the aim to specify the most parsi-monious best fitting model. The first of these models involved only nine first-order uncorrelated factors, each of them constrained to be related to its corresponding pair of half-scores. The fit of this model was very poor, $\chi^2(144) = 2016.942$, p = .001, CFI = .582, GFI = .727, AGFI = .676, SRMR = .201, RMSEA = .125.

A second model involved these nine first-order factors and three second-order uncorrelated factors. Specifically, the first three first-order factors (i.e., ambition, impulsivity, and systematicity) were regressed on a second-order factor which may be taken to represent self-representation in terms of how the individual would like himself to be and how he generally tends to organize his activities when dealing with problems. In Sternberg's terms, this factor is close to the form of self-government. In more traditional terms, this factor represents general self-representations about personality dispositions. The next four factors (i.e., professional responsibility, and executive, legislative and evaluative style) were regressed on another second-order factor which may be taken to represent the individual's system of concepts underlying his tendency to prefer one type of activity or style over another. In Sternberg's terms, this factor is similar to the function of self-government. The logical reasoning factor and the learning factor were regressed on another second-order factor referring to self-representation of general ability to reason and learn. The fit of this model, although significantly better than the fit of the first model, was still very poor, $\chi^2(135) = 1463.247$, p = .001, CFI = .703, GFI = .836, AGFI = .792, SRMR = .175, RMSEA = .108.

The third model involved the nine first-order factors and one general second-order factor on which all of the first-order factors were regressed. The fit of this model, $\chi^2(135) = 818.088$, p = .001, CFI = .847, GFI = .900, AGFI = .873, SRMR = .076, RMSEA = .078, was much better than the fit of both the other models.

A fourth model involved all three types of factors. That is, the nine first-order factors, the three second-order factors and the general third-order factor to which all second-order factors were regressed. The fit of this model did not differ significantly from the fit of the model which involved the first-order and the general factor, $\chi^2(132) = 812.730$, p = .001, CFI = .948, GFI = .900, AGFI = .871, SRMR = .076, RMSEA = .078. Therefore, the model involving the nine first-order factors and the general second-order factor is preferable over all other models tested here because, although equally good in statistical terms, it is simpler. The fit of this model reached statistical acceptability when several of the error variances of the variables were allowed to correlate $\chi^2(86) = 107.272$, p = .06, CFI = .995, GFI = .986, AGFI = .972, SRMR = .029, RMSEA = .017. This is the model shown in Figure 3.4.

This finding suggests that the person's self-representations about personality characteristics and activity styles are organized in two instead of three levels. That is, they are organized at the level of characteristic-specific representations and at the level of general self-representations. Thus, the intermediate realm-specific level that was found to be present in both cognitive performance itself and the self-representation of cognitive performance was lacking from self-representations of personality characteristics and style. The

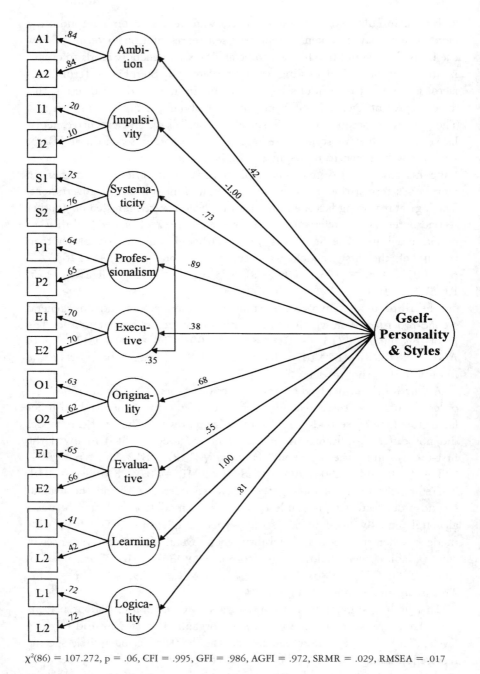

$\chi^2(86) = 107.272$, p = .06, CFI = .995, GFI = .986, AGFI = .972, SRMR = .029, RMSEA = .017

Figure 3.4 The model of self-representation of general personality characteristics, general cognitive functions, and thinking and activity styles

models to be presented below will explore further the nature of the different forms of self-representation and their dynamic interrelationships.

Dynamic relationships among domains, dimensions, and levels of the mind

To specify the relationships among cognitive abilities, their representation in the hypercognitive system, and the various aspects of social and personal strategies, characteristics and styles, a series of models was fitted on the entire set of: (a) the 14 half-scores representing the seven cognitive factors (see Figure 3.1); (b) the 14 half-scores representing the factors abstracted from the cognitive abilities questionnaire (see Figure 3.3); and (c) the 10 half-scores representing the first five factors abstracted from the comprehensive analysis and the eight half-scores representing the four job preferences factors (see Figure 3.4). These models are discussed below.

The general hierarchical model

The first model aimed to integrate the three specific models (see above) into a comprehensive model that would specify directly the relationships among the various dimensions and hierarchical levels identified therein. Thus, this model comprised all factors in the three specific models, in addition to a fourth-order factor on which the general cognitive self-image factor of model 3 (Figure 3.3) and the general personality and styles factor of model 4 (Figure 3.4) were regressed. This factor, which is taken to represent the hypercognitive level of the mind, was allowed to correlate with the general cognitive performance factor of model 1 (Figure 3.1) so as to specify the relationship between the environment-oriented and self-oriented levels of the mind. Based on a first run of this very complex model, a number of direct relationships between some factors were introduced into the model (see below). Thus, the model was retested with these relationships built into it, providing a complete model with an excellent fit, $\chi^2(835) = 901.125$, p = .060, CFI = .995, GFI = .955, AGFI = .941, SRMR = .040, RMSEA = .010. This is the model shown in Figure 3.5.

Validating this model suggests the following conclusions. First, the model clearly indicates that the human mind involves strong local organizations at both performance and self-representation levels. The organizations at the level of self-representation, when related to performance itself, mirror the performance-level organizations to an impressive degree; even the clusters of organizations are identical at the two levels of the mental architecture. This clearly substantiates hypotheses 2.3 and 2.5.

Second, it seems that there are mechanisms allowing the transfer of

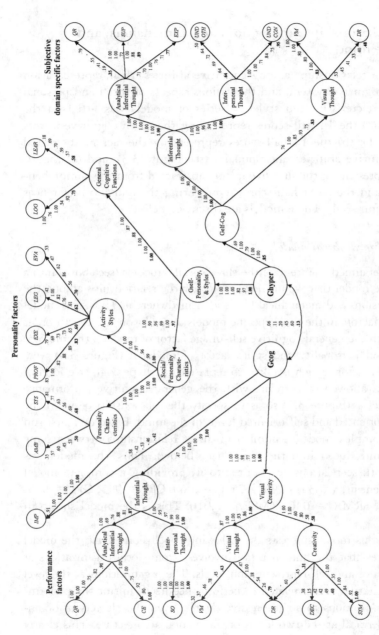

$\chi^2(835) = 901.125$, p = .06, CFI = .995, GFI = .955, AGFI = .941, SRMR = .040, RMSEA = .010

Figure 3.5 The general hierarchical model applied on all tasks and inventories

Note
Numbers in bold in each column refer to the model applied on the whole sample. The other five numbers refer to the model applied on each of the five groups. From top to bottom, the numbers refer to age groups 10.5–14.5, respectively.

influences between the levels of the mind. That is, the direct relationships among factors located in different realms and levels suggest that some abilities and processes are more important in this transfer of influences, which leads from actual performance to self-representation and vice versa. One such (negative) relationship is that which directly connects the general cognitive performance factor with the impulsivity factor. Obviously, these relationships suggest that actual cognitive efficiency is projected directly onto some privileged dimensions of the self-image. From these dimensions these effects are diffused into the self-system through interconnections among these privileged dimensions and other dimensions of the self-system. The models to be presented below will further clarify the interrelations among the levels and structures of the mind and their change with development.

Direct structural relationships among domains

A series of structural equation models were tested in order to specify both direct and indirect relationships among the various aspects of mind identified by our analyses. These models included 19 of the 23 pairs of scores in the general hierarchical models, differing from them in two crucial respects. First, each pair of scores representing a domain or module was constrained to be related to only one factor, such that, by definition, this factor must be taken to represent the domain or the module concerned. Second, each factor was regressed directly onto one or more of the other domain- or module-specific factors on the basis of theoretical or technical criteria, which will be specified below. Thus, technically speaking, the underlying connections among domains or modules were defined as direct structural relationships among factors in the present models and as higher-order factors in the hierarchical models. This implies that the structural models must be considered complementary to the hierarchical models in that they show how the domain- or module-specific factors interact directly rather than through the higher-order factors, which represent these interactions indirectly and grossly.

We built a prototype model to use as a starting point for the process that would lead to a good approximation of the structural relationships among factors (see Figure 3.6). The factors in this model were organized into five groups. The first group included five cognitive performance factors, i.e. factors representing the quantitative-relational SCS, the causal-experimental SCS, social thought, visual memory, and drawing. The other cognitive performance factors (i.e. the two ideational fluency factors and the mental rotation factor) were excluded from these models for technical and substantive reasons. Specifically, these factors did not have a counterpart at the level of the self-image factors to be included in the model. The second

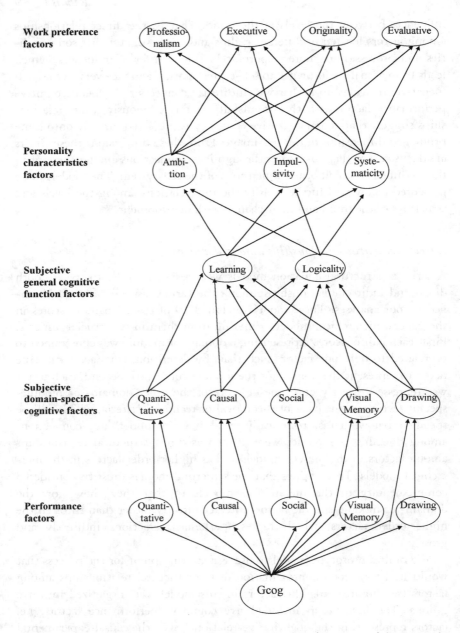

Figure 3.6 The prototype model of the dynamic relationships between modules across the
different levels of the mental architecture

group included five of the seven self-representation factors abstracted from the questionnaire on abilities. For the same technical reasons referred to above, of the two causal thought factors only the suppositional thought factor was included, and of the two social thought factors only the understanding others factor was involved. The third group comprised the two self-image factors representing general cognitive characteristics, the learning ability, and the logical reasoning factors. The fourth group included the three self-image factors representing general personality characteristics, that is, ambition to excel, impulsivity, and systematicity. Finally, the fifth level comprised the four activity-specific factors, that is, the factors representing professional responsibility, the rule-abiding activities, the activities requiring originality, and the evaluative professions.

The arrows on the model indicate how the causal relationships among factors were initially defined (see Figure 3.6). First, the five cognitive performance factors were regressed on a second-order factor that can be taken to represent the general cognitive ability (G_{cog}). This manipulation was necessary to allow the specification of influences exerted on each ability-specific, self-representation factor by both the general cognitive ability and its corresponding domain-specific performance factor. That is, each ability-specific, self-representation factor was regressed on both the second-order G_{cog} and the residual of its corresponding cognitive performance factor. Regression of the self-representation factors on the residual of the corresponding performance factor rather than on the factor itself is a method that enables the dissociation of the effects exerted on the self-representation factors by the corresponding domain-specific ability from the effects on the self-evaluation factors by general cognitive abilities, which in the model are captured by the G_{cog} factor. This is so because the residual of each of a number of factors regressed on a higher-order factor represents what in each of the specific factors is not captured by this higher-order factor. Second, each of the two factors standing for one's self-representation in regard to general cognitive functions (i.e. the learning and the logical reasoning factors) was regressed on all five ability-specific, self-representation factors to see how the ability-specific, self-representation factors contribute to the formation of self-representations regarding general cognitive characteristics. Third, each of the three factors representing general personality characteristics (i.e. ambition, impulsivity, and systematicity) was regressed on both of the two general cognitive characteristics self-image factors (i.e. the learning and the logical reasoning factors). This set of relationships would reveal how the formation of general personality characteristics is affected by self-representations of general cognitive attributes. Finally, each of the four activity style factors was regressed on each of the three factors representing general personality characteristics. These relationships would show how

preferences for different types of activity are affected by one's general personality characteristics. From a strictly technical point of view, all factors
included in this model are of the same order. However, from a substantive
point of view, each of the five groups of factors can be considered to represent a different layer in the edifice of dynamic relationships among the
dimensions of ability and self-image represented by the various factors.

The fit of this model was not very good $\chi^2(620) = 1871.360$, p = .001,
CFI = .881, GFI = .882, AGFI = .859, SRMR = .099. The Lagrange
multiplier test attributed the rather poor fit to the direction of the causal
relationships between the general and the domain-specific cognitive self-
image factors. Specifically, this test suggested that the paths between the
two general and the five domain-specific cognitive self-representation factors
would have to be inverted so as to run from the general to the specific rather
than vice versa. Implementing this change resulted in a very large improvement in the model fit, $\chi^2 = (617) = 1508.895$, p = .001, CFI = .916,
GFI = .909, AGFI = .891, SRMR = .068; $\Delta\chi^2(3) = 362.465$, p = .001.
Therefore, the two factors representing general cognitive functioning in the
self-image seem to play a rather privileged role in the organization of the
person's self-image system as they appeared to exert causal effects both on
the domain-specific, cognitive self-image factors and the factors representing
self-representation of personality characteristics. To fully accommodate this
role, these two factors were defined as independent factors, and were allowed
to correlate with the second-order G_{cog} factor. As assumed, this modification
resulted in a further large improvement of the model fit,
$\chi^2(616) = 1401.856$, p = .001, CFI = .926, GFI = .915, AGFI = .897,
SRMR = .058; $\Delta\chi^2(1) = 107.039$, p = .001. This result is in full agreement with the assumption put forward in the introduction that self-
representations of general cognitive efficiency result directly from general
cognitive processes. In this model two parameters were added following the
Lagrange multiplier test: specifically, the impulsivity factor was regressed on
the G_{cog} factor, and the ambition factor was regressed on the impulsivity
factor. This slight modification has also resulted in an impressive improvement to the model fit, $\chi^2(614) = 1274.580$, p = .001, CFI = .937,
GFI = .920,   AGFI = .903,   SRMR = .048,   RMSEA = .003;
$\Delta\chi^2(2) = 127.276$, p = .001. This was determined as the final model
because subsequent deletion or addition of parameters resulted in a deterio-
ration of the model fit.

The inspection of this model (see Figure 3.7) suggests the following conclusions about the relationships among the various factors. First, all five
domain-specific cognitive self-image factors depend primarily on the logical
reasoning factor and secondarily upon the G_{cog}. The learning factor was
found to affect only the quantitative-relational self-attribution factor. Inter-

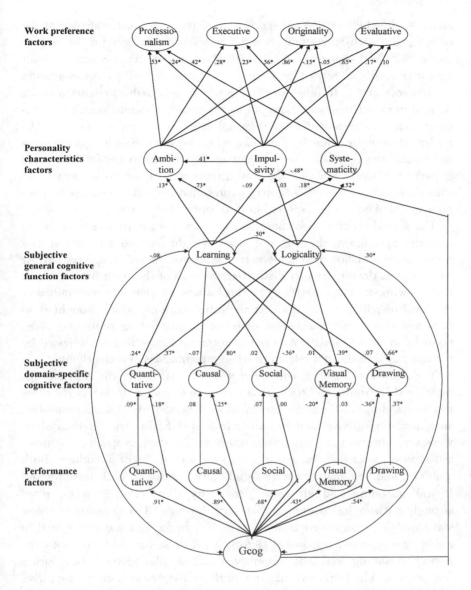

Work preference factors

Professio-nalism · Executive · Originality · Evaluative

.53* .24* .42* .28* .23* .56* .86* -.15* -.05 .65* .17* .10

Personality characteristics factors

Ambi-tion · .41* · Impul-sivity · -.48* · Syste-maticity

.13* .73* -.09 .03 .18* .52*

Subjective general cognitive function factors

-.08 · Learning · .50* · Logicality · .30*

Subjective domain-specific cognitive factors

.24* .37* -.07 .80* .02 -.56* .01 .39* .07 .66*

Quanti-tative · Causal · Social · Visual Memory · Drawing

.09* .18* .08 .25* .07 .00 -.20* .03 -.36* .37*

Performance factors

Quanti-tative · Causal · Social · Visual Memory · Drawing

.91* .89* .68* .43* .54*

Gcog

$\chi^2(614) = 1274.580$, p = .001, CFI = .937, GFI = .920, AGFI = .903, SRMR = .048, RMSEA = .003

Figure 3.7 The final model of the dynamic relationships between modules across the different levels of the mental architecture

estingly, the effect of domain-specific cognitive performance factors on the corresponding self-representation factor was significant only for the quantitative SCS and drawing; the social thought self-representation factor appeared totally unrelated to both the G_{cog} factor and its corresponding performance factor. In other words, domain-specific self-representations are derived from self-representations of more general or dynamic cognitive functions and, to a certain degree, they reflect general cognitive ability. The reader may wonder here why the relationships between the self-representation factors and the G_{cog} factor were negative. This is due to the fact that with growth, self-representations about ability become more conservative and thus they decrease whereas cognitive scores increase with growth. This phenomenon will be further explored in the chapters following.

The second conclusion is concerned with the peculiarities of some of the domains. Specifically, drawing and social thought seem to have very special properties that define their idiosyncratic status in the self-image system. At one extreme, drawing is very distinctive in terms of the skills involved such that drawing-related experiences or capabilities are generally maintained at the level of self-representation. At the other extreme, social thought is so pervasive that an overestimation of social understanding skills may often occur by most individuals. As a result, social understanding as addressed by the tasks used here is not related to self-representations of social thought.

The third conclusion is concerned with the pattern of the relationships between the learning and the logical reasoning factors with each of the three factors standing for the self-representation of personality characteristics (i.e. ambition, impulsivity, and systematicity). Specifically, these relationships were very similar with the relationships to the domain-specific cognitive self-representation factors in some respects and different in others. Both ambition and systematicity were significantly related to both learning and logical reasoning and all these personality dimensions correlate more strongly with logical reasoning than with learning. The impulsivity factor was closely and negatively related to the G_{cog} factor, but was not related to either two cognitive self-image factors. Thus, it seems clear that both the logical reasoning and the impulsivity factor play pivotal but rather independent roles in the organization of the self-image at both the cognitive and the personality level. For instance, they both contribute strongly to the formation of ambitions. However, systematicity is formed in relation to logicality but independently of impulsivity. It is equally interesting that general cognitive ability directly affects self-image in regard to dominant ways of responding to pressures or incoming information; i.e. individuals with stronger general ability do not represent themselves as impulsive.

Finally, when factors representing activity preferences were regressed on the three factors representing personality characteristics most correlations were significant and some were very high. Thus, it is clear that statements related to activity preferences are generated in close relation with self-representation of personality characteristics which, in turn, are based on self-representation as a learner and a reasoner. However, the pattern of relationships between activity preferences and personality factors suggest several more specific conclusions. First, the ambition factor exhibited the strongest effect on three of the four activity preference factors. This suggests that the dimension represented by this factor is as important in the formation of a person's choices as the logical reasoning factor is in the organization of the cognitive aspects of one's self-image. Second, the pattern of the relationships between personality and activity preference factors gives some evidence of how personality characteristics affect activity preferences. Specifically, the factor representing the rule abiding or executive activities was more closely related with systematicity than with the two other factors representing personality characteristics. The factor representing activities requiring originality was related highly with ambition, but unrelated to systematicity and negatively related to impulsivity. The factor representing evaluative activities was related highly with ambition, much lower but positively with impulsivity, and to a very low degree with systematicity. It seems, therefore, that ambitious individuals who do not consider themselves impulsive are oriented to activities requiring originality; if they think of themselves as both ambitious and impulsive they tend toward evaluative activities; systematic individuals who also believe themselves to be impulsive appear to orient themselves to the rule-abiding activities. Finally, it is noteworthy that the factor representing professional responsibility was positively related to both ambition and systematicity, but negatively related with impulsivity.

Decomposing the on-line experience of problem solving

The analyses so far presented here focused on identifying constellations and levels in the organization of cognitive and personality processes and their interactions. Although relevant, these analyses do not highlight directly how the various structures of the mind are involved in the formation of the subjective experience generated when working on cognitive tasks and how this experience contributes to the formation and consolidation of these structures. This question is highly important because it is directly concerned with the dynamic interplay of the mind and reality, and also with the dynamic interplay between the various modules, dimensions, and levels of the mind in real time. Although this issue was considered by early scholars of the classic theory of intelligence (Cattell, 1930), systematic empirical evidence related to these phenomena is still lacking. The present study was designed to provide directly relevant evidence. To this purpose, it generated evidence regarding the on-line experience of problem solving, actual problem-solving, and the participants' long-term self-representation about problem solving.

Specifically, we recall that participants were to solve problems representing several cognitive domains (quantitative, causal, social, imaginal thought, and drawing) and also to twice evaluate the difficulty of tasks and their solution success, both before and after actually working on the tasks. These subjective evaluations represent the functioning of working hypercognition, because they are shaped during on-line problem-solving. The self-representations of ability on the questionnaire addressed to the cognitive self-concept (e.g. I am good in visualizing mentally objects that I see; I am good in adjusting mathematical rules to solve new problems; I can easily decipher similarities between phenomenally unrelated phenomena) represent long-term hypercognition, because they reflect preconceived representations of these domains more than actual performance and experience attained on particular tasks at a particular moment. Moreover, the pre- and post-evaluations allows to test directly the effect of actual experience on working hypercognition. This is so because it is plausible to assume that evaluations effected before performance derive from ready-made self-representations and feelings; evaluations effected after working on a task directly derive, at least to a certain extent, from this very recent experience.

To specify the relative contribution of actual performance and long-term hypercognition to subjective evaluations which represent working hypercognition, a complex structural model was built using the scores used in the previous models (see Figure 3.1 and Figure 3.3). These scores made it possible to construct one first-order factor for each of the five problem-solving domains in the four dimensions of interest, that is, actual performance, difficulty and success evaluation (which represent working hypercognition), and self-representations of ability (which represent long-term hypercognition). Moreover, the five domain-specific factors within each of the four dimensions were regressed to a second-order factor, which can be taken to represent the dimension as such. Specifically, the five performance factors were regressed on a factor representing general cognitive ability. The five success evaluation factors were regressed on a general success evaluation factor representing the processes activated during performance self evaluation (e.g. comparison between the outcome/solution and task-related criteria; one's attitudes in regard to self-evaluation, etc.). The five difficulty evaluation factors were regressed on a general difficulty evaluation factor representing experiences generated during problem solving (such as uncertainty regarding procedures, feelings of mental effort, etc.). The five self-attribution of ability factors were regressed on a general factor that reflects general cognitive self-image (such as feelings of general cognitive efficiency etc.). This model was tested separately on the pre-performance and the post-performance evaluation, because this would allow to specify the possible effects of the experience of solving the tasks addressed to each of the SCSs.

The primary objective of this analysis was to specify how, if at all, performance and long-term hypercognition influence working hypercognition. Therefore, each of the five pre-performance and post-performance domain-specific success evaluation factors was also regressed on the general cognitive performance factor, the general cognitive self-image factor, the residual of the corresponding domain-specific performance factor, and the residual of the corresponding domain-specific self-image factor. The success evaluation factors were also regressed on the residual of the corresponding domain-specific difficulty evaluation factors. Using the residual of domain-specific factors rather than the factors themselves in this model allows their relative influence on the factor of interest to be more fully specified.

The regression coefficients of the success evaluation factors on all the above-mentioned factors show a highly interesting pattern of effects. Specifically, panel A of Table 3.1 shows the influence of the various factors on success evaluation before solving the tasks addressed to each SCS. It can be seen that the influence of all three general second-order factors on pre-performance success evaluation is reliable and significant across all five domains (most effects are circa .3–.4), although the magnitude of influence varies across domains. The corresponding domain-specific factors are also involved, although variation in their case is even greater, ranging from .0 (the imaginal SCS) to .684 (the quantitative SCS). The effect of the domain-specific self-image was very low in all domains (circa .1) but drawing (.555). The effect of difficulty evaluation was also very reliable and strong (negative, i.e. inverse co-variation), indicating the interrelationships between the two types of self-evaluation. This, in turn, testifies to the operation of working hypercognition as a system.

The conclusion suggested by these findings is clear: pre-performance evaluations are a function of actual general cognitive ability, self-representation of general cognitive ability, domain-specific ability, self-representation in regard to this specific ability, and also their evaluation of the difficulty of the task in consideration. The relative contribution of each of these factors varies across domains. Specifically, the highest effects in the case of quantitative thought came from general cognitive ability and the corresponding domain-specific ability. This is of course consistent with our previous findings presented here and elsewhere (Demetriou *et al.*, 1992; Demetriou *et al.*, 1993a) that mathematical thought is transparent to awareness and that evaluations of it reflect directly the condition of general cognitive ability. In the case of causal thought, the highest effects came from the self-representation of general cognitive ability. Attention is drawn to the very low (and negative)

Table 3.1 Regression of the pre- and post-performance success-evaluation factors on the general and domain-specific performance, self-image, and difficulty-evaluation factors

	Quantitative	Causal	Social	Imaginal	Drawing
A. Pre-performance evaluation					
Gself-evaluation	.213	.377	.581	.310	.395
Gcognitive	.403	.308	.312	.310	.103
Gself-image	.107	.449	.233	.341	.489
Quantitative					
Performance	.684				
Self-image	.118				
Difficulty	−.460				
Causal					
Performance.		−.140			
Self-image		.081			
Difficulty		−.553			
Social					
Performance			.157		
Self-image			.081		
Difficulty			−.631		
Imaginal					
Performance				.000	
Self-image				−.056	
Difficulty				−.832	
Drawing					
Performance					.046
Self-image					.555
Difficulty					−.286
B. Post-performance evaluation					
Gself-evaluation	.201	.632	.585	.614	.527
Gcognitive	.537	.057	.233	.194	−.003
Gself-image	.038	.396	.194	.304	.350
Quantitative					
Performance	.808				
Self-image	.060				
Difficulty	.118				
Causal					
Performance		−.157			
Self-image		−.125			
Difficulty		−.605			
Social					
Performance			.686		
Self-image			−.011		
Difficulty			−.087		
Imaginal					
Performance				.000	
Self-image				−.197	
Difficulty				−.396	
Drawing					
Performance					.236
Self-image					.243
Difficulty					−.396

Note
Gself-evaluation is a second-order factor loading on all of the domain-specific pre- or post-performance self-evaluation factors. Gcognitive is the second-order factor loading on all of the domain-specific performance factors. Gself-image is the second-order factor loading on all domain-specific factors abstracted from the cognitive self-representation inventory. The three domain-specific factors refer to actual performance on the respective tasks, self-representation about these tasks, and self-evaluation of difficulty of these tasks. General factors were taken as such, whereas the residual of each domain-specific factors was used in the model in order to disentangle the effects of the domain-specific factors from the effects of the general factors on domain-specific success evaluation.

effect of the actual performance on the causal tasks. This pattern of effects is fully consistent with our previous finding that causal thought is opaque to awareness. As a result, the thinker cannot produce performance-relevant evaluations in regard to it. Thus, he derives his evaluations of performance on causal tasks primarily from his general cognitive self-image. The pattern of effects regarding the social domain is similar, although in this case the strongest effect came from the second-order self-evaluation factor. This is taken to indicate that evaluations of performance on the social tasks, being also opaque to awareness, are constructed on the spot as derivations of the general self-evaluation attitudes of the person. The imaginal SCS was about equally and moderately related to the three general factors (circa .3); however, it was highly affected by the corresponding evaluation of difficulty, indicating the presence of a very specific task effect. That is, probably because of the lack of experience related to mental rotation tasks such as those used here, the pre-performance evaluation of success was geared on the subjective feelings of the possible difficulty of these tasks. In the case of drawing, the effect of general cognitive ability was very low; the strongest effects came from self-representation of general cognitive ability and self-representation of the corresponding domain-specific ability. This pattern suggests that drawing is, on the one hand, subjectively independent of cognitive ability; on the other hand, it seems to have an eminent and clear position in the thinker's cognitive self-image.

How is success evaluation affected by the experience of working on the tasks? To answer this question we would have to compare the results presented in panels A and B of Table 3.1. It can be seen that there are some clear changes from pre- to post-performance evaluation. Specifically, the effect of the general self-evaluation factor increased considerably in three (i.e. causal, imaginal, and drawing) of the five SCSs and it remained basically the same in the other two (i.e. quantitative and social). The effect of the domain-specific performance factors was in the same direction. That is, it increased in all but one SCS (i.e. the imaginal). On the contrary, the effect of the general cognitive performance factor decreased considerably in all but the quantitative SCS; the effect of the general cognitive self-image decreased in all five SCSs. This pattern of results indicates that working on a task leads the thinker to change the focus of his evaluations from general cognitive ability and general cognitive self-image (i.e. long-term hypercognition) to the experience of working on the tasks as such (whereby the increase of the effect of domain-specific performance) and to on-line self-evaluation criteria (whereby the increase of the effect of the general self-evaluation factor which stands for working hypercognition). These changes explain why domain-specific organizations are preserved on both the level of performance and the level of self-representation. That is, each new person-task encounter sharpens the differentiation of the task-domain affiliated to the task encountered from other domains. Moreover, these changes also indicate that the recent experience of problem solving activates general attitudes to self-evaluation which are engrafted in working hypercognition (for instance some persons are systematically strict and others are systematically lenient to themselves). Thus, the experience of problem solving contributes to both the refinement of domain-specific mental maps that persons have of their mind and the strengthening of personal attitudes to self-evaluation. We will return to this issue many times in the following chapters.

CONCLUSIONS

The results presented in this chapter suggest a number of clear conclusions related to the structure of cognitive functions and processes, and their projection in the self-evaluation and self-representation systems. Specifically, it is clear that this study provided further evidence to support the presence of the SCSs described by our theory. However, the present study suggests that the structural assumptions of the theory must be extended in two important respects.

First, social thought and drawing are indeed domains that stand as autonomous systems together with the SCSs we found in the past. Of course, further study is required to specify their relationships with the other SCSs. It needs to be noted, for instance, that the five SCSs uncovered by our previous research differ between each other in their domain of application and the basic mental operations involved. However, drawing and social thought may refer to any of the domains affiliated to the other five SCSs. Thus, we need to specify what is particular to each of these two systems in terms of mental operations and skills and study how each of them is used to express the relations involved in the other SCSs.

Second, no SCS is an isolated island of functions and abilities; in fact, all analyses presented in this chapter have suggested strongly that the SCSs belong to broader families or systems, according to their dominant ways of functioning. Specifically, the causal, quantitative, and social SCSs were found to belong to what one might call the *inferential thought systems*. Drawing, and imaginal thought, and the creative processes involved in the ideational fluency tasks were found to be associated with another family *of creative thought processes*.

For the most part, the hypercognitive system reflects the architecture of the environment-oriented systems at both the level of the domains and the level of domain families. The reader is reminded that both levels of the organization of mental functions were found operative in the self-evaluation system that directs the self-evaluations of several aspects of online cognitive functioning as well as long-term self-representations. Moreover, we found very systematic relationships between performance, self-evaluation, and self-representation, which revealed how experience continually contributes to the formation of the mental maps of abilities sparing the representation of particular domains. That is, these maps, although continually updated preserve the peculiarities and dynamics of each of the particular systems of the mind that deal with different types of relationships in the environment.

Our findings related to social/personality dimensions studied here indicated that these dimensions are equally robust, particularly in their effects on real-life decisions, such as preferences for different types of activities. Moreover, these social/personality dimensions are interrelated with actual cognitive abilities and their self-representation through some privileged dimensions (learning, logicality, and impulsivity) which seem to function as the go between agents that connect these two levels of the mind and the self. The following chapter will focus on development and individual differences, highlighting what develops and what remains stable in the various dimensions of the hypercognitive system for differing categories of individuals (e.g. gender, SES).

4 Results II

Development and individual differences
in cognitive abilities, self-evaluation,
and self-representation

The development of the cognitive abilities investigated in this book has been
charted in other studies (Demetriou and Efklides, 1985, 1989; Demetriou *et
al.*, 1991, 1993a; 1993b); thus, developmental changes in the participants'
task performance will be described here briefly. The reader is reminded that
our study has two major objectives in regard to development: first, to clarify
and extend our previous research related to possible changes in the relationships between cognitive performance and cognitive self-awareness; second, to
reveal any relationships among this awareness and the various dimensions of
the cognitive self-image. We first present results about the influence of age,
SES, and gender on the general architecture of the mind. We then present
results indicating the main developmental trends related to task performance,
and then focus on cognition-hypercognition relationships and their effects on
certain dimensions of the cognitive self-image.

Age, SES, and gender effects on the general architecture
of the mind

Age effects

To study possible changes in the architecture of the mind with growth we
tested the fit of the general hierarchical model shown in Figure 3.5 separately on each of the five age groups. To run this analysis, the covariance
structure of the scores involved in the model above was estimated separately
for each of the age groups tested. The older age group was excluded from
this analysis because the number of subjects involved (N = 56) was limited
relative to the number of variables involved (46). Impressively, the same
constructs were found for all three measures (performance, self-awareness of
performance, and thinking styles) across all five age groups. It can be seen in
Figure 3.5 that even the factor loadings and the coefficients indicating structural relationships between factors *within* each of the three sets of scores were

largely the same across age groups. One very interesting difference between age groups was found, however, and it seems to have captured a systematic developmental trend. Specifically, the correlation between the higher-order factor representing the environment-oriented level of the mental architecture (which accounted for the variance of the various domain-specific constructs) and the higher order factor representing the self-oriented or the hypercognitive level (which accounted for the variance of the self-representation factors corresponding to the domain-specific constructs and various personality and thinking styles constructs) was practically nil at the age of 11 years, but it increased systematically and became strong at the age of 15 years (i.e. the correlation between these two higher order factors was .06, .11, .20, .45, and .60 at the age of 10.5, 11.5, 12.5, 13.5 and 14.5 years, respectively).

This finding indicates that many of the changes traditionally associated with the transition from childhood to adolescence may primarily affect the communication between the two knowing levels of the mental architecture, rather than the modules and actual processes at each level. Thus, self-monitoring and self-representation at the environment-oriented level become increasingly accurate and detailed. The results to be presented below will corroborate this conclusion.

Gender effects

To test if there are any effects of gender on this general structure, the covariance structure of the scores involved in the model above was estimated separately for all of the females (N = 414) and the males (N = 426) involved in the study. The model above was then tested on each of the genders under the constraint that all factor loadings would be equal across genders. It needs also to be noted that in all of these models the factor variances were fixed to unity in all groups. Thus, finding that the constraints of equality of factor loadings hold true would imply that the factors are identical across groups. The fit of this model was good $\chi^2(1870) = 2546.781$, p = .001, CFI = .951. This finding indicates strongly that there are no differences between genders in the organization of the abilities and characteristics represented in this study.

SES effects

To run the analysis addressed to SES, the covariance structure of the scores involved in the model above was estimated separately for the low (N = 424), the middle (N = 181) and the high SES subjects (N = 235) involved in the study. Thus, the model above was tested under the constrain that all of the factor loadings would be equal across the three groups. Given the many constraints under which this model was tested, the fit obtained was satisfactory, $\chi^2(2905) = 3925.047$, p = .001, CFI = .925. Therefore, the architecture of the aspects of mind studied here seems not to be affected by the various socioeconomic or educational factors that differentiate the various SES groups.

Developmental changes in cognitive performance

To specify the effect of the various factors on the cognitive abilities represented in the study, a MANOVA was run on the five domains for which subjects had provided hypercognitive self-evaluations. For this analysis, a mean was computed for each of the five domains; apart from the quantitative SCS (where the second of the three algebra items was excluded), this mean included all items addressed to a domain. To ensure comparability across domains, performance on all items was reduced to a 0–2 scale, which was the scale used to evaluate performance on most cognitive tasks. Thus, this was a 5 (the five ages) × 3 (the three SES groups) × 2 (the two genders) × 5 (the five thought domains-called SCSs hereafter) analysis, with repeated measures on the last factor. The means and standard deviations are shown in Table A4.1 in the Appendix; major trends revealed by the analysis are shown in Figure 4.1. The α level for this and all the MANOVAs to be presented below was set to .01, according to Bonferoni.

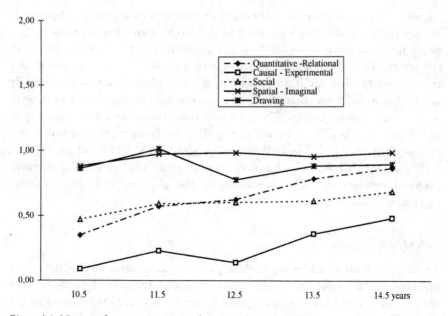

Figure 4.1 Mean performance scores as a function of age and SCS

Regarding the between-subject factors, the effect of age was highly significant, F (4, 754) = 31.68, p < .001, indicating that older subjects performed better than younger subjects overall. The effect of SES was also significant, F (2, 754) = 60.45, p < .001, indicating that higher SES subjects performed better than lower SES subjects. Finally, the effect of gender was also significant, F (1, 754) = 12.29, p < .001, indicating that females performed better than males. The age × SES interaction was significant, F (8, 754) = 5.48, p < .001, indicating that the performance of the low SES subjects was consistently lower than the performance of the two other SES groups over all ages, whereas the performance of the middle SES group varied.

The effect of the SCS factor was highly significant, F (4, 3016) = 372.28, p < .001. This effect reflected the fact that performance on the causal tasks was much lower than performance on the other tasks, and that performance on the quantitative and the social tasks was similar and lower than performance on the spatial-imaginal and drawing tasks, which were also similar.

With respect to the between × within-subject interactions, the significant age × SCS interaction, F (16, 3016) = 8.77, p < .001 indicated that performance improvement with age was most pronounced for the quantitative and the causal SCSs. In fact, there was no improvement after age 11 years for the spatial SCS, and performance on the drawing tasks varied with age. These results are consistent with other cognitive developmental research (Case *et al.*, 1996; Demetriou *et al.*, 1993, Fischer and Aboud, 1993; Fischer and Pipp, 1984). The significant SCS × SES interaction, F (8, 3016) = 12.46, p < .001, indicated that SES differences were more pronounced for some SCSs (the quantitative-relational and the causal-experimental, in particular) and very limited for one SCS, the spatial-imaginal in particular. Likewise, the significant gender × SCS interaction, F (4, 3016) = 11.56, p < .001, indicated that females scored noticeably higher on social thought and the drawing tasks, but both genders received very similar scores for the other three task categories. In fact, the significant age × SES × SCS interaction, F (32, 3016) = 3.38, p < .001, indicated that low SES subjects' performance was lower than that of the other two SES groups across all SCSs and ages, but middle SES group performance approached or even exceeded high SES group performance at some ages for some SCSs, indicating that these two groups were very close to each other.

Developmental changes in self-evaluation

Subjects had been asked to evaluate the success of solution and the difficulty of two tasks per domain two times (i.e. before and after solving each of the two tasks). These evaluations were taken to represent the hypercognitive system's ability to register and represent the dynamics of the factors underlying cognitive organization and functioning. In fact, our structural analyses (see Chapter 3) confirmed that the hypercognitive system does possess these properties. Now we will examine to what extent these properties are affected by development. In other words, does the accuracy of the hypercognitive system in terms of these properties change with increasing general experience as indicated by the progression of age *per se,* or with the development of actual cognitive abilities, as indicated by the level of task performance? Evidently, this question must be reduced to several more specific questions related to the effects of certain factors such as the kind of evaluation (i.e. success versus difficulty), the experience of working on the tasks (i.e. pre- versus post-performance measures), and the domain of thought.

To answer these questions, the hypercognitive accuracy index (HAI) was devised. The estimation of this index was a rather complicated procedure. This procedure is described below.

1   First, for each subject, each of the five sets of performance scores, pre-performance and corresponding post-performance success evaluation scores, and their corresponding pre-performance and post-performance difficulty evaluation scores were reduced to mean scores. Thus, there was one performance score, two success evaluation scores (one pre- and one post-performance), and two difficulty evaluation scores (one pre- and one post-performance) for each domain of thought.

2   Second, each of these mean scores was standardised for the whole group of 840 subjects involved in the study. This was effected by transforming each mean score into a z-score. Standardisation was necessary to ensure comparability of performance scores and evaluation scores which were measured on different scales.

3   Step # 2 above yielded a z-scale for each of the 25 measures. Each of these scales was first defined to span over the six intervals following: <-2, -2 to -1, -1 to 0, 0 to 1, 1 to 2, >2.

4   Then the values 1 to 6 were ascribed to the six intervals above, respectively. For reasons of convenience, let these new scales be called the "specification scales" (Sp).

5   The reader is reminded that the difficulty evaluation in the original battery varied in opposite direction to the direction of success evaluation and the scoring of performance. To ensure comparability between the HAIs for success and difficulty evaluation the Sp scales for difficulty were inverted, so as to vary in the same direction with the Sp scales for performance and success evaluation.

6   The HAIs were then estimated on the basis of equation # 1 shown below:

$$\mathrm{HAI} = (\mathrm{Sp}_{\mathrm{performance}} - \mathrm{Sp}_{\mathrm{evaluation}}) \tag{1}$$

That is, the difference between a subject's Sp performance score and this subject's corresponding success or difficulty evaluation Sp score can be taken to indicate the degree of correspondence between the two scales. The smaller the difference the greater the correspondence. That is, the equation above gives HAIs ranging from -5 to 5, with 0 indicating absolute accuracy of self-evaluation, values below 0 indicating positive or lenient self-evaluation, and values above 0 indicating negative or strict self-evaluation. Applying this equation here yielded a total of 20 HAIs; that is, two success HAIs (one pre- and one post-performance), and two difficulty HAIs (one pre- and one post-performance) for each of the five domains of thought represented in the present study. Each of these HAIs is a direct measure of the accuracy of the hypercognitive system to register and represent a different aspect of the experiences generated by cognitive functioning, such as the feelings of difficulty caused by a problem during processing or the feelings of adequacy regarding the solution given to this problem.

These 20 HAIs were subjected to a 5 (age) $\times$ 3 (SES) $\times$ 2 (gender) $\times$ 2 (time) $\times$ 2 (evaluation) $\times$ 5 (SCS) MANOVA, with repeated measures on the last three factors. The mean HAIs and standard deviations resulting from this analysis are shown in Table A4.2 of the Appendix; Figure 4.2 illustrates some of the main trends revealed by this analysis.

Regarding the between-subject factors, the effect of age was highly significant, $F (4, 754) = 6.31$, $p < .001$. The association between age and mean accuracy (see Figure 4.2) requires clarification in two respects. First, this result reflected the fact that self-evaluation accuracy was associated with age in a sigmoid fashion; i.e. it was more lenient at age 10 years, becoming more strict at age 11 years, then shifting to perfect accuracy for the next two years, and finally deviating towards the strict side at age 15 years. This pattern of association between age and self-evaluation accuracy is interesting in that it reflects the association between age and the other dimensions of performance and self-image studied here. We have confirmed earlier that major changes in performance occurred at ages 10–11 and 14–15 years. Now we will show these are precisely the ages at which we observe major changes in the self-attribution of cognitive or social abilities/characteristics and even work preferences. These findings are consistent with our structural modelling data (see Chapter 3) in suggesting that the on-line self-evaluation system is directly connected to both the level of performance itself and all other dimensions of self-representation. Thus, the connection to performance enables the hypercognitive system to register the changes that affect ability and adjust the self-image accordingly. It is interesting to note, however, that these adjustments initially make self-evaluation more strict, which is to be expected. At the beginning of a new developmental cycle the individual has not yet fully mastered his newly acquired abilities and skills; as a result we

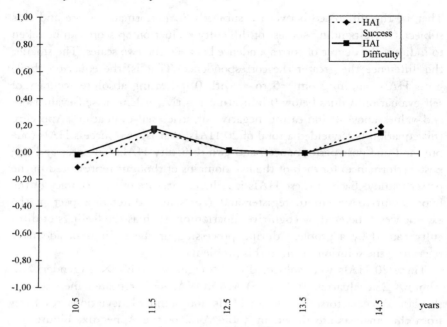

Figure 4.2 Mean hypercognitive accuracy as a function of age and type of evaluation

have the apparent paradox of a spurt in cognitive functioning and a drop in self-confidence regarding cognitive functioning.

The second aspect of the present findings is equally important. Specifically, the presence of a systematic self-evaluation accuracy-age trade-off does not diminish the significance of the fact that accuracy was impressively high across the entire age spectrum represented; in fact, the mean HAI was very close to perfect accuracy for all ages (Figure 4.2). When contrasted with the highly significant improvement in performance across all SCSs suggested by our analysis, this finding indicates that the hypercognitive system can accurately register cognitive functioning independent of the level at which the cognitive system itself tends to function. Evidently, this finding is consistent with the results of structural modelling (see Figure 3.2), which indicated that the various domains are accurately reflected at the level of self-evaluation.

The effect of the SES factor was highly significant, F (2, 754) = 9.46, p < .001, indicating overall that low SES subjects (M = −.040) were more accurate than middle SES (M = .200) and high SES (M = .140) subjects, which both tended to be on the strict side of the scale. In combination with the differences in cognitive performance between SES groups noted earlier, this finding indicates that higher cognitive performance tends to be associated with a more conservative self-evaluation, which is consistent with the finding that developmental changes in ability are initially associated with a shift toward more negative self-evaluation.

The effect of gender was also significant, F (1, 754) = 7.06, p < .008, replicating the same pattern of relationships between performance and self-evaluation. That is, females, who were found to perform better than males on cognitive tasks were also more strict (M = .12) than males (M = .00) in their self-evaluations. This finding is consistent with many other studies which have found that girls underestimate their abilities (see Phillips and Zimmerman, 1990). Interactions among these three between-subject factors were not significant.

Regarding the within-subject factors, evaluation exerted no significant effect, F (1, 754) = .01, p = .928. This result indicated that, overall, success (M = .050) and difficulty evaluation (M = .065) were equally accurate.

The effect of time was not significant, F (1, 754) = 3.23, p = .071. However, time interacted significantly with SES, F (2, 754) = 17.56, p < .001, and gender, F (1, 754) = 36.74, p < .001, indicating that the various groups were affected differently by the experience of solving the tasks. Specifically, the first of these interactions indicated that the pre-performance evaluations for all three groups were on the strict side (M = .03, .14, and .08 for the low, the middle, and the high SES group, respectively). However, after solving the tasks, the low SES shifted to the lenient side and the other two groups became even stricter (M = −.11, .26, and .21 for the low, the middle, and the high SES group, respectively); as a result, the difference increased between the low SES subjects and the two other SES groups. Likewise, the second interaction indicated that females (M = .06) and males (M = .07) were at approximately the same point on the HAI scale before solving the tasks, but they deviated considerably after solving them; that is, females became stricter (M = .18) and males became more lenient (M = −.07). Of the various higher order interactions between time and the between-subject factors only one was significant. Specifically, the significant age × SES × time interaction, F (8, 754) = 2.77, p < .005, indicated that the shift from the strict to the lenient side of the HAI scale exhibited by the low SES group referred to 11, 12, and 13-year old subjects.

The effect of the SCS factor was highly significant, F (4, 3016) = 20.39, p < .001, indicating that evaluations concerning the various SCSs were differentially accurate. Specifically, drawing (M = .01) and social tasks (M = .05) were found to generate the most accurate evaluations. Interestingly, evaluations of the experimental tasks (M = −.22) were on the lenient side of the scale, whereas evaluations of the quantitative (M = .25) and the rotation tasks (M = .20) were on the strict side. The age × SCS,

F (16, 3016) = 2.27, p < .003, SES × SCS, F (8, 3016) = 8.99, p < .001, and gender × SCS, F (4, 3016) = 6.16, p < .001 interactions were significant, indicating that the accuracy of evaluations generated by the various SCSs varied somewhat as a function of age, SES, or gender. These results suggest that the various systems are not equally transparent to hypercognitive monitoring. Similar to the results of structural modelling, drawing appeared to be the most transparent domain. Moreover, in agreement with our earlier findings (Demetriou *et al.*, 1993a; Makris, 1995), quantitative tasks were evaluated as most difficult. Mental rotation seems to generate similar feelings of difficulty and as a result, these tasks led to conservative evaluations. Interestingly, the causal domain received lenient evaluations, although performance on causal tasks was no higher than other tasks, even quantitative tasks.

The three interactions between the within-subject factors were significant. Specifically, the evaluation × SCS, F (4, 3016) = 17.93, p < .001, the time × SCS, F (4, 3016) = 7.783, p < .001, and the evaluation × time × SCS interactions, F (4, 3016) = 11.47, p < .001, indicated that the exact position of each SCS on the HAI scale varied to a certain extent as a function of the type of evaluation, or time, or both. Specifically, the first of these interactions indicated that, overall, success and difficulty evaluation were practically identical for quantitative and causal tasks, and somewhat different for social, mental rotation, and drawing tasks. The second interaction indicated that, overall, the experience of solving the tasks variably affected the five domains: post-performance evaluations remained the same as pre-performance for quantitative and social tasks; they became stricter for rotation tasks; and they were more lenient for causal and drawing tasks. However, according to the third interaction, this shift affected difficulty evaluation in some SCSs and success evaluation in others.

In conclusion, the subjective evaluation of success and difficulty proved to be impressively accurate. Moreover, it appeared to be systematically related to age in a way that was consistent with the developmental changes of certain cognitive and hypercognitive dimensions. At the same time however, it was also found that subjective experiences of working on the tasks were clearly distinct and also, to a certain extent, related to various factors such as age, SES, and gender. These results clearly confirm our predictions (see Introduction) on self-evaluation. Next we will demonstrate in some detail how subjective evaluation of performance is related to the various dimensions of cognitive and social self.

Developmental changes in self-representation

This study was planned as a three-year longitudinal study which aimed to investigate both the dynamic interactions between cognition and hypercognition during development, and also how parents' and teachers' representations of the developing adolescent might affect the adolescent herself. A total of 294 participants, almost equally sampled from each combination of age and SES, were selected from the total of the 840 participants analysed above. Participants belonged to one of the following combinations of cognitive performance and success evaluation: (1) low performance-low success evaluation; (2) low performance-high success evaluation; (3) high performance-low success evaluation; and (4) high performance-high success evaluation. For reasons of convenience, the four groups will henceforth be called *low-accurates* (LA), *low-inaccurates* (LI), *high-inaccurates* (HI), and *high-accurates* (HA), respectively.

To form the four categories, for each participant, first, the sum of performance scores for items which had been evaluated for success and difficulty was computed, and also the sum of post-performance success evaluation scores was computed. Then for each combination of age and SES five participants were selected for each of the four combinations of cognitive performance and hypercognitive accuracy. We note here that approximately equal numbers of females and males were represented within each subgroup, whenever possible. Specifically, for each combination of age and SES, the LA were defined as the five participants having the lowest cognitive performance sum and the lowest post-performance success evaluation sum; the LI were defined as the five participants having the lowest cognitive performance sum and the highest post-performance success evaluation sum; the HI were defined as the five participants having the highest cognitive performance sum and the lowest post-performance success evaluation sum; and the HA were defined as the five participants having the highest cognitive performance sum and the highest post-performance success evaluation sum. This would give a total of 300 participants: 5 age groups × 3 SES groups × 4 person categories × 5 participants; however, six participants were lost because of the restriction on categories, i.e. categories only held subjects whose sums did not fall into the range of the sums of another category. The composition of this sample and the means of the two critical sums are shown in Table A4.3 in the Appendix.

This sample was used to investigate the development of the various dimensions of cognitive self (tapped by the questionnaires used in this study) because it allowed the influences of the dynamic relationships between cognitive performance and cognitive self-awareness to be specified. If these evaluations are filtered through a more general system which also underlies the dimensions of cognitive and social self-image (represented in the various questionnaires used in this study), one should expect to find obvious differences among the four groups on all dimensions represented in these questionnaires.

Developmental changes in self-representation of cognitive abilities

Seven factors were included in the questionnaire on cognitive abilities: one for the quantitative-relational SCS, two for the causal-experimental SCS (one for suppositional thought and one for experimentation), two for social thought (one for understanding others and one for understanding the social context of behaviour), one for visual memory, and one for drawing. For the present purposes, the two causal-experimental and the two social thought factors were combined. A mean score was computed for each subject for each of the five self-attribution of ability factors to represent all items related to the factor concerned. The five mean self-representation of ability scores were then subjected to a 5 (age) × 4 (the four person categories specified above) × 2 (gender) × 5 (the five ability-specific factors) with repeated measures on the last factor. It should be noted here that the SES as a factor was excluded from this analysis because preliminary analyses indicated that it did not exert any effect on the factors under consideration. The means and standard deviations involved are shown in Table A4.4 in the Appendix. Figure 4.3 illustrates some of the main trends revealed by this analysis.

The effect of age was highly significant, $F (4, 254) = 6.41$, $p < .001$, reflecting a decrease in self-representation of abilities from age 10–11 years, followed by first an increase, and finally a decrease again from age 13–14 years. It is noteworthy (see Figure 4.3) that 10-year olds gave the highest, and 15-year-olds gave the lowest scores across all five SCSs. It must be noted, however, that the significant age × SCS interaction, $F (16, 1016) = 2.66$, $p < .001$, indicated that the tendency of the self-representation of ability scores to decrease with age fluctuated to a certain extent among the SCSs in the three intermediate age groups.

The effect of the person category was highly significant, $F (3, 254) = 18.37$, $p < .001$. No other interactions between this factor and any other factor ever approached significance, indicating that this effect was very consistent. This result reflects the fact that, on the one hand, the LA scored considerably lower than the HA on all five factors (see Figure 4.3), which is consistent with the findings that the hypercognitive system is generally accurate in its representation of the cognitive system. Thus, in the present case, those who performed low on the cognitive tasks and had evaluated their own performance as relatively unsuccessful also ascribed to themselves less of the abilities represented by the five ability-specific factors than those who had high performance and had also highly evaluated their performance. However, this effect also indicated that the LI scored considerably higher than the HI on the five ability-specific factors. In other words, the low-performing subjects, who thought that they succeeded on the cognitive tasks, also tended to ascribe to themselves more of the abilities represented

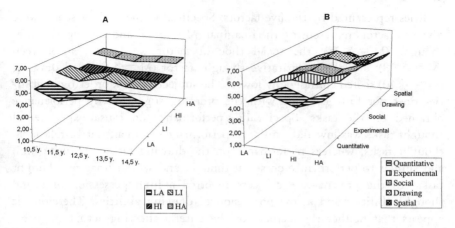

Figure 4.3 Self-attribution of ability scores as a function of age and person category (panel A) and person category or thought domain (panel B)

by the five factors than the highly performing subjects who had given themselves strict self-evaluations.

This finding is highly interesting in its implication that the various self-awareness functions of the hypercognitive system are internally consistent and, once in place, tend to function independently of actual performance to a considerable extent. In more practical terms, this assumption implies that lenient or strict self-ascriptions will tend to be stable over quite different occasions (e.g. evaluation of performance attained on a particular task, or the self-ascription of more general characteristics that depict the image that one has about oneself as a cognitive being). Evidently, this finding confirms the operation of the general hypercognitive factor identified by the structural analysis. The practical and theoretical implications of this assumption will be discussed after the presentation of the results related to other aspects of the self-image investigated by this study.

The effect of gender was non significant, $F (1, 254) = 6.16$, $p < .014$, indicating that overall, females ($M = 5.056$) and males ($M = 4.980$), ascribed to themselves about the same levels of ability. However, the significant gender $\times$ SCS interaction, $F (4, 1016) = 5.98$, $p < .001$, indicated that females scored higher than males on the social ($M = 5.29$ versus $M = 4.88$, respectively), the imaginal ($M = 5.53$ versus $M = 4.15$, respectively), and the drawing factors ($M = 4.49$ versus $M = 4.32$, respectively), and they scored lower than males on the quantitative ($M = 4.51$ versus $M = 4.87$, respectively) and the experimental thought factors ($M = 5.46$ versus $M = 5.68$, respectively).

Finally, the effect of ability was highly significant, $F (4, 1016) = 47.70$, $p < .001$, indicating that subjects reported differential possession of the abilities represented by the five factors. Specifically, the highest scores were given to factors representing the imaginal (M = 5.34) and the experimental thought (M = 5.25); the social thought factor was scored in-between (M = 5.08); and the quantitative thought factor (M = 4.69) and drawing (M = 4.40) scored considerably lower. The subjective rank ordering of abilities does not fully coincide with the ordering suggested by performance obtained on the tasks. Specifically, performance on causal-experimental thought tasks was low and similar to performance on quantitative-relational thought tasks, whereas performance on the drawing tasks was quite high and similar to performance on social thought and spatial-imaginal thought tasks. In the present case subjects reported a high possession of causal thought abilities and a low possession of drawing abilities. Therefore, it appears that neither the factors nor the criteria affecting actual cognitive performance are entirely identical with the factors or the criteria guiding the self-representations effected by the hypercognitive system.

Developmental changes in self-representation of general strategies and characteristics

Five factors were abstracted from the common factor analysis applied on the three sections of the general personal strategies and characteristics questionnaire which aimed to probe self-image in regard to a number of general cognitive, social, and emotional characteristics. These factors, which were included in the structural models, were as follows: ambition for personal success and social desirability, impulsivity, learning, planning and systematicity, and logical reasoning and discourse. The present analysis was applied on these five factors. This was a 5 (age) $\times$ 4 (person category) $\times$ 2 (gender) $\times$ 5 (the five characteristics) MANOVA with repeated measures on the last factor. The means and standard deviations derived from this analysis are shown in Table A4.5 in the Appendix. Figure 4.4 illustrates some of the main trends revealed by this analysis.

The results for the between-subject factors were very similar to our findings on the self-representation of cognitive abilities. Specifically, the effect of age, was significant, $F (4, 257) = 3.34$, $p < .01$, indicating, consistent with our previous findings that increasing age was associated with more conservative evaluations about all five factors. The effect of the person category factor was highly significant, $F (3, 257) = 9.48$, $p < .001$, although in this analysis the person category $\times$ characteristics interaction was also significant, $F (12, 1028) = 4.59$, $p < .001$. Taken together, these results indicate that the pattern of self-attributed characteristics across the four person categories was not entirely identical to that found for cognitive abilities. In the previous analysis, higher scores were given to the five abilities by

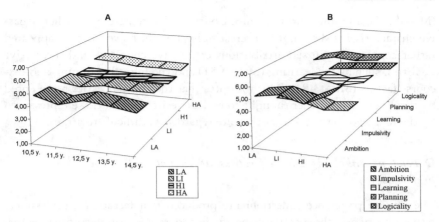

Figure 4.4 Mean self-attribution scores for general cognitive and personality characteristics across age and person category (panel A) or across person category and characteristics (panel B)

the HA than the LA, and LI scores were higher than HI scores. In the present case there were two deviations from this pattern. The scores given to the impulsivity factor by the four groups were ordered, from low to high, as follows: HI (M = 3.20), HA (M = 3.38), LI (M = 3.79), and LA (M = 3.86), indicating that low-performers tended to self-ascribe more impulsivity than high-performers independent of their performance evaluations. A second deviation was found for the logical reasoning and discourse factor. In the present case, the HI gave a higher score than the LI so that the four groups were ordered, from low to high, as follows: LA (M = 3.57), LI (M = 3.78), HI (M = 3.92), and HA (M =4.07), which indicates that the association between this factor and cognitive performance is the opposite of that between cognitive performance and impulsivity. That is, low-performers tended to self-ascribe less of this characteristic than high-performers. Together, these findings are consistent with the structural models presented above in their implication that logicality and impulsivity constitute dimensions of self-image which correlate directly with general cognitive ability. Thus, these two dimensions appeared to vary as a function of cognitive performance rather than success evaluation. This concurrence of structural modelling and the present more traditional analysis is noteworthy.

Finally, the effect of the characteristics factor was highly significant, F (4, 1028) = 252.67, p < .001, indicating that overall subjects did not self-ascribe the five characteristics equally. Understandably, they provided high scores for positive and generally highly valued characteristics, such as planning and systematicity (M = 5.63) and ideal self and social acceptance

(M = 5.26), and low scores for impulsivity, which represents a rather negative characteristic (M = 3.56). Interestingly enough, however, they appeared rather conservative in self-attributions of positive cognitive and interactive qualities, such as the learning (M = 4.51) and the logical reasoning and discourse factors (M = 3.81). This indicates that the characteristics represented by these factors are either thought to be less desirable than those represented by the first two factors, or that they are regarded as difficult to attain.

Developmental changes in self-representation of professional preferences

The activity preferences questionnaire produced four factors: (1) professional responsibility and three activity-specific factors representing activities requiring; (2) conformity to rules (executive style); (3) originality (legislative style); and (4) evaluation of others (judicial style). Following the same approach as previous analyses, a 5 (age) × 4 (person category) × 2 (gender) × 4 (the activity preferences factors) MANOVA with repeated measures on the last factor was run to specify the effects of the various between-subject factors on job preference. The means and standard deviations are shown in Table A4.6 in the Appendix; and Figure 4.5 highlights some of the main trends revealed by this analysis.

The between-subject effects were identical to the corresponding effects yielded by the analysis of self-attributed cognitive abilities. Specifically, the age effect was significant, $F (4, 257) = 3.50$, $p < .008$, indicating that increasing age was associated with decreasing preference scores across all factors. The person category factor was also highly significant, $F (3, 257) = 5.02$, $p < .002$, indicating that activity preference scores of the HA subjects were higher than the corresponding scores of all three other groups, and that the scores of the LI subjects were higher than the corresponding scores of the HI subjects and very similar to those of the HA subjects. Finally, the gender effect was marginally significant, $F (1, 257) = 5.39$, $p < .021$, indicating that males (M = 5.273) tended to be more conservative than females (M = 5.417) in stating activity preferences. None of the interactions between these factors ever approached significance.

Finally, the activity preference effect was highly significant, $F (3, 771) = 66.88$, $p < .001$, indicating that subjects exhibited differential preferences for the four factors. Specifically, from more to less preferred, the factors were ordered as follows: professional responsibility, (M = 5.65), conformity to rules (M = 5.07), originality (M = 5.06), and evaluation of others (M = 4.59). No interaction between this factor and any other factors ever approached significance, indicating that this ordering was the same across age groups, person categories, and genders.

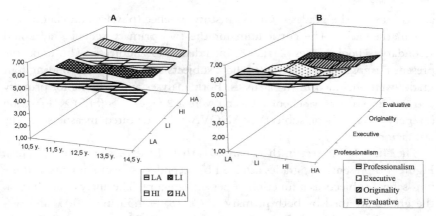

Figure 4.5 Mean preference scores across age and person category (panel A) or across person category and occupation type (panel B)

In conclusion, the results presented in the three sections above suggest clearly that self-evaluation of success on cognitive tasks is generally a better predictor of self-representations regarding several personality and social characteristics than is cognitive performance itself. At the same time, however, some cognitive and personality characteristics, such as logicality and impulsivity, appeared to have a privileged correlation with cognitive performance. That is, these dimensions appeared to function as agents intervening between cognitive functioning as such and the other components of self-image. An interesting question here is how these dimensions interact, if at all, with important aspects of cognitive functioning, such as school achievement which are independent of the design and manipulations of the present study. Evidently, the validity of the assumptions advanced here would be strengthened if this interaction could be demonstrated. The findings to be presented in the section below are a step in this direction.

Self-evaluation and school performance

To investigate the above question, school grades of the four subgroups of subjects (i.e. LA, LI, HI, and HA) were recorded and analysed. We note here that we were able to record grades for only 266 out of the 294 subjects. We also note that the grade system is different between primary and secondary school in Greece, ranging from 0–10 in primary school and from 0–20 in secondary school. Thus, the data from the two levels of education were analysed separately. Finally, school subjects vary across grades both at the primary and the secondary school level with only four common subjects across most of the grades – Greek, history, science (physics and chemistry), and mathematics. The curriculum for the two primary school grades and secondary school grades 2 and 3 included these subjects. Thus, for the present purposes only these four school subjects and their corresponding four grades were included in the analysis. Both analyses applied (one for primary and one for secondary school subjects) were a 2 (age) × 3 (SES) × 4 (person category) × 4 (school subject) MANOVA with repeated measures on the last factor.

The effect of interest in this analysis is that of the person category. Thus, Figure 4.6 presents the grades attained by secondary school students at these four school subjects as a function of person category. The analysis applied on the grades attained by both primary, $F (3, 78) = 4.55$, $p < .005$, and secondary school subjects, $F (3, 88) = 10.10$, $p < .001$, indicated that the effect of the person category was highly significant. Analysis revealed that at both school levels the two groups of participants who performed highly on the cognitive tasks (that is, the HI and the HA) attained higher school grades than the two groups of participants whose cognitive performance on the cognitive tasks was low (that is, the LA and the LI) across all school subjects. We emphasise that no interactions between person category and any other between- or within-subject factors ever approached significance.

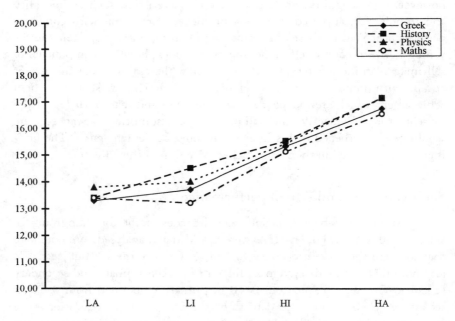

Figure 4.6 School grades obtained by high school second graders (13.5 years of age) as a function of age and school subject

Therefore, the superiority of high cognitive performers in school attainment was stable over age, SES, gender, and school subject.

At first reading, there seems to be a tendency for the HA to attain lower grades than the HI at primary school and higher grades at secondary school. A post hoc comparison of these two subject categories indicated that this difference was nonsignificant at primary school, $F (1, 39) = .85$, $p = .362$, but highly significant at secondary school, $F (1, 44) = 9.10$, $p < .004$. This may indicate that differences in self-evaluation and self-representation are established in adolescence rather than in childhood.

The reader is reminded that the person category was found to relate differently to the various dimensions of self-image, i.e. overall, the LIs self-ascribed the dimension characteristics to the same degree as the HAs. This indicates that it was self-evaluation of cognitive performance rather than cognitive performance itself which was the most important factor in the formation of the various dimensions of self-image. The results above indicated that for school achievement, however, the actual performance is more significant than performance self-evaluation. In other words, cognitive ability *per se* determines the individual's success at school rather than how she perceives her ability. This finding is obviously not surprising.

However, an alternative interpretation may also hold. Specifically, this pattern of results may indicate real differences in cognitive ability between the HI and the HA subjects which are accurately represented in their corresponding self-representations. That is, it might be the case that these subjects do differ in broad domains related to school performance, such as other cognitive abilities, motivation or interest related to academic achievement, but they do not differ in regard to the abilities underlying performance on the tasks used here. However, these other broad domains affect self-evaluation together with the abilities underlying performance on our tasks. In this case, the lower self-evaluations of the HI subjects, as compared to the self-evaluations of the HA subjects, reflect real differences in ability and achievement. The results to be presented in the following section will shed some light to this issue.

However, self-evaluation may also influence achievement and thinking. The significantly lower grades of the HIs as compared to those of the HAs at secondary school may indicate that individuals who underevaluate themselves may tend to attempt less and as a result to achieve less. Other interpretations cannot be ruled out however. For example, one might assume that the difference between these two groups is due to a complex interaction between cognitive and educational factors. That is, individuals who underevaluate themselves often convey a negative image that is independent of their actual ability. This negative image (held by the teacher) is fed back through lower grades, which, in turn, may cause further disengagement from the school learning process, which then leads to actual under-performance and even lower grades, etc. Because this difference is seen at secondary school but not primary school, we might conclude that subtle differences in self-evaluation are more possible or more important later rather than earlier in development. Evidently, these interpretations are not incompatible. They are both interesting in their implication that everyday achievement is a complex function of ability *per se*, self-representation, and factors external to the individual, which may affect and be affected by both ability and self-representation. Future research will have to disentangle the web of these interactions.

The stability of self-evaluation and self-representation

It is beyond the scope of this book to delve into the longitudinal part of the study. This would require a full monograph. However, some longitudinal findings need to be presented in order to strengthen the findings and conclusions of the main study. A crucial question is concerned with the stability of individual differences in self-evaluation and self-representation. Examining the self-evaluations of the four groups of persons who participated in the longitudinal study across the three testing waves would provide evidence directly related to this question. If these differences are stable, we would have to expect that the pattern of self-evaluations produced by the low accurate, the low inaccurate, the high inaccurate, and the high accurate subjects would remain the same at the second and the third testing wave. In other words, the subjects must continue to provide the same type of self-evaluations despite the fact they develop cognitively. To test this assumption, the performance attained on the five SCSs and the corresponding self-evaluations of success produced after solving the tasks were subjected to two separate multivariate analyses of variance.

Longitudinal findings about cognitive growth

To examine the development of the cognitive abilities involved in this study, a 5 (the five age groups) × 4 (the four person categories) × 3 (the three testing waves) × 5 (the five SCSs, i.e. quantitative, causal, imaginal, social, and drawing) with repeated measures on the last two factors was applied on performance attained at each of the three testing waves on each of the five SCSs. The table of means and standard deviations involved in this analysis is shown in Table A4.7 in the Appendix. To facilitate the inspection of the effects of primary interest here we prepared Figure 4.7. This Figure shows performance averaged across the five SCSs as a function of person category, testing wave, and age. The most interesting effect here is the effect of the person category. This effect was highly significant, $F (3, 210) = 54.73$, $p < .001$, indicating that the subjects ascribed to the low performance groups always performed lower than the subjects ascribed in the high performance groups across all three testing waves. As expected, the effect of age was also significant, $F (4, 210) = 6.66$, $p < .001$, indicating that older subjects performed better than younger subjects. The effect of wave was highly significant, $F (2, 420) = 139.81$, $p < .001$, indicating that performance improved systematically from the one testing wave to the next. The person category $\times$ wave interaction was significant, $F (6,420) = 8.85$, $p < .001$, indicating that the differences between the four person categories, although always present, tended to diminish from the one wave to the next. It can be seen in Figure 4.7 that the performance of the two lower groups improved more than the performance of the two higher groups at the last two testing waves, particularly from the first to the second wave. Similar is the meaning of the significant age $\times$ wave interaction, $F (8, 420) = 4.85$, $p < .001$. Overall, there was more change from the first to second rather than from the second to the third testing wave. However, there was some variation across age groups in the size of this change. Specifically, the pattern of change described above is very clear for the three younger age groups; however, there was practically no change from the second to the third testing wave among the subjects of the two older age groups.

As expected, the effect of the SCSs was also highly significant, $F (4, 840) = 263.53$, $p < .001$, indicating that performance varied across the five

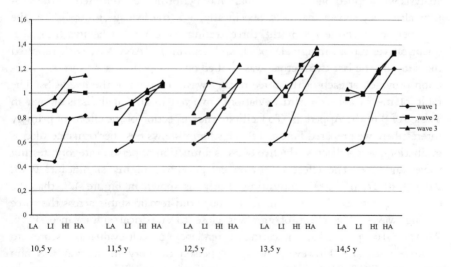

Figure 4.7 Cognitive performance averaged across SCSs as a function of age, person category, and testing wave

SCSs. Specifically, performance was lower on the causal SCS and drawing and higher on the imaginal and the social SCSs, the quantitative being in between. The interaction between person category and SCSs, $F (12, 840) = 3.19$, $p < .001$, and age and SCS, $F (16, 840) = 6.20$, $p < .001$, indicated that the difference between the performance attained by the four person categories or the five age groups varied across the five SCSs. Likewise, the significant wave $\times$ SCS interaction, $F (8, 1680) = 23.16$, $p < .001$, indicated that the size of performance improvement from each testing wave to the next varied across the five SCSs. For example, the experimental and the quantitative SCS improved much more that the imaginal and the social SCS. Moreover, the significant person category $\times$ wave $\times$ SCS interaction, $F (24, 1680) = 2.28$, $p < .001$, indicated that some groups of person (e.g. the low inaccurate persons) improved more on some SCSs (e.g. the imaginal SCS) from the first to the second testing wave whereas some other groups (e.g. high inaccurate persons) improved more from the second to the third testing wave in regard to others SCSs (e.g. the experimental).

Longitudinal findings about changes in self-evaluation

The stability of the differences between the four person categories makes their comparison in regard to their self-evaluation and self-representation highly interesting. Are the differences between the four groups also preserved across the three testing waves? That is, is the initial sigmoid relation between self-evaluation and person category also stable? To answer this question the same type of analysis was applied on the self-evaluation of performance attempted by the subjects after they solved the tasks. Specifically, a 5 (the five age groups) $\times$ 4 (the four person categories) $\times$ 3 (the three testing waves) $\times$ 5 (the five SCSs, i.e. quantitative, causal, imaginal, social, and drawing) MANOVA, with repeated measures on the last two factors, was applied on post-performance success evaluation provided at each of the three testing waves on each of the five SCSs. The table of means and standard deviations involved in this analysis is shown in Table A4.8 in the Appendix. To facilitate the inspection of the effects of primary interest here we prepared Figure 4.8. This figure shows post-performance success evaluation averaged across the five SCSs as a function of person category, testing wave, and age. The effect of person category was highly significant, $F (3, 210) = 49.27$, $p < .001$, indicating clearly, as shown in Figure 4.8, that the expected differences between the four groups did remain stable across the three testing waves. The effect of age was close to statistical significance, $F (4, 210) = 3.16$, $p < .015$, indicating a tendency of self-evaluation scores to increase with age. However, the age $\times$ person category interaction was non significant, $F (12, 210) = .86$, $p = .592$, indicating that differences between the four person categories remained stable across the five age groups.

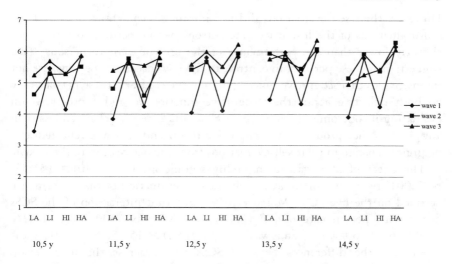

Figure 4.8 Post-performance success evaluation averaged across SCSs as a function of age, person category, and testing wave

The effect of testing wave was highly significant, F (2, 420) = 65.18, p < .001, indicating that self-evaluation scores increased from the one wave to the next, particularly from the first to the second wave. This increase may be taken to reflect the performance improvements revealed by the above analysis. The significant person category × wave, F (6, 420) = 25.72, p < .001, and person category × age interaction, F (8, 420) = 2.76, p < .006, indicated that the differences between the four person categories tended to diminish from the one wave to the next or with increasing age, respectively.

The highly significant person category × wave interaction requires special mention. It can be seen in Figure 4.8 that this effect reflected the fact that the increase in self-evaluation scores was limited to two of the person categories: namely the low accurate and the high inaccurate persons. This is an interesting developmental finding, if coupled with the changes in cognitive performance discussed above (see Figure 4.7). Specifically, it is reminded that the low accurate subjects improved across testing waves more than any other person category. Provided that these persons are accurate in their self-evaluations, it is to be expected that their self-evaluation would improve to match the actual cognitive changes brought about by development. The low inaccurate persons also developed considerably from the one testing to the next. However, their self-evaluations did not change accordingly because they were already very high. The high inaccurate persons did change cognitively and their self-evaluations improved accordingly.

However, their self-evaluations did not improve so much as to exceed the self-evaluations of the low inaccurate persons, whose performance was consistently lower than the performance of the high inaccurate persons. This suggests that these persons, in contrast to the low inaccurate persons, are not insensitive to their cognitive functioning; on the contrary, these persons may be both reflective about their cognitive functioning and conservative in evaluating its outcomes. Finally, the high accurate persons changed less than any of the other groups in the cognitive realm and this was reflected as a negligible change in their self-evaluations from the one testing to the next.

The effect of SCS was again highly significant, $F (4, 840) = 151.53$, $p < .001$, reflecting differences in the success evaluation of the performance attained on the five SCSs. Moreover, the significant interaction of the SCSs factor with person category, $F (12, 840) = 5.21$, $p < .001$, age, $F (16, 840) = 6.28$, $p = .001$, and wave, $F (8, 1680) = 15.05$, $p < .001$, indicated that the differences between SCSs varied across the four person categories, the five age groups and the three testing waves.

Longitudinal findings about changes in self-representation

A series of analyses explored the effects exerted by the person category and testing wave on all of the various personality factors and thinking styles investigated by this study. Space considerations do not allow a full presentation of the findings generated by these analyses. Only one of them is presented here, which involved children's self-representations about one of the general cognitive characteristics, namely learning ability, and one of the personality factors, namely impulsivity. Results about these dimensions were selected for presentation here for two reasons. First, these dimensions are special in that they have a central position in the organization of the self-system. The reader is reminded that, according to the structural models presented above, these two dimensions are directly connected to general cognitive abilities and they influence self-representations at a number of levels within the self-representation system. Second, they are directly related to the results concerning mothers' representations which are to be presented in Chapter 5. It needs to be stressed, however, that the results of the analyses applied on all other factors were very similar to the results of the other analyses presented in this section. That is, the effects of person category and testing wave on all self-representations about cognitive abilities, personality factors, and thinking styles were very strong and similar to their effects on self-evaluation.

The analysis mentioned in the above paragraph was a 4 (the four person categories) × 2 (self-representations about learning ability versus impulsivity) × 3 (the three testing waves) MANOVA with repeated measures on the last two factors. The means and standard deviations involved in this analysis are shown in Table A4.9 in the Appendix. The results of this analysis are summarized in Figure 4.9. It can be seen that the effect of the person category was significant, F (3, 226) = 7.76, p < .001, indicating that the four person categories differ in the self-representations they hold about learning ability and impulsivity. The effect of the two types of self-representation was also highly significant, F (1, 226) = 498.93, p < .001, indicating, in accord with expectations, that adolescents ascribe to themselves more learning ability than impulsivity. Specifically, the sigmoid relationship holds in regard to learning ability whereas a U-shaped relationship holds in regard to impulsivity. This last relationship requires special mention because it indicates clearly that persons low in cognitive ability regard themselves to be more impulsive than persons high in cognitive ability. The effect of wave was also significant, F (6, 452) = 13.28, p < .001. This effect requires special attention because the trend it represents is the opposite of the trend found by the analyses above which involved self-evaluations about domain-specific cognitive abilities. That is, self-representation scores about both learning ability and impulsivity tended to decrease from the one testing wave to the next. This is taken to indicate that, with cognitive growth, persons generally become more conservative in how they represent their general cognitive powers underlying learning. This may also indicate that, with growth, adolescents become more reflective and, as a result, less impulsive. The net result of these changes is the decrease in the scores given to both, learning ability and impulsivity.

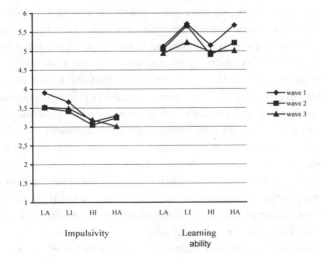

Figure 4.9 Self-attribution scores for impulsivity and learning ability as a function of person category and testing wave

In conclusion, the first of the analyses presented above showed clearly that the difference in performance between the four groups of persons are preserved over the period of the three years of this study, although all groups improved considerably from year to year in degrees varying from SCS to SCS. The findings of the second and third analysis complemented those of the first nicely. Specifically, differences in a person's attitude towards self-evaluation are also preserved. That is, individuals who are accurate, strict, or lenient in their self-evaluations tend to remain so despite changes in actual performance caused by development. These findings are important because they indicate that initial differences in ability or self-evaluation are not offset by development. Thus, on the one hand, self-evaluation cannot block cognitive development. All types of persons develop. At the same time, however, self-evaluation may be a factor in the determination of the relative standing of individuals on the developmental ladder. It is reminded that the four person categories remained consistently ordered in their cognitive performance, with the low and the high accurate persons to occupy the two extremes and the two groups of inaccurate persons to stand in the middle. This might suggest that the orientation of a person to himself or herself is related to how this person capitalizes on the individual and social resources available. We will return to this issue in the next chapter, when we will focus on the role of the two parents on development.

It also needs to be noted, however, that development does cause pervasive changes in self-representation. Specifically, all persons become more self-aware of the difficulties of problem-solving and understanding. This makes them more conservative in their self-representations about general cognitive abilities and also more careful in how they act. As a result, with growth, persons justifiably think of themselves as becoming less impulsive.

To cut a long story short, these findings suggest that self-evaluation and self-representation remains generally consistent in time. That is, persons may remain accurate, lenient, or strict to the output of their cognitive functioning and other dispositions. This implies the operation of a kind of internal monitor that adjusts evaluations and representations in regard to particular behaviours or events to stay consistent with one's self-definitions despite variations caused by changes in the environment or in the developmental status of the cognitive abilities and tendencies themselves. Thus, this internal mechanism seems to be rescaled as one moves from the one environment to the other or during development, in order to accommodate these changes. In fact, this rescaling is balanced enough so as to integrate into one's self-image the real and frequently large differences caused by cognitive development and also preserve one's self-profile despite these changes.

These interpretations bear an important implication in regard to the fact that the hypercognitive maps of all persons may accurately represent the architecture of their mind and self and still be accurate or inaccurate in regard to the evaluation of personal performance and behaviour. Specifically, the accuracy of the hypercognitive maps refers to relative differences between cognitive and personality functions and abilities within persons. The moderation mechanism mentioned here refers to something like a personal constant that is consistently applied across the board of cognitive and personality functions and abilities. Thus, assuming this constant we can explain why both types of differences are generally stable. That is, relative differences between abilities and tendencies within persons and relative differences in self-evaluation and self-representation across persons vis-à-vis each of the abilities and tendencies.

CONCLUSIONS

First of all, the findings presented in this chapter suggest clearly that the architecture of the mind proposed here is stable across different groups of the population, such as males and females or various SES groups. Even more important: This architecture is basically the same across different age groups. Only the communication between the two fundamental levels of this architecture was found to change with growth. It seems reasonable to conclude, therefore, that the various dimensions of the mental architecture proposed here can be used as standard yardsticks in order to evaluate and compare groups and individuals in development or other aspects of everyday functioning.

Another implication of our findings comes from the generalized impact that self-evaluation was found to have on the various dimensions of personality and thinking styles. That is, this impact implies that the self-awareness system involves a general moderation mechanism that defines the tone of many different aspects of self-awareness. This mechanism moderates both the on- or near on-line self-evaluations (regarding various aspects of performance on particular tasks at particular moments) and also the various aspects of self image, such as cognitive, social, and personality characteristics or even work preferences. This mechanism appeared to be "driven" by a factor that may be termed *personal constant*. That is, the individual adopts a particular attitude to his or her performance and ability which is consistently applied across different domains. This constant is used to adjust any signals regarding his or her functioning to a level which is personally characteristic.

It is important to emphasize that this personal constant is not developmentally invariable. Both the results of structural modelling regarding the effects of age on the communication between the environment-oriented and the self-oriented level of the mind and the developmental changes in the various dimensions of the self-concept indicated clearly that this personal constant undergoes major changes which start at about 11 years of age and continue well into adolescence. That is, the gradual establishment of relationships between the level of cognitive abilities and the hypercognitive level, together with the initial drop and subsequent rise in self-ascribed abilities and characteristics, indicate that the value of the constant is somehow redetermined or rescaled with development. As a result, the adolescent starts to evaluate or represent herself in reference to each of the various dimensions investigated here in a way which is at one and the same time accurate in regard to their organization but also consistent with one's particular type of self-definition and self-regard. The rescaling of the personal constant is obviously related to the fact that the effects of this constant remain more or less stable in time despite changes in cognitive development. These assumptions have both theoretical and practical implications.

An important theoretical implication is that the self-awareness system must be taken as a coherent construct that functions according to principles and forces which are to a certain extent independent of those forces defining the functioning of cognitive processes themselves. Thus, it can simultaneously preserve an accurate structure of cognitive processes in the mental maps it constructs and also involve a strong personal element in terms of how these processes are effected (or are thought to be effected) in the real world.

Moreover, these findings bear clear implications for the process of identity formation which is supposed to take place in adolescence (Erikson, 1963). That is, they suggest that establishing a sense of self or an identity is a process of tuning the various levels and dimensions of mind with each other. This process leads to an identity because it makes a person sufficiently aware of his or her strengths and weaknesses, talents, dispositions, and preferences. Of course, developmentalists (Campbell and Bickhard, 1986; Case, 1992; Fischer and Pipp, 1984; Harter, 1999) would argue that this tuning results, eventually, into a higher-order integration that defines the person as a whole. We would agree with this argument as it is fully consistent with our notion of a personal constant that undergoes rescaling with development.

In so far as practical implications are concerned, the personal constant may be important at a number of levels, because it may influence how the individual uses her cognitive and self-awareness skills and resources. That is, it may affect such functions as persistence toward the attainment of mental and other goals, or sensitivity to feedback. For example, persons who are low in ability but who think highly of themselves may not work as hard as needed to achieve certain goals or they may ignore signs of failure because they consider themselves sufficiently successful. Moreover, they may not allow themselves to fully engage in activities, so as to compensate for their comparatively low ability. On the other hand, persons who are high in ability but negative in their self-evaluations, may transmit an image which underscores their true potentialities and capabilities; in turn, this may cause their exclusion from the distribution of otherwise available resources. Thus, they deprive themselves of developmentally valuable nutrients which, if available, would cause a faster or more stable developmental pace. In other words, the self-awareness moderation mechanism becomes a factor of personal development in two distinct but interrelated respects: as a moderator of one's self-actualization of potentials and as a moderator of others' attitudes to any self-actualization endeavour. Our findings related to school achievement fully concur with these assumptions.

5 Study 2

Families of mind: relationships between children's self-representations and parents' representations about them

The evidence presented so far was limited to the individual. However, individuals do not develop alone but in groups with other individuals. As noted in the Introduction, the mind in general and the self-system in particular may be a social construction as much as it is an individual construction. Therefore, obtaining evidence about the relationships between the developing child's self-representations and the representations held by others about the child is necessary if we are to understand how the mind and the self-system are formed. This chapter will focus on the following questions:

1   How do the children's actual cognitive abilities and self-representations about them relate to their parents' respective representations? That is, how children's abilities and self-representations contribute to the formation of their parents' representations and how the parents' representations feed back and influence children's abilities and self-representations? How do the two parents' representations about the child interact with each other? How do these relations change over time?

2   Self-representations and the representations that persons have about each other may interact indirectly and implicitly. That is, they may interact through the behaviours that they cause without any awareness about them. However, these representations may also interact directly and explicitly. That is, persons may be aware of the representations that they have about each other. Even more: persons may have representations about the representations that others have about them. This higher-order awareness may influence the interactions between persons, their self-representations, and the representations they develop about each other. Thus, in this chapter we will provide some evidence about how aware children are of their parents' representations about them and how aware parents are of their children's self-representations.

To answer these questions, we decided to examine the parents of the participants who participated in the longitudinal part of the study. We may recall that four categories of persons participated in the longitudinal study. These were selected on the basis of their performance on the cognitive tasks and their self-evaluation of their performance. That is, they were persons: (1) low in cognitive performance who also evaluated their performance as being low (low-accurate persons); (2) low in performance but with high scores in their self-evaluations (low-inaccurate persons); (3) high in performance but with low scores in self-evaluation (high-inaccurate persons); and (4) high in performance and with high scores in self-evaluation (high-accurate persons). The sample of concern to the present chapter is described below.

METHOD

Participants

Most of the 294 participants who were selected to participate in the longitudinal study were tested twice after their first testing which involved the whole sample of 840 participants. Specifically, 275 and 230 participants were tested at the second and third testing wave, respectively (see Table 2.2). A period of 12 months intervened between each testing.

The ideal was to test both parents of these 294 participants. Unfortunately, not all parents were available. Specifically, 192 mothers and 95 fathers participated in the second testing and 95 mothers and 35 fathers participated in the third testing wave. The exact distribution of these parents in the various categories of participants is shown in Table 5.1.

Batteries

Second testing

The children were examined on all of the task batteries and the self-evaluation and self-representation inventories used at the first testing.

The parents were first presented with one of the tasks addressed to each SCSs and they were told that their child was asked to solve them. They were then asked to state how well they think that their child can solve each of these tasks. The 7-point scale was again used (with 1 indicating no ability to solve a task and 7 indicating full possession of this ability). This manipulation was employed for two reasons. First, to enable the parents to focus their representations on the cognitive abilities examined by the present studies rather than on their own subjective interpretation of them. Second, to provide direct evaluations of the children's abilities. These evaluations can be compared with children's corresponding actual performance, self-evaluation, and self-representation and also with the parents' representations as evoked by the cognitive abilities inventories described above.

Table 5.1 Composition of the sample of mothers and fathers

Age group	SES	Gender	2nd wave Mothers N	Fathers N	3rd wave Mothers N	Fathers N
10.5	Low	F	7	5	4	–
		M	7	4	7	2
	Middle	F	4	1	3	1
		M	5	3	4	2
	Upper middle	F	6	2	3	1
		M	5	2	4	2
11.5	Low	F	9	2	6	1
		M	2	–	1	–
	Middle	F	6	2	2	1
		M	6	2	5	–
	Upper middle	F	5	2	3	2
		M	7	2	4	2
12.5	Low	F	11	9	6	4
		M	8	7	3	2
	Middle	F	7	6	3	1
		M	10	7	6	3
	Upper middle	F	4	2	1	–
		M	7	3	1	–
13.5	Low	F	5	2	2	1
		M	3	2	1	1
	Middle	F	2	–	–	–
		M	5	2	2	2
	Upper middle	F	7	4	5	2
		M	8	1	3	–
14.5	Low	F	5	3	2	–
		M	5	5	5	3
	Middle	F	5	3	3	1
		M	3	1	1	–
	Upper middle	F	7	4	3	1
		M	5	1	2	–
15.5	Upper middle	F	12	5	–	–
		M	4	1	–	–
Total			192	95	95	35

To examine the parents' representations about their children, all self-representation inventories (that is, the inventory addressed to cognitive abilities, general personal strategies and characteristics, and thinking and activity styles) were restated to refer to the children. The parents were asked to state (using the same 7-point scale) how much each of the items applies to their own child.

Third testing

The children were again examined on all task batteries and inventories. The parents were tested on all of the child-centred inventories used during the second phase.

Moreover, during the third wave, both children and parents were examined on the reflected appraisals inventory. This inventory was constructed to represent all of the dimensions found in the various self-representation inventories described above. That is, we included in this inventory the first four best-loading items on the factor standing for a dimension (according to the exploratory factor analysis presented in Chapter 3). These are the items shown in Table 2.3, 2.4, and 2.5 to load on each of the various factors used in all of the analyses presented in Chapters 3 and 4. Specifically, children were asked to answer this inventory from the perspective of each of their parents (that is, answer how you think your mother – and father – each answered about you). Parents were asked to respond from their child's perspective (that is, answer how you think your child answered about himself or herself). Thus, this inventory, together with the other inventories, can show how family members represent themselves, each other, and each other's representations about themselves.

Procedure

Children were tested in groups during school hours according to the procedures described in Chapter 2. Each of the parents was tested individually at home by especially trained interviewers.

Hypotheses to be tested

The literature reviewed in the Introduction, together with the findings of the main study presented in Chapters 3 and 4, justify stating the following hypotheses:

5.1 The various dimensions of self representation must also be present in the parents' representations of the children. This hypothesis reflects either or both of two possibilities. On the one hand, the information emitted by the child to others is framed according to these dimensions. On the other hand, these dimensions organize the parents' mind and self as well. Therefore, they organize their observations and evaluations of their children's abilities and tendencies according to these dimensions.

5.2 Some dimensions must be more important than others as sources of influence on the parents' representations. General cognitive ability must be more important than particular domains and domains transparent to awareness (such as drawing) must be more important than opaque domains (such as social thought).

5.3 The mother is found to be a very sensitive and accurate observer and evaluator of the child – often more accurate than the child herself

(Miller, 1988, 1995). This justifies the assumption that the mother would somehow influence both the self-representations of the child and the father's representation of the child.

5.4 Despite their interdependencies, children and parents are autonomous persons. Therefore, the relations between dimensions or the successive states of a dimension over time must be considerably stronger within rather than across individuals. However, there should be an interplay of influences between children and parents over time whose exact nature cannot be anticipated due to lack of relevant research and theorizing.

5.5 The child's reflected appraisals of their parents' representations about them reflect, at least in part, the view that children have about their own public image. The parents' reflected appraisals of their children's self-representations reflect, at least in part, how sensitive the parents are to differences between what the children think of themselves and what they themselves think of the children. Unfortunately, the evidence available does not provide the basis for formulating exact predictions about the relations between these four kinds of measures (that is, children's self-image and reflected appraisals and parents' representations about the children and their reflected appraisals of children's self-representations). However, there is a particular pattern of relations among these measures, which seems more plausible than other patterns. On the one hand, it can be expected that the relation between the children's reflected appraisals of their two parents' representations must be stronger than the relations between each of these two types of reflected appraisals and their own self-representations. This would indicate that self-image and public image are distinct from each other in the mind of the children, and this is considered a condition of good adaptation and mental health (Brown, 1998). On the other hand, a close relation between parents' representations and their reflected appraisals can also be expected. This would reflect parents' conviction that their image of the child is accurate and, therefore, it would have to be espoused by the child too.

RESULTS

A full presentation of the longitudinal part of the study concerned with parents is beyond the scope of this book. The aim of this chapter is to present results related only to the hypotheses stated above so that the evidence presented in the other chapters is put in the perspective of broader social influences.

The children-parents' interactions

To answer the first two of the above hypotheses a model is needed that would involve factors standing for children's abilities and self-representations and also factors standing for the parents' representations about these abilities. In this model the relations between the factors can be estimated both within and across persons. The model shown in Figure 5.1 is a first attempt in this direction. This model included only three of the various cognitive abilities examined in the study. We reduced the number of abilities to be analyzed here only to a representative sample of them because these analyses include three persons (the child and the two parents). Including all of the abilities would increase the number of dimensions to be dealt with in the model beyond technically manageable levels. Thus, we chose three abilities that represent different types of thought, that is, quantitative thought, social thought, and drawing. For each of these abilities two half scores were created according to the procedures described in Chapter 3 above. This model was applied on the 95 families from the second testing wave for which complete examinations were available.

Following hypothesis 5.1, this model involved four sets of first-order factors and each set involved one factor for each of the three SCSs. That is, there were three SCS-specific factors representing children's performance on the tasks addressed to three SCSs mentioned above, three SCS-specific factors representing children's self-representations about these SCSs, and, finally, two sets of three SCS-specific factors representing the two parents' representations about these three SCSs. The three factors in each of the four sets were regressed on a second-order factor. As far as the child is concerned, the meaning of these factors was discussed in Chapter 3. As far as the parents are concerned, these higher order factors may be taken to stand for the parents' overall representation of the child as a thinker.

Moreover, the following structural relations were built into the model. First, each of the child's three self-representations factors were regressed on: (i) the residual of the corresponding SCS-specific factor representing actual performance and, for the reasons stated in hypothesis 5.3; (ii) the corresponding SCS-specific factor of the mother. Second, all three factors of the mother and the father were regressed on the child's general cognitive ability factor for the reasons stated in hypothesis 5.2. Moreover, each of the SCS-specific factors of the mother and the father was regressed on the corresponding SCS-specific performance factor of the child. Third, each of the three factors of the father was also regressed on the corresponding factor for the mother. Finally, the three second-order factors (that is, the child's general self-representation factor and the two general factors of the parents) were allowed to correlate.

The fit of this model was excellent, $\chi^2(214) = 229.053$, p = .23,

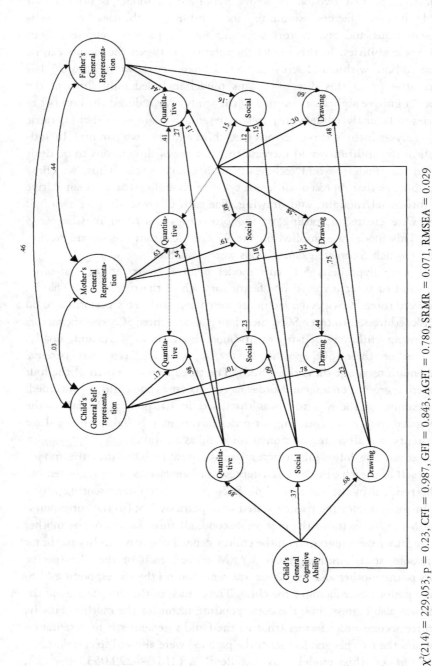

$X^2(214) = 229.053$, p = 0.23, CFI = 0.987, GFI = 0.843, AGFI = 0.780, SRMR = 0.071, RMSEA = 0.029

Figure 5.1 The model of the interrelationships between children's abilities and self-representations and parents' representations of children's abilities

CFI = .987, GFI = .843, AGFI = .780, SRMR = .071, RMSEA = .029. Validating this model suggests a number of interesting conclusions. First, in agreement with hypothesis 5.1, all cognitive domains are present in performance, in self-representation, and in other persons' representations of other persons. This is an important finding because, technically speaking, it justifies further exploring the interactions between persons vis-à-vis these constructs. It also has important theoretical implications, which will be discussed in the concluding section below.

The second conclusion is equally interesting. That is, in line with hypothesis 5.3, the mother does influence the formation of the child's self-representations and the father's representations of the child. It can be seen that the mother's representations about the child are based on two complementary sources. That is, in line with hypothesis 5.2, the mother's representations about all domains reflect the child's general cognitive ability. Moreover, the mother's representations about transparent domains reflect the actual condition of these domains in the child. This indicates that the mother is sensitive to the child's general efficiency as a problem solver as reflected in the child's speed, accuracy, and general strategies. It may also indicate, however, that the mother somehow averages over different activities so that the child's strengths and weaknesses are pulled together into a general representation for the child. At the same time, some domains, that are transparent to awareness, such as mathematics or drawing, are reflected directly and clearly in the mother's system of representations about the child. Then the mother's representations influence both, the self-representations of the child herself and the father. It can be seen that the child's self-representations in some domains are influenced by the mother's corresponding representations as much or more than they are influenced by the actual state of the corresponding domains.

Do the same relationships hold for the realm of personality? To answer this question, a similar model was applied on three of the personality factors identified by the study, that is the factors of ambition, impulsivity, and systematicity. This model is shown in Figure 5.2. It can be seen that this model involved the three characteristic-specific factors and a general second-order factor related to the specific factors for each of the three persons. Moreover, the following direct structural relations between the domain-specific factors were build into the model: (1) Each of the three factors standing for the mothers' representations about the child was regressed on the corresponding factor standing for children's self-representations. (2) Each of the three factors standing for the fathers' representations was regressed on both the corresponding factor of the mother and the corresponding factor of the child. The fit of this model was excellent, χ^2 (117) = 109.435, p = .68, CFI = 1.000, GFI = .894, AGFI = .846, SRMR = .080, RMSEA = .000.

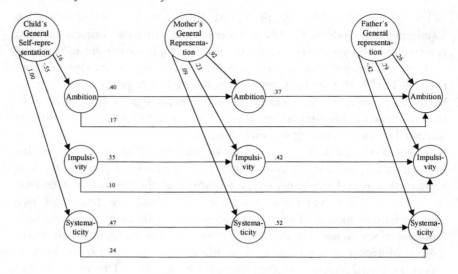

$\chi^2(117) = 109.435$, p $=$ .679 CFI $=$ 1.000, GFI $=$ .894, AGFI $=$ .846, SRMR $=$ .080, RMSEA $=$ .000

Figure 5.2 Model of the interrelationships between children's and parents' representations of children's position on the dimensions of ambition, impulsivity, and systematicity

This model suggests a number of conclusions about the parent's representations of the personality characteristics of their children. First, these representations are organized along the same dimensions that organize the children's self-representations themselves. Second, both parent's representations about their children are very accurate in their reflection of the condition of children's self-representations. As in the case of the cognitive abilities, the mother plays an interfacing function between the child and the father as this is suggested by the fact that direct relationships between the mother's and the father's representations were always higher that the corresponding child-father relationships. However, it needs to be noted that the effects of the mother's representations of the personality of the child on the child's respective representations seem weaker than those concerning the cognitive realm.

Dynamic relations along time

To test the fourth of the hypotheses above, a complex model was constructed which involved the three SCS-specific factors to represent children's actual performance and the corresponding self-representations across all three testing waves and also the mothers' corresponding representations across the second and the third testing. In order to have a sufficient number of subjects, this model was applied on the set of 95 families for which there were complete examinations of the mothers across both the second and the third testing wave.

In a first run, implementing hypothesis 4.4, each SCS-specific factor at each testing wave was initially regressed on its corresponding factor of the previous testing wave. That is, each of the three performance and the three self-representation factors from the third testing wave was regressed on its corresponding factor from the second wave and each of these factors was regressed on its corresponding factor from the first wave. Moreover, each of the self-representation factors at each testing wave was also regressed on its corresponding performance factor. In as far as the mother is concerned, each of the third wave factors was regressed on the corresponding second wave factor. Then, following the modification indexes, some paths were deleted and others were added as appropriate. The final model, which was found to have a good fit, $\chi^2(982) = 1053.256$, p = .056, CFI = .971, GFI = .726, AGFI = .672, RMSR = .087, RMSEA = .030, is shown in Figure 5.3. It can be seen that self-regressions (i.e. regressions of a factor of a subsequent testing wave on the corresponding factors of an earlier wave) are generally high both within the child and within the mother. This indicates considerable stability of individual differences over time in actual performance, self-representations about it, and the mother's representations about it. This stability, together with the finding that both performance and representations change over time (see the results presented in Chapter 4), indicates that the child's self-representations and the mother's representations about the child are continually adjusted over time to accommodate developmental changes in the abilities concerned.

How do the child and the mother interact over time? In general, there are fewer interactions between mothers and children and these are weaker than the interactions between factors within persons. This being said, it is also clear that there are systematic interactions between mother and child along with time. Specifically, it can be seen that the child's general self-representation and one of the SCSs at time 1 influences directly some of the mother's representations at time 2. These representations of the mother then influence some of the child's self-representations at time 2, and these self-representations at time 2 influence self-representations at time 3. In other words, it seems that actual abilities and self-representations in the family form very complex loops which span over time and in which everybody's condition affects and is affected by everybody else's condition. In this system of complex dynamic interactions some abilities or functions play a more crucial role than other abilities or functions.

To test if these relationships apply to personality as well, a similar model

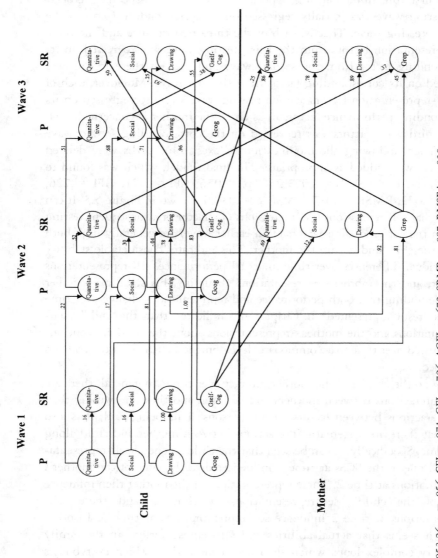

$\chi^2(982) < 1053.26$, p = .056, CFI = .971, GFI = 726, AGFI = .672, SRMR = .087, RMSEA = .030

Figure 5.3 The model applied to three performance factors (P), their corresponding self-representations (SR), and corresponding representations of the mother across three testing waves

was tested on three of the personality factors abstracted by this study, namely the factors standing for ambition, impulsivity, and systematicity. This model is shown in Figure 5.4, $\chi^2(374) = 519.251$, p $= .001$, CFI $= .897$, GFI $= .750$, AGFI $= .690$, SRMR $= .100$, RMSEA $= .065$. The inspection of this model makes it clear that the same pattern of relationships interconnects the factors both within and across persons. That is, the self-regressions are very high in both the children and the mothers across all three personality factors included in the analysis. Relationships between the two persons are much weaker and these concern only a few of all possible relationships tested. Specifically, the only significant (but moderate) causal paths running from children's self-representations to the corresponding representations of the mothers go from the impulsivity and the systematicity factor of children's first wave of testing (time 1) to the corresponding factors of the mother's first wave of testing (time 2), which took place one year later. It is noted that negative correlations in these longitudinal models are taken to stand for the fact that self-representations become stricter with age, during the age-phase studied here.

These findings are clearly incongruent with the looking glass model. That is, they clearly suggest that, on the one hand, development within persons is by and large self-propelled and self-sustained; on the other hand, it gets interleaved with other persons at some privileged times and in relation to some privileged domains. This state of affairs is of course a reasonable one. It ensures at one and the same time the autonomy of the individual and its rapport with important others in his environment.

Reflected appraisals

The research summarized so far was concerned with first-order self-representations or representations about other persons. Thus, to test hypothesis 5.5 about higher-order representations or reflected appraisals, the results generated from the reflected appraisals inventory at the third testing wave were used together with the child's self-representations and the parents' representations at the same wave. Due to the limited number of fathers examined at this wave only results from children and mothers are used. Moreover, because even the number of children and mothers is small relative to the large number of dimensions represented in these inventories, the items representing a dimension were pulled together to a mean score and the zero-order correlations between the various dimensions were calculated. These correlations are shown in Table 5.2.

The correlations in Table 5.2 illustrate the interrelationships among

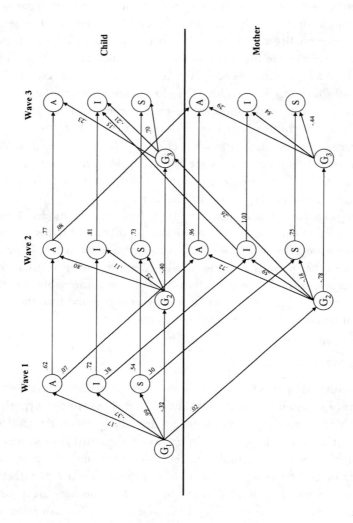

$\chi^2(374) = 519.251$, p = .001, CFI = .897, GFI = .750, AGFI = .690, SRMR = .100, RMSEA = .065

Figure 5.4 The model of the relationships between the dimensions of ambition (A), impulsivity (I), systematicity (S), as represented by the child and the mother across three testing waves

representations both within and across persons. These interrelationships suggest the following conclusions.

First of all, attention is drawn to the very high correlations between the children's reflected appraisals for their mother and their father (actually out of a few tens of correlations of this kind none was below .6). This finding clearly implies that children believe that they have a "public image", which is transmitted to their parents. Thus, they think that their two parents' images of them are very similar to each other.

The second conclusion is concerned with the relations between self-image and public image. The correlations between the various dimensions of self-image and the children's reflected appraisals of their parents' representations are relevant in this regard. It can be seen that these correlations were significant in most of the cases. This suggests that these two images are related. At the same time, it needs to be noted that the size of these correlations varied across domains and persons. It can be seen that children's self-representations are closer to representations they think their parents have about them when they refer to domains transparent to awareness, such as quantitative or imaginal thought rather than in regard to domains opaque to awareness, such as social thought. That is, while these correlations are satisfactory (circa .4) for transparent domains, they are very low for opaque domains. Moreover, children think that their mother's representations about them are more similar to their own self-representations than their father's corresponding representations for all dimensions. It needs to be stressed, however, that, although related, self-image and public image are clearly distinct. This is strongly suggested by the fact that the correlations between the child's reflected appraisals ascribed to each of the two parents were always considerably higher that the correlations between the various self-image dimensions and the corresponding reflected appraisals.

Finally, we examined the question: how are the mothers' reflected appraisals of the children self-representations related to these self-representations? The last row of Table 5.2 indicates that correlations are again very satisfactory for transparent domains but weak for opaque domains. It is also interesting to note that the correlations between the mother's representations of the child and her reflected appraisals of the child's self-representations are impressively high – even higher than the correlation between the child's self-representations and the child's representations of her mother's representations. This indicates that in the mother's mind her actual opinion of the child and what she believes that the child thinks of himself are less differentiated than the child's self-representations and the representations that she believes her mother holds. These findings are in full agreement with hypothesis 5.5.

To verify the constructs and dimensions discussed above, the same model

Table 5.2 Correlations between self-representations, mother's representations about the child, and reflected appraisals across different dimensions

	1	2	3	4	5
1 Child's self image					
Quantitative					
Social					
Imaginal					
Ambition					
Impulsivity					
Originality					
2 Child's reflected appraisal for the mother					
Quantitative	.61**				
Social	.42**				
Imaginal	.54**				
Ambition	.56**				
Impulsivity	.36**				
Originality	.47**				
3 Child's reflected appraisal for the father					
Quantitative	.54**	.68**			
Social	.30*	.77**			
Imaginal	.47**	.74**			
Ambition	.47**	.82**			
Impulsivity	.37**	.87**			
Originality	.49**	.74**			
4 Mother's image of the child					
Quantitative	.42**	.36**	.32**		
Social	.20	.01	.06		
Imaginal	.17	.23	.37**		
Ambition	.17	.15	.05		
Impulsivity	.18	.32**	.37**		
Originality	.06	.05	.06		
5 Mother's reflected appraisal for the child					
Quantitative	.52**	.40**	.33**	.77**	
Social	.14	.06	.06	.57**	
Imaginal	.13	.21	.24*	.52**	
Ambition	.18	.19	.15	.83**	
Impulsivity	.18	.27*	.35**	.53**	
Originality	.07	.00	.12	.59**	

Note

Quantitative thought is regarded as transparent to awareness and social thought is regarded as opaque to awareness. Ambition seems to fall in-between (N = 95, p <.05 and p <.01 for one and two asterisks, respectively).

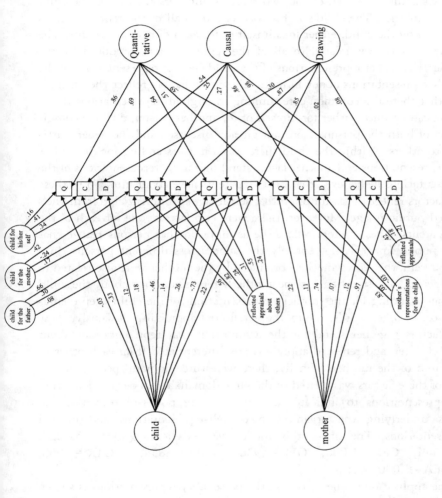

$\chi^2(53) = 51.222$, p = .544, CFI = 1.000, GFI = .936, AGFI = .854, SRMR = .068, RMSEA = .000

Figure 5.5 The model of self-representations of the child, mother's representations about the child, and reflected appraisals about each other's representations in regard to quantitative (Q), causal (C), and drawing (D) SCS

was tested two times, one on cognitive and another on personality representations. The application of the model on the cognitive representations is shown in Figure 5.5. This model was applied on the representations about the quantitative, the causal, and the drawing domains. It can be seen that the following constructs were built into the model. There were two factors standing for each of the two representing persons, that is the child and the mother. The child's factor was related to all of the representations produced by the child, either for himself or for each of his two parents. The mother's factor was related to all of the representations produced by the mother, that is her representations of the child and her representations of the child's representations about himself. These two factors reflect the assumption that there is a common core running through all representations that a person can produce, either for himself or for another person, due to a combination of both the personal constant already discussed and the general attitude to others. Within the child there was a factor standing for the child's self-representations and another factor standing for his representations of the representations he believed that his two parents have about him. Thus, these two factors reflect the assumption that self-image is differentiated from one's alleged public image. Moreover, there were two factors, one for each of the two parents. These factors reflect the assumption that persons realize that their public image is not entirely the same across different persons. In a similar vein, the representations produced by the mother were also related to two factors, one standing for the mother's representations about the child and one standing for the mother's representations of the child's representations or, in other words, the mother's reflected appraisals. Obviously, these two factors together stand for the assumption that representations about their children and reflected appraisals are differentiated from each other in the mind of the mothers. Finally, there were three domain-specific factors; each of these factors was related to the same domain across persons and types of representations to indicate that domains are powerful organizational forces underlying the organization of self-representations and mutual representations. The fit of this model was excellent, $\chi^2(53) = 51.222$, p $= .544$, CFI $= 1.000$, GFI $= .936$, AGFI $= .854$, SRMR $= .068$, RMSEA $= .000$.

The application of the model on the personality representations is shown in Figure 5.6. It can be seen that the representations about the ambition, impulsivity, and systematicity were included in this model. Inspection of Figure 5.6 shows that this model involved exactly the same constructs as the model applied on the representations about cognitive ability. The fit of this model, although not as good as the fit of the model applied on the cognitive representations, was very satisfactory, $\chi^2(52) = 70.418$, p $= .05$, CFI $= .975$, GFI $= .915$, AGFI $= .804$, SRMR $= .079$, RMSEA $= .062$.

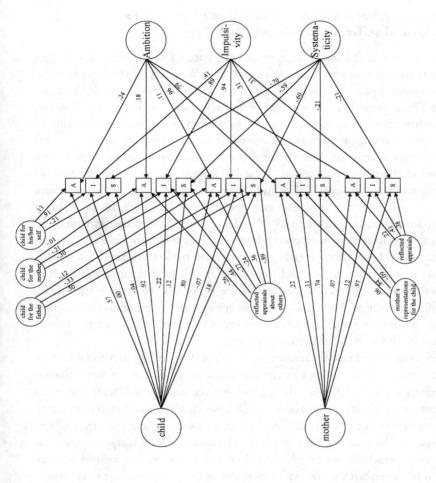

$\chi^2(52) = 70.418$, $p = .05$, CFI = .975, GFI = .915, AGFI = .804, SRMR = .079, RMSEA = .062

Figure 5.6 The model of self-representations of the child, mother's representations about the child, and reflected appraisals about each other's representations in regard to ambition (A), impulsivity (I), and systematicity (S)

The results above make it very clear that persons do differentiate clearly between themselves and others and also between their various public images as held by different persons. Interestingly, this differentiation within and between persons goes together with the fact that the various self-images and public images as well as the images about others that we hold are organized along the same dimensions. The implications of this pattern are discussed below.

Mothers' representations as a function of children's abilities and self-representations

The results presented above suggest that the parents' representations of their children are not accurate across the board. The accuracy of these representations depends upon the ability or characteristic concerned. That is, it is satisfactory in regard to transparent domains and general cognitive or personality characteristics but rather weak in regard to opaque domains or more specialized characteristics. To provide further support to this conclusion, a series of analyses were performed on the representations given by the mothers at their first testing (that is, at the second testing of the children) as a function of the cognitive ability and the self-representation of their children. That is, these analyses aimed to examine if the four categories of children involved in the longitudinal study (that is, low in cognitive performance and low in self-evaluation (low accurate); low in cognitive performance and high in self-evaluation (low inaccurate); high in cognitive performance and low in self-evaluation (high inaccurate); and high in cognitive performance and high in self-evaluation (high accurate subjects)) are differentiated in the representations of the mothers. These analyses were applied on the representations given by the mothers at their first testing in order to have a sufficient number of subjects in each of the four person categories.

A 4 (the four person categories) × 5 (the five SCSs) MANOVA with repeated measures on the last factor was first applied on the mothers' characterizations of their children's ability to solve the tasks which were presented to them as representative of the five SCSs. Neither the main effect of person category nor any of the interactions between this factor and the other factors involved in the analysis ever reached significance. This indicates that the mothers' representations of their children's abilities are not refined enough so as to be tuned with variations of performance attained on particular tasks.

A second MANOVA was performed on the mothers' representations as specified through the inventory addressed to the same domain-specific cognitive abilities. Thus, this was also a 4 (the four person categories) × 5 (the five SCSs) MANOVA with repeated measures on the last factor. This analysis aimed to test if children's differences in ability and self-evaluation are somehow reflected in mothers' more broad representations (the means and standard deviations involved in this analysis are shown in Table A5.1 in the Appendix). The α level for the analyses applied on this study was set to .05. Again, the main effect of the person category factor was non significant, F (3, 135) = 1.46, p = .229. The effect of the SCS was highly significant, F (4, 540) = 27.02, p < .001, indicating that mothers ascribed to their children more ability in some SCSs (such as the social and the imaginal SCS) rather than in others (such as the quantitative SCS or drawing). However, in this analysis, the person category × SCS interaction was marginally significant, F (12, 540) = 1.70, p = .06. This indicated the fact that the differences between the four children's categories were differentially represented in mothers' representations. It can be seen in Figure 5.7 that the ascription of ability in regard to mathematical ability (that is, the quantitative SCS) increased linearly from the LA to LI to HI to HA, indicating that mothers' representations are affected by both children's actual mathematical ability and the respective self-evaluation. In the case of drawing, the lowest score was ascribed to LI and there was no clear trend in regard to the other domains. The results are generally in line with the conclusions suggested by structural modelling. That is, the person category was found to exert an effect on mothers' representations only in the most transparent of the cognitive domains, namely mathematics and drawing, although this effect was not entirely the same as in children's representations themselves.

A series of analyses aimed to explore the possible effects of children's category on all of the mother's representations concerning the cognitive abilities, personality characteristics, and thinking styles of the children. It needs to be stressed that this factor affected significantly only the mother's

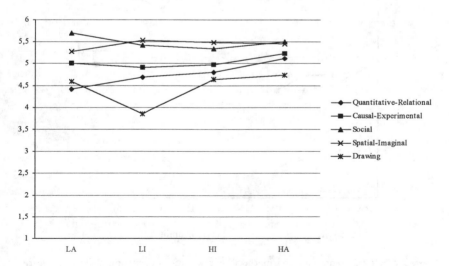

Figure 5.7 Mother's representations about children's cognitive abilities

representations about the learning ability of the child. Likewise, of the various personality and thinking style factors only one appeared to be affected, namely impulsivity. Thus, a 4 (the four person categories) × 2 (the factor standing for the learning ability versus the factor standing for impulsivity) MANOVA with repeated measures on the last factor was run to specify these effects (see Table A5.2 in the Appendix). The effect of the person category was non significant, $F (3, 135) = 1.32$, $p = .269$. The difference between the representations about the two characteristics was highly significant, $F (1, 135) = 309.43$, $p < .001$, indicating that the scores for learning ability were much higher than the scores for impulsivity. However, the interesting part of this analysis, from the point of view of the present discussion, lies in the interaction between the category of children and the representations. This interaction was significant, $F (3, 135) = 3.60$, $p < .036$, indicating that the scores given to learning ability increased and the scores given to impulsivity decreased as a function of the person category of the children. This interaction is shown in Figure 5.8.

To compare children's self-representations with mothers' representations in regard to these two important dimensions, a 4 (the four person categories) × 2 (children versus mothers) × 2 (learning ability versus

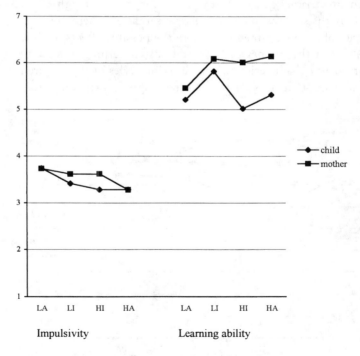

Figure 5.8 Self-representations and mothers' representations about impulsivity and learning ability in children as a function of person category

impulsivity) MANOVA with repeated measures on the last factor was performed on the children's self-representations at their second testing wave and the mothers' respective representations at their first testing wave (that is, contemporaneous scores were analyzed) (the means and standard deviations involved in this analysis are shown in Table A5.2 in the Appendix). The main findings of this analysis are summarized in Figure 5.8. The effect of the person category was non significant, $F (3, 135) = 1.79$, $p = .152$. The difference between children and mothers was highly significant, $F (1, 135) = 25.86$, $p < .001$, indicating that mothers' scores were generally higher than those of the children. Expectedly, the difference between learning ability and impulsivity was highly significant, $F (1, 135) = 336.02$, $p < .001$, indicating that the scores given to learning ability by both children and mothers were much higher than the scores given to impulsivity. The interaction between the person category and the learning versus impulsivity factor was significant, $F (3, 135) = 2.74$, $p < .046$ indicating that scores given to learning ability tended to increase whereas scores given to impulsivity tended to decrease as we move from low to high cognitive performance and self-evaluation. Moreover, the interaction of the comparison between mothers and children with (i) the person category, $F (3, 135) = 2.92$, $p < .036$, and also with (ii) the two types of representation, $F (1, 135) = 8.77$, $p < .004$, was significant.

These findings are interesting because they suggest that the differences between the four categories of children are not reflected in the representations of the mothers. Specifically, Figure 5.8 shows that, in as far as learning ability is concerned, there were systematic differences between children and mothers. That is, the sigmoid relation between representations and the four person categories holds for children but not for mothers in regard to learning ability. This was caused by the fact that there was no difference between the representations of the mothers of the two inaccurate groups of children, namely the low inaccurate and the high inaccurate children. Thus, it seems that the mothers of the low inaccurate children are, like their children, lenient and they ascribe to them more ability than they have. The mothers of the high inaccurate children are accurate in their representation of the children's learning ability. That is, the representations of these mothers reflect the actual state of cognitive ability rather than the (strict) self-representation of their children. This may interpreted in the following two ways.

On the one hand, one might assume that the mothers of children with low cognitive ability and high self-representations are deceived by them. That is, these children create in their mothers the impression that they are better than they really are. Alternatively, it might be the case that it is the mothers that they are responsible for the inaccuracy of these children. That is, the mothers of low inaccurate children pass a lenient attitude towards self-representation. On the other hand, the mothers of the children who are high in cognitive ability but they are conservative in how they represent it do not affect their children's self-representations in the direction of coming closer to their actual abilities. In regard to impulsivity, the differences between children and mothers were much weaker than their differences regarding learning ability. This suggests that impulsivity is probably more visible to others than cognitive ability.

It is to be concluded, therefore, that the more general an ability or process is the more accurately the parents can take notice of and represent it. Thus, general learning ability can be represented more accurately than general representations of particular domains and these can be represented more accurately than performances on particular tasks. As a result, representations about learning reflect more accurately children's actual cognitive ability and related self-evaluations than representations about other abilities. In concern to personality, it is impulsivity that is more visible to others than other personality characteristic. In fact, its relationship with the person's general cognitive ability and self-evaluation (both within the children themselves and the parents) indicates that persons think of it as a direct reflection of cognitive functioning. Given its centrality in self-representations and mutual representations, it may affect how persons behave to each other in important ways.

CONCLUSIONS

The findings of this study bear directly on the issues raised in the introduction about the contribution of important others in the formation of the developing person's self-image. A first implication of these findings is concerned with the dimensions that organize the representations that persons hold about each other. The first of the models discussed above indicated clearly that the dimensions described by this theory are present in both the individual's self-representations and the others' representations about the individual. This indicates that the structures described by this theory are not just latent constructs underlying individual behaviour. They also organize the representations that individuals hold about themselves and each other. Because of this very fact, these structures have a shared or an inter-personal dimension that enables the persons to formulate and negotiate the views and representations that they have about each other.

Another implication of the present findings is concerned with the looking glass model of the symbolic interactionists. Clearly, the present findings suggest that reality is much more complex than how it was depicted by the interactionists. Specifically, our findings suggest that the parents' image of the child does represent the child's actual abilities to a considerable extent. However, developmental changes within persons reflect intra-individual dynamics much more than inter-personal interactions. This was clearly suggested by the pattern of the longitudinal results presented above. Thus, if we would accept that parents do function as a looking glass for their children, as the interactionists posit, we would also have to accept that what children see in this looking glass is, to a large extent, what they themselves project onto it. That is, the individual is a much more powerful agent of self-development than what is suggested by the looking glass model.

Of course it is to be noted that others, for their own reasons, may somehow transform what they see in the child, both at the level of the child's actual ability and at the level of the child's self-representation. This is the meaning of the finding that the mother differentiates her own representation of the child from the child's self-representation less well than the child differentiates his self-representations from his public image. Thus, what they reflect back to the child is coloured by these transformations. The differences between transparent and opaque domains indicates that the extent of these transformation varies as a function of how accessible the different domains are to awareness, both intra-individually and inter-individually.

These findings are complementary to Kenny and DePaulo's (1993) recent review of relevant literature on the relations between self-perceptions and reflected appraisals. On the one hand, our findings suggest that people strongly project their own self-image on others so that they see in others what they are capable of or what they think of themselves. This is in agreement with Kenny and DePaulo and contrary to symbolic interactionists. On the other hand, others do add up into the image they project back and how this is done seems to depend on the social/developmental role that they have. For instance, the mother tends to ascribe to (and probably impose on) the child her representation of him more than the child tends to project on the mother his own self-concept.

And a final but no less important conclusion: All of these exchanges between persons are differentiated according to the various levels and systems of the architecture of the mind. That is, some domains are more important than others as systems of reference used by people in their reciprocal representations and ascriptions of ability and worth. In agreement with this conclusion, van Aken *et al.*, (in press) have recently found that some of the Big Five factors of personality (e.g. openness to experience) are more important than others (e.g. extraversion and emotional stability) as dimensions for the construction of reciprocal representations.

6 Study 3

From processing speed to
self-representation

The studies presented so far have clarified the relationships between the domains of thought represented by different specialized structural systems and the various dimensions of self-representation and self-evaluation involved in the hypercognitive system. The present study will attempt to highlight some of the possible relationships between the various dimensions of the processing system and the SCSs and/or the hypercognitive system. We will focus on how the three dimensions of the processing system invoked by the theory, namely speed of processing, control of processing, and short-term storage, influence the various SCSs, and examine their role in the formation of the self-image.

As noted earlier in the Introduction, to our knowledge this issue has not been directly investigated. We noted, however, that one is justified assuming that feelings of general cognitive efficiency that one may have as part of his or her general self-concept may stem directly, at least to a certain extent, from the functioning of the processing system itself. Of course, the contribution of the SCSs to the formation of these feelings may not be excluded. Although our findings on the relationships between the SCSs and the self-image (see Figure 3.7) are only indirectly related, they proved to be in line with this assumption. That is, our model (again, see Figure 3.7) suggested a direct relationship between both cognitive and social self-image and general cognitive abilities. The reader is reminded that the second-order G_{cog} factor was directly correlated to three self-image dimensions which reflect cognitive self-efficiency, that is learning, logicality, and impulsivity. However, this model did not stipulate to what degree the G_{cog} factor represents the processing system as such nor to what extent this factor explains commonalities between the SCSs and the processing system. Therefore, it is unclear whether the direct correlations between that G_{cog} factor and the self-image dimensions were due to those portions of the G_{cog} factor representing the processing system or those representing general problem-solving skills. The present study will resolve these issues.

This study additionally focused on the possible intervention of symbolic representation in the interaction between the processing system and the various systems and functions included in the other levels of the mental architecture. Specifically, our earlier studies have shown that the functioning of the processing system, however general it may be, is affected by the symbol system (e.g. words versus numbers versus figures) in which the to-be-processed items are expressed. For example, it was found that the time needed to recognize simple geometrical figures, such as a circle or a triangle, under Stroop-like conditions, differs from the time needed to recognize single words or numerical digits. It was also found that acoustically received information is stored differently and recalled better than visually presented information. Interestingly, all three dimensions of the processing system (speed, control, and storage) were found to be sensitive to the effects of "cultural biases" toward different symbol systems. For example, we found that Chinese are faster than Greeks under those Stroop-like conditions in which practice with pictorial information is relevant (Demetriou, Platsidou, and Sirmali, in preparation; Platsidou, 1993; Platsidou, Demetriou, and Zhang, 1995). Thus, a question in this regard may be as follows: To what extent is the transfer of effects from one level of the mental architecture to the other confined within symbol system-specific channels?

To answer the two questions above, all tasks and questionnaires used in the first study were given to a number of subjects participating in another project which aimed to investigate the structure and development of the processing system. The participants involved in this project were examined by a very large array of tasks addressed to speed of processing, control of processing, and short-term storage under three different symbol systems: verbal, numerical, and imaginal. These participants were also examined by tasks addressed to four SCSs, specifically the qualitative-analytic, the verbal propositional, the quantitative-relational, and the spatial-imaginal. Attention is drawn to the fact that two of these SCSs, the quantitative-relational, and the spatial-imaginal, were involved in the other studies presented here. The other two SCSs are involved in this study only. Moreover, it will be seen below that a different set of tasks was used in this study due to the younger age of the participants. Combining the two studies provided the unique opportunity of studying the hierarchical structure of mind from speed of processing to self-image. Next we will describe only those tasks which are of relevance to the present study.

METHOD

Participants

A total of 83 participants were involved in this study. They were at grades 6 (13 females and 16 males), 8 (15 females and 14 males) and 10 (13 females and 12 males). Their mean age was 11.1 (range 10.6–12.5), 13.1 (range 12.5–13.4), and 15 (range 14.5–15.8) years, respectively. All subjects represented upper middle SES Greek families living in Thessaloniki.

Batteries

In addition to all tasks and questionnaires used in the first study, the tasks described below were also employed.

Speed and control of processing tasks

A series of Stroop-like tasks were devised to measure speed and control of processing under different symbol systems. Specifically, three stimuli were used for each of the two dimensions of the processing system (i.e. speed and control of processing) for each of the three symbol systems, giving a total of 18 reaction times. Each stimulus was written on a separate card made of white cardboard (21 × 15 cm).

To measure verbal speed of processing, participants were asked to read a number of words denoting a colour written in the same ink-colour (for example the word "red" written in red) as described below. For verbal control of processing, subjects were asked to recognize the ink-colour of words denoting a colour different than the ink (for example, the word "red" written in blue ink). Both tasks employed the following three Greek words, which have the same number of letters: κόκκινο (red), πράσινο (green), κίτρινο (yellow).

To measure the two dimensions of numerical processing, several "large" number digits were prepared which were composed of "small" digits. This task involved the numbers 4, 7, and 9. In the compatible condition, the large digit (e.g. 7) was composed of the same "small" digit (i.e. 7). In the incompatible condition, the large digit (e.g. 7) was composed of one of the other digits (e.g. 4). To measure speed of processing, the subjects were asked to recognize the large number digit of the compatible stimuli. To measure control of processing the subjects were asked to recognize the small digit of the incompatible stimuli. Examples of these tasks are shown in Figure 6.1.

The tasks addressed to the imaginal system were similar to those used for the numerical system (see Figure 6.1), and comprised three geometrical figures: circle, triangle, and square. In the tasks addressed to speed of processing the large geometrical figure was composed of the same small figure. For the control of processing tasks, the large figure was composed of one of the other figures.

Reaction times to all three types of the compatible conditions described above were taken to indicate speed of processing for the follow-

Compatible   **Incompatible**

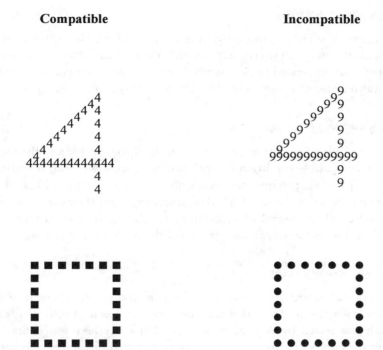

Figure 6.1 Examples of the stimuli used in the Stroop-like tasks addressed to the numerical and the figural symbol system

ing three reasons: (i) subjects are asked to provide a familiar and well practiced response to a perceptually dominant and familiar stimulus; (ii) ideally, nothing interferes in the encoding of this stimulus or the production of the response; and (iii) the encoding of this dominant and familiar stimulus is facilitated by the fact that the secondary stimulus is the same. Reaction times to the incompatible conditions can be considered indicative of the individual's efficient control of processing because he must inhibit the tendency to react to the perceptually dominant but irrelevant stimuli in order to encode and respond to the secondary but relevant stimuli. In fact, the difference between reaction time to the incompatible and the corresponding compatible condition is a measure of the individual's efficiency in suppressing the processing of the irrelevant stimulus in order to process and respond to the relevant one (see Demetriou *et al.*, 1993a; Jensen and Rohwer, 1966).

Scoring of speed of processing

Six measures of speed of processing were used, two for each symbol system. They were the two fastest errorless response times attained as a response to the three items addressed to each symbol system. Then each pair of response times was reduced to a mean score for each symbol system.

Scoring of control of processing

The difference between the response time in the incompatible and the corresponding compatible condition for each symbol system was seen to indicate control of processing. Thus, six such difference scores were calculated by subtracting the six measures of speed of processing from their corresponding items addressed to control of processing. As above, these six scores were reduced to three mean scores, one for each of the three symbol systems.

Short-term memory tasks

Three tasks addressed storage in short-term memory, one for each of the three symbol systems. The *verbal task* combined six levels of difficulty, each of which was tested by two different trials. Difficulty here was defined in terms of the number of the words; thus, from easy to difficult, the number of words ranged from 2–7 concrete nouns. All of them were two-syllable words. A 1-item level was not included as it was judged too easy for all participants. The two trials within a level were differentiated in terms of the grammatical complexity of the words, i.e. in the easy trial the nouns were presented in the singular nominative case and in the difficult trial both singular and plural Greek nouns in various different cases were used (see Appendix, Table A6.1).

The *numerical task* was structurally identical to the verbal task, including six levels of difficulty defined by the number of the to-be-stored numbers (i.e. 2–7 for the six successive difficulty levels). Each level was tested in two different trials, each of which involved two-digit numbers of variable complexity. Specifically, in the easy trial only decade numbers were involved (60, 40, etc.); in the difficult trial the two digits of the numbers were different (32, 57, etc.) (see Appendix, Table A6.2).

In the *imaginal task* the stimuli were presented visually and they had to be reproduced visuo-spatially; specifically, in each of the items, the participants were shown a card (21 × 15 cm) on which a number of geometrical figures were drawn (e.g. a rectangle and a triangle, see Figure 6.2). Participants were shown the target card for 2 seconds per figure (e.g. 2-figure cards were shown for 4 seconds) and were given twice as many ready-made cardboard figures from which to choose the figures they saw on the target-card.

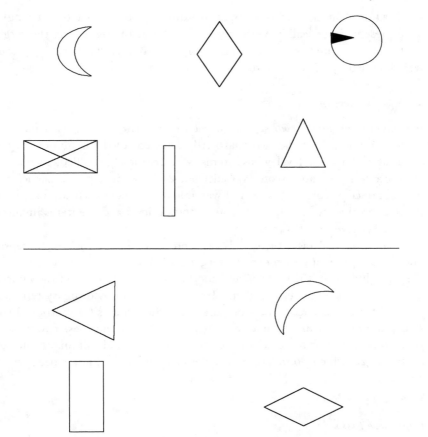

Figure 6.2 Examples of the stimuli used in the memory tasks addressed to visual short-term memory

That is, participants were to fully reproduce the target card by choosing the appropriate figures among several ready-made cardboard geometrical figures which were identical in size and shape to the figures drawn on the target card, and then placing them on a white card, also identical in size and shape with the target card. Thus, instructions were to place on the white card the figures seen on the target card in exactly the same position and orientation.

The imaginal task was designed to be structurally similar to the verbal and numerical tasks as much as possible. Thus, this task also included six levels of difficulty, each defined in reference to the number of the to-be-recalled items (i.e. from the lowest to the highest difficulty level the target cards involved 2–7 geometrical figures), and each difficulty level also involved two trials. In the easy trial all of the figures were presented in their standard orientation relative to the three dimensions of space (e.g. triangles were presented vertically: Δ). In the difficult trial the figures on the target card were presented in orientations diverging from the standard (e.g. they were inclined by $45°$ relative to their vertical axis).

Scoring of memory tasks

Participants obtained two scores for each of the three short-term memory tasks, one for each of the two trials. All scores equalled the number of the items at the highest level whose items were errorlessly recalled, so that all six short-term memory scores varied from 2–7. For instance, a participant who obtained a score of 4 on a trial was able to recall correctly all four items involved in the given trial of the corresponding level and the items involved in all lower levels of this trial.

In the imaginal task, each trial was scored twice in regard to the reproduction of figures appearing on the target card. That is, a score was given for the reproduction of the position and another of the orientation of the figures. The two scores were independent of each other. This scoring system was adopted for this particular task because our earlier studies (Demetriou, Platsidou, and Sirmali, in preparation; Platsidou, 1993) found these two dimensions to be the most representative of visual memory and minimally affected by language, which dominates when the identity of the figures needs to be recalled.

Cognitive tasks

The cognitive tasks were designed to tap verbally encoded and processed reasoning, quantitative reasoning, and spatial reasoning. The aim was to map the three symbolic systems (i.e. verbal, numerical, and imaginal systems) which were represented in the tasks addressed to the three dimensions of the processing system. Thus, verbal reasoning was addressed by a verbal analogies task, which represents the qualitative-analytic SCS and a syllogistic reasoning task, which represents the verbal-propositional SCS. Quantitative reasoning was addressed by an arithmetic operations task and a proportional reasoning task, which both represent the quantitative-relational SCS. Finally, spatial reasoning was addressed by a mental rotation and the tilted bottle task, which both represent the spatial-imaginal SCS. The tasks addressed to each SCSs were systematically manipulated to achieve variation in complexity. The structure and affiliation of the tasks is explained below.

The *qualitative-analytic SCS* was addressed by the following four verbal analogies:

1   ink : pen :: paint :: – [colour, *brush*, paper].
2   bed : sleep :: – [paper, *table*, water] : – [*food*, rain, book].
3   (children : parents :: family) ::: (students : teachers :: – [school, *education*, lesson])
4   {(tail : fish :: feet : mammals) :::: – [*movement*, animals, vertebrates]} :::::
    {(propeller : ship :: wheels : car) ::: – [vehicles, *means of transportation*, transport]}

The participant's task was to choose the correct word (italicized in the examples above) among the three alternatives provided for each missing element.

It can be seen that in this task difficulty was primarily manipulated in terms of abstractness of the relationships involved. Second-, third-, and fourth-order relationships would have to be abstracted for the solution of analogies 1 and 2, 3, and 4, respectively. The number of the missing elements was also manipulated in the case of the first two analogies, both of which were of the same order. The first analogy required completion of the target pair, whereas the second required analogy construction which aimed to differentiate between children at the lower end of the developmental continuum.

The *verbal-propositional SCS* was addressed by four syllogisms, each of which comprised two premises and three alternative conclusions. They were as follows:

1   If animals live in a cage then they are not happy. The bird is happy ⇒ [the bird lives in the cage, *the bird does not live in the cage*, none of the two].
2   If peacocks have more beautiful feathers than cocks and sparrows have more ugly feathers than cocks ⇒ [sparrows have more beautiful feathers than peacocks, *sparrows have more ugly feathers than peacocks*, none of the two].
3   If the bird is in the nest then it sings; the sparrow sings ⇒ [the sparrow is not in the nest, the sparrow is in the nest, *none of the two*].
4   If elephants are heavier than horses and if elephants are heavier than dogs ⇒ [horses are heavier than dogs, elephants are heavier than dogs, *none of the two*].

For all syllogisms, two alternatives were conceptually related to the content of the premises and a third was "undecidable". In pairs, the four tasks addressed implication and transitivity, and in each pair one task was decidable and the other undecidable. Many studies suggested that implication is generally more difficult than transitivity and that decidable tasks are more difficult than undecidable ones (see Efklides, Demetriou, and Metallidou, 1994).

The *quantitative-relational* SCS was addressed by two tasks. The first examined the participants' facility to execute the four arithmetic operations, one in combination to each other. This task involved the following four items:

1    $9 * 3 = 6$.
2    $(2 \# 4) @ 2 = 6$.
3    $(3 * 2 @ 4) \# 3 = 7$.
4    $(3 \# 3) * 1 = (12 @ 3) \$ 2$

The participants were told that the symbols in each of the equations above stand for an operation and they were asked to specify all of them in each of the equations. Thus, difficulty here was manipulated in reference to the number of the operations missing from each equation as one, two, three, and four operations were missing from items 1–4, respectively.

The second task addressed proportional reasoning. This task involved six items of $w : x :: y : ?$ type. They were as follows:

1    $6 : 12 :: 8 : ?$
2    $6 : 3 :: 8 : ?$
3    $3 : 9 :: 6 : ?$
4    $3 : 1 :: 6 : ?$
5    $6 : 8 :: 9 : ?$
6    $6 : 4 :: 9 : ?$

It can be seen that difficulty here was manipulated in reference to the type of the mathematical relationship. Specifically, in three of the items the numbers increased and in the other three they decreased; numbers in both sets increased or decreased by a factor of 2 (items 1 and 2, respectively), 3 (items 3 and 4, respectively) or 1/3 (items 5 and 6, respectively). Evidence suggests that increase can be estimated more easily than decrease and that changes by a factor of 2 are more easily specifiable than changes by a factor of 3 and these are more easily specifiable than fractional changes (Demetriou et al., 1993a).

The *spatial-imaginal* SCS was also addressed by two tasks. The first of them was a mental rotation task comprising six items (see Figure 6.3). Each item depicted a clock with one hand always pointed to the 12:00 position and the other pointed to either: 12:15, 12:30, or 12:45. There always was a figure drawn on the arm pointing to the 12:00 position. The participant's task was to draw on the other arm how this figure would look like when the 12:00 position arm was going to meet this other arm. Thus, difficulty in this task was manipulated in relation to the degree of mental rotation. Research has established that rotations of different degrees exhibit differential difficulty and

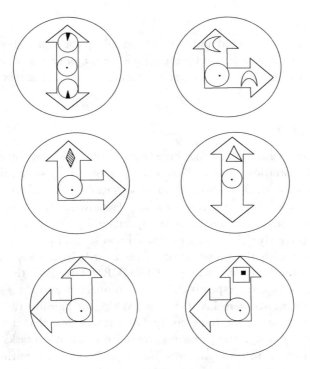

Figure 6.3 The items included in the task addressed to mental rotation

that the more information one needs to integrate into an image the more difficult the task is (Shepard and Cooper, 1982).

The second task was a version of the classical Piagetian (Piaget and
Inhelder, 1967) water-level task in which a picture of a half-full bottle was
presented and the subject's task was to draw the line indicating the water
level when the bottle was inclined first by 45° and then 90° degrees. There
is vast literature on this task, indicating that it is a good test of the person's
ability to integrate multiple systems of reference in space (see Thomas and
Lohaus, 1993).

Scoring of cognitive tasks

All items in the cognitive battery were scored on a pass-fail basis (0 and 1).
The mean scores used in the analyses below were computed by averaging
over the items involved in each battery.

Procedure

Each participant was tested individually on all of the tasks. Testing took place in a quiet room provided by the school for the purposes of this experiment. Experimenter and participant sat facing each other across a normal table.

The Stroop-like tasks

The experimenter introduced the three tasks to the child, one by one, using first the demonstration cards and then the practice cards to familiarize the child with the tasks. The aim was to make clear to the subjects that the cards in the main task were going to be presented in succession and that their task was to name the attribute specified by the instruction word quickly and correctly. The instruction word was stated by the experimenter simultaneously with the presentation of each card. In the verbal task the instruction words were WORD and COLOUR for reading the word and naming the ink-colour, respectively. In the numerical and the figural task the instruction words were LARGE and SMALL for naming the large and the small number or figure, respectively. Once it was clear that the child was able to follow the instructions, testing proceeded to the main tasks described above. For practical reasons, the presentation order of items within symbol systems was the same across subjects. However, the presentation order of the three symbol systems was counter-balanced across subjects.

Testing on the main tasks was tape-recorded. The records of each subject were then loaded into a computer with special hardware and software enabling response reaction time to be specified. In this process, reaction time was defined as the time between the first phoneme of the instruction word and the first phoneme of the subject's response. The reaction time to a stimulus was not used for incorrect responses; however, incorrect responses were very rare, varying from .07% to 1.04% in the compatible conditions and from 1.9% to 3.2% in the incompatible conditions.

The memory tasks

For verbal and numerical tasks subjects were instructed to recall the words or the numbers in the order of presentation as soon as the experimenter finished stating a series, as indicated by a nonverbal sign. Items within a series were presented at a rate of one item per second. The presentation order of the two trials within each of the six difficulty levels was randomized across levels; the presentation order of difficulty levels was the same across subjects, going from easy to difficult. Administration of a task stopped if the subject failed to recall errorlessly the two trials involved in a level. In the imaginal task the participant was instructed to carefully reproduce the figures on a target card in exactly the same position and orientation.

The cognitive tasks

The cognitive tasks were presented in a paper-and-pencil form but they were individually administered. The presentation order of tasks was counterbalanced across participants but the items within tasks were always presented according to difficulty; that is, simpler tasks were presented before complex tasks. The experimenter explained each task and was available to answer questions as needed.

RESULTS

The results to be presented below do not aim to highlight the processing system *per se*. This has been attempted in a series of other publications (Demetriou *et al.*, 1993a; Demetriou *et al.*, in preparation; Platsidou, 1993; Zhang, 1995). Rather, our aim is to clarify how the processing system is related to the various dimensions of self-image which is the focus of this book.

Structural modelling was used as a first approximation to the specification of the relations between the various dimensions of the processing system and the dimensions of the other systems involved in the study. A total of 23 mean scores were used as follows: nine means representing performance on each of the three dimensions of the processing system (i.e. speed and control of processing and storage) across the three symbol systems (i.e. verbal, numeric, and spatial); four means representing performance on each of the cognitive domains used in the present study (i.e. verbal analogies, syllogisms, quantitave-relational and spatial-imaginal thought); four means representing performance on the tasks addressed to the four SCSs in the first study (i.e. quantitative-relational, causal-experimental, social, and drawing); four means indicative of the corresponding domain-specific dimensions of self-image and two means representing the two general dimensions of cognitive self-image (i.e. learning ability and logical reasoning). These means were created by averaging over all items addressed to an SCS or found to be related to a self-image dimension according to the descriptions given in Chapter 3.

Only one mean score was used to refer to each dimension, function, or component in our structural analyses due to the limited number of subjects in the present study. It has been established that limited sample size can make the application of structural modelling difficult, especially in cases (such as the present one) where the number of dimensions involved is relatively large (Tanaka, 1987). Therefore, the number of scores was kept to a minimum. These means were used to test the fit of two models, one referring to the processing system alone, and one involving all of the means specified above.

The first was a nested-factor model, which included only the nine scores related to the processing system and is presented primarily for indicative purposes as it demonstrates the validity of our claims (see Introduction) related to the structure of the processing system. Thus, this model is useful for the interpretation of the overall model in terms of the structural relationships among the variables to be presented below. The reader is reminded that, according to the theory, the processing system involves speed and control of processing and storage. Moreover, it is also assumed that these dimensions are affected by the symbol systems in which the information to be processed is presented. The model tested (see Figure 6.4) is the end-product of a series of analyses presented elsewhere (Demetriou *et al.*, in preparation; Platsidou, 1993; Zhang, 1995). The fit of this model is excellent, $\chi^2(18) = 23.208$, p = .183, CFI = .972, GFI = .946, AGFI = .865, SRMR = .070, and comprises the following factors: (1) Speed of processing factor defined by the speed of processing measures and weakly related to the memory variables; (2) Weaker control of processing factor mainly related to the corresponding measures and to a lesser extent to the memory measures; (3) Very strong auditory memory factor related only to the measures representing verbal and numerical memory; (4) A visualization factor strongly related to the visual memory score and also to the numerical and figural control of processing measures (the reader is reminded that in these two measures the subject is required to recognize a small secondary figure by inhibiting the recognition of the dominant large figure, and thus, requires visual processing); (5) Finally, there were three symbolic system-specific factors. Each of these factors was related to the two Stroop-like tasks addressed to the same symbol system. These factors represent the encoding processes activated when information is to be processed in each of the three symbol systems involved in the study.

The second model comprised the nine means representing the three dimensions of the processing system in each of the three symbol systems, the four means representing the four SCSs in the present study (i.e. the means representing performance on the verbal analogies, the propositional reasoning, the quantitative-relational, and the spatial-imaginal tasks), four means representing all but one of the domains or SCSs involved in the first study (i.e. social thought, the causal-experimental and the quantitative-relational SCS and drawing), the corresponding self-image dimensions resulted from the questionnaire on abilities, and the two self-image dimensions represent-

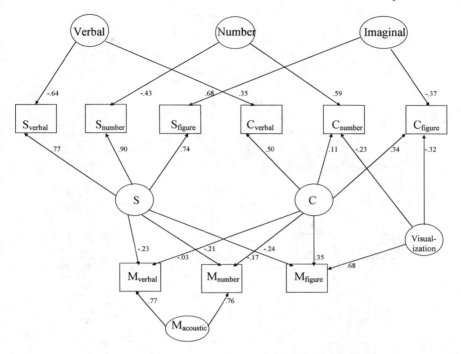

$\chi^2(18) = 23.208$, p = .183, CFI = .972, GFI = .946, AGFI = .865, SRMR = .122, RMSEA = .070

Figure 6.4 The best fitting model to the structure of the processing system

Note
The symbols S, C, M and Vis stand for speed, control, memory and visualization respectively.

ing general cognitive abilities (learning and logicality). These means were used in a path model which directly investigated the structural relationships among the variables, rather than in a factor model that would identify the factors first. This path model was selected over the factor model because of the rather limited number of subjects involved in this study. However, it is noted that what is lost in measurement power in structural models fitted on observed rather than on latent variables is compensated for by the fact that these models remain closer to the real data involved.

The prototype model (see Figure 6.5) has been based on the relationships revealed by an earlier corresponding model (Figure 3.7). Thus, the following relationships are built in this model: (1) It was assumed that causal effects run from the lower to the higher hierarchical levels of mind (i.e. from speed, to control of processing, to storage, to SCSs, to the general dimensions of self-image, to the specific dimensions of self-image); (2) It was also assumed

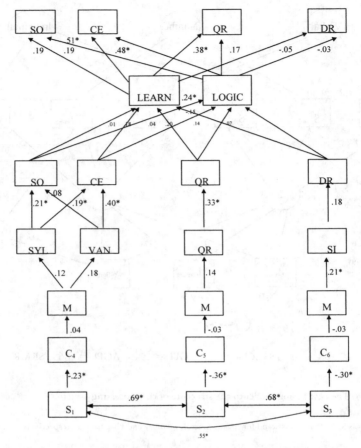

$\chi^2(193) = 347.727$, p $= .001$, CFI $= .745$, GFI $= .738$, AGFI $= .626$, SRMR $= .167$, RMSEA $= .102$

Figure 6.5 The prototype path model of the relation between the processing system, the SCS, and the self-image dimensions

Note

The symbols S, C and M stand for speed, control and memory respectively. The symbols SYL, VAN, QR, SI, SO, CE, and DR stand for syllogistic reasoning, verbal analogies, quantitative-relational, spatial-imaginal, social, causal-experimental, and drawing respectively.

that causal effects run from simpler to more complex measures. That is, from SCS-specific measures representing performance on the tasks used in this study to the SCS-specific measures representing performance on the tasks used in the first study. The reader is reminded that the tasks used in the first study include the processes required for performance on the tasks used in the present study. For example, it is plausible to assume that the syllogistic and analogical reasoning processes are involved in the processes required for the processing of the social or causal thought tasks. In a similar vein, the processes required to execute the arithmetic operations and the proportional reasoning tasks or the visualization tasks of the present study are part of the processes required by the quantitative or the drawing tasks used in the first study; (3) The assumption was also tested that causal effects are confined within each of the three symbol systems (i.e. verbal, numerical, and imaginal); (4) Finally, to remove any covariance between the variables shown by previous analyses to pertain to the same factor, the residual variances of all variables on the same level (see point # 1 above) were allowed to correlate. This manipulation was necessary because there was no factor in this model to capture this covariation. However, if this variance were left unaccounted for, the structural relationships among those variables the model intends to specify might be unclear due to covariation related to within-factor variance.

The fit of the model as specified above was poor, $\chi^2(193) = 347.727$, p = .001, CFI = .745, GFI = .738, AGFI = .626, SRMR = .167, RMSEA = .112, due to both within-symbol system relationships between nonadjacent levels and inter-symbol system relationships not represented in this model. Following the modification indexes generated by the programme, the prototype model was modified in the model shown in Figure 6.6. This model was found to have a very good fit, $\chi^2(186) = 208.175$, p = .127, CFI = .963, GFI = .832, AGFI = .751, SRMR = .040, RMSEA = .017. Three major conclusions are suggested by this model. First, there are strong relationships progressing from lower to higher levels throughout all three symbol systems. Interestingly, however, there are connections between adjacent levels as well as long distance connections between levels which are remote in the hierarchy. Noteworthy among the long-distance connections are those ones which extend directly from the speed of processing measures to the various SCS-specific measures and also to the measure representing self-ascribed logicality. Second, it is also noteworthy that the dimension of logicality in one's self-image also correlated with both syllogistic reasoning and verbal analogies, the latter in particular. The dimension of learning was found to correlate with the quantitative-relational SCS and memory. Thus, these two dimensions of self-image derive from experiences at different levels of the mental architecture and also from different modules or functions within hierarchical levels. Finally, we note that, concurring with corresponding results of the first study, the SCS-specific dimensions of self-image are generated from learning and logicality (general self-image dimensions) rather from the corresponding SCS-specific performance.

There are two points to note particularly: self-representation in relation to social and causal thought derives more from the dimension of logicality than

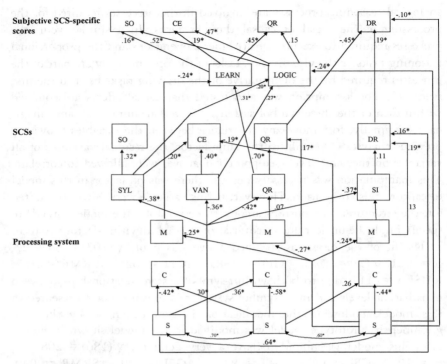

$\chi^2(186) = 208.175$, p = .127, CFI = .963, GFI = .832, AGFI = .751, SRMR = .040,
RMSEA = .017

Figure 6.6 The path model of the relations between the processing system, the SCS, and the
self-image dimensions

Note
The symbols S, C and M stand for speed, control and memory respectively. The symbols SYL, VAN, QR,
SI, SO, CE, and DR stand for syllogistic reasoning, verbal analogies, quantitative-relational, spatial-
imaginal, social, causal-experimental, and drawing respectively.

learning. The relationship between self-representation regarding mathematical thought and these two dimensions is the opposite. However, self-
representation related to drawing is totally unrelated to these two
dimensions of self-image, but is directly derived from actual drawing
performance and is negatively related to the quantitative SCS. These results
suggest, confirming our findings in the first study, that drawing occupies a
very special position in both actual performance and the self-image.

In conclusion, we find that the present model validates and extends the
model (see Figure 3.7) suggested by the results of the first study. Specifically, cognitive self-image involves a few pivotal dimensions, which are
directly linked to both the processing system and to logical reasoning *per se*.

In fact, our findings enable us to conclude that these self-image dimensions directly reflect the efficiency of both cognitive hardware (represented by the speed of processing measures) and logical reasoning software (represented by syllogistic and, particularly, analogical reasoning). They are employed as systems of reference when more specialized self-descriptions representing efficiency in relation to the various environment-oriented SCSs are required.

Admittedly, the models above are built on statistical relationships rather on experimental manipulation of variables which is the only method able to directly reveal causal relationships among variables. Thus, one might object that these models do not directly demonstrate causal relationships between the dimensions of self-image and other dimensions which reside at lower levels of the mental architecture. To approach this ideal a quasi-experimental design was used. Specifically, in order to specify the effects of processing speed and analogical reasoning on the various dimensions of self-image, the two first variables were treated as independent variables with two levels, i.e. slow and fast for performance on the speed of processing tasks and low and high for performance on the verbal analogies task. Then four groups of participants were organized for each of the possible combinations: slow-and-low, slow-and-high, fast-and-low, and fast-and-high.

These four groups were formed as follows. First, the average of the three symbol-system specific speed of processing scores was calculated for each participant. Then, for each age group, the three participants with the highest speed of processing average (hence they were slow) and the lowest score on the verbal analogies task were placed in the slow-and-low group. The three participants with speed of processing means comparable to those placed in the slow-and-low group, but with a high verbal analogy score (one of the best six in their age group) were placed in the slow-and-high group. The participants placed in the fast-and-low group had obtained one of the best six speed of processing averages in their age group but their verbal analogies score was comparable to the subjects placed in the slow-and-low group. Finally, the three participants with the lowest speed of processing average (hence, they were fast) and the highest verbal analogies score were placed in the fast-and-high group. The means and standard deviations attained by these four groups on these variables are shown in Table A6.3 in the Appendix. Two MANOVAs were run to test the effects of these independent variables on the various dimensions of self-image revealed by the path model. Processing speed and analogical reasoning were selected as the criterion variables because the path model revealed them as the best predictors of self-image dimensions. The α level for these analyses was set to .05.

In the first MANOVA, age (i.e. the three age groups involved in this study) and the combination between performance on the speed of processing and the verbal analogies tasks (i.e. the four person categories specified above) were taken as between-subject factors; the two general dimensions of cognitive self-image (i.e. learning and logicality) were taken as within-subjects factor. Of interest here is the effect exerted by the person category on self-image which, based on the path model, would be expected to be significant. As expected, this effect was highly significant, $F (3, 24) = 10.65$, $p < .001$. Confirming the corresponding analysis applied to the performance of the participants in the first study, the effect of age was also significant, $F (2, 24) = 4.55$, $p < .021$. Neither the effect of the self-image dimensions factor nor any of the various interactions between the three factors ever approached significance. Our illustration (Figure 6.7) of the person category's effect on each of the two self-image dimensions shows an almost linear relationship. Thus, the slow processors and weak reasoners rated themselves low, and the fast processors and strong reasoners rated themselves high in terms of learning and logicality. The other two groups rated themselves in between these two extremes.

The second analysis involved the same between-subject factors and one within-subject factor; that is, the mean scores representing performance on the five SCS-specific self-representations. This analysis gave identical results for the between-subject factors. In agreement with the path model which suggested that there are no direct relationship between the processing system or the SCSs and these dimensions of self-representation, this analysis showed that there was no significant effect of the person category on these dimensions, $F (3, 24) = .47$, $p = .705$. Moreover, none of the interactions between the person category and any of the other factors was statistically significant.

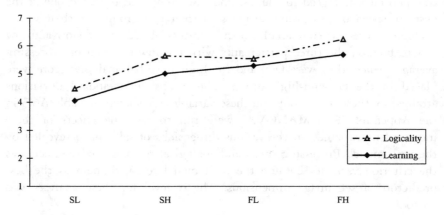

Figure 6.7 Self-attribution of learning and logicality scores according to the combination of performance on the speed of processing and the verbal analogies tasks

CONCLUSIONS

The results of these two parametric analyses are fully consistent with the models which were found to fit the various dimensions of cognitive perform-ance and self-representation investigated by both the first and the second study. In fact, the results of the present study clarified and extended the results of the first study in revealing which of the influences exerted by the G_{cog} factor on self-representation derive from the processing system and which derive from the environment-oriented systems. To reiterate briefly, the results of the present study indicated that, of the dimensions involved in the processing system, it is speed of processing which is directly connected to the dimension of self-image representing logicality; of the various environment-oriented systems, it is mainly the reasoning processes associ-ated with analogical reasoning which are also connected to this dimension of self-representation. More interestingly, the effect of these two dimensions on logicality are by and large cumulative. That is, the more the individual has of what each of these two dimensions represent, the more logical and – to a lesser extent – the more able to learn he feels. Finally, it also must be noted that, to a certain degree, the flow of these effects runs through symbol-specific channels.

These findings are in agreement with the assumption advanced in the Introduction that self-representation of cognitive efficiency is directly related to the functions and processes involved in the processing system of the mind. Validating this assumption indicates that the famous construct of *g* of psychometric theories of intelligence (Jensen, 1998), on the one hand, and the recently revitalized constructs of global self-worth (Harter, 1998, 1999) and self-efficacy (Bandura, 1989) of self- and personality-psychology, on the other hand, may to a large extent be the two sides of the same coin. We will return to this issue in the concluding chapter.

7 Study 4

Cognitive self-image, thinking styles and the big five factors of personality

The studies presented so far focused on cognitive performance, self-representations about cognitive performance, thinking styles, and personality. However, personality was rather under-represented in these studies, because our tests did not address directly the dimensions of personality which are considered dominant by current personality theory (see Costa and McCrae, 1997; Graziano, Jensen-Campbell, and Finch, 1997). Moreover, our inventory of cognitive self-image did not address some important dimensions of the mind as specified by our theory. To remedy this limitation, a series of new studies were designed. The present study is the first of this series. In this study personality was examined by one of the classical inventories addressed to personality. Specifically, this was the Greek version of an inventory addressed to the "Big Five" factors of personality (Besevegis, Pavlopoulos, and Mourousaki, 1996; Kohnstamm, Mervielde, Besevegis, and Halverson, 1995). This inventory was used together with a new version of our inventories addressed to cognitive self-image and thinking styles. In the present version of our two inventories only the four items best representing a dimension were retained. That is, the items retained in the present version of the inventories were those having the four highest loadings on a factor, according to the results of factor analysis shown in Tables 2.3–2.5.

Moreover, a series of new items were added to the cognitive self-image inventory to address processes and functions which were not represented in the version used in the previous studies. That is, the new items addressed self-image in regard to various aspects of: (i) speed of processing; (ii) working memory; (iii) self-monitoring and self-regulation; and (iv) deductive and inductive reasoning. Thus, in its present version, the cognitive self-image inventory addressed most dimensions of each of the three levels of the mind (i.e. the processing system, the environment-oriented systems, and the hypercognitive system). Thus, this study was designed to reveal the relations between the various dimensions of the cognitive self-image, thinking styles, and personality more adequately than the previous studies.

METHOD

Participants

Three hundred and twenty two students from the faculties of arts and social sciences of the University of Cyprus were examined. The mean age of this group was 19.3 years; 265 of them were females and 57 were males. These students came from all over Cyprus and from different socio-economic groups of the population. However, they belong to the top 10–15% of the population, in as far as school performance is concerned.

Inventories

The cognitive self-image inventory

This inventory involved the 53 items shown in Table 7.1. It can be seen that this version of the inventory included all of the various dimensions represented in the first version. That is, it included quantitative, causal, social, verbal, imaginal thought, drawing, learning, and reasoning. In addition, it included items addressed to the processing system (that is, speed of processing, understanding and decision making and working memory), working and long-term hypercognition (that is, self-monitoring of thought processes, emotions, bodily functions and self-representation of thought and social functions and abilities), and relational thought which underlies the categorical SCS.

The thinking styles inventory

This inventory involved a total of 24 items; these are shown in Table 7.2. In sets of four, these were the items best representing the six of the seven factors of thinking styles and personality identified by the first study. That is, this inventory addressed the ideal self and social desirability, systematicity, impulsivity and the legislative, the executive, and the judicial style.

The personality inventory

This inventory included a total of 99 items; these are shown in Table 7.3. The items involved in this inventory addressed the facets involved in each of the Big Five factors of personality. Specifically, the factor of emotional reactivity/neuronticism included items addressed to manageability/neuroticism and emotional instability. The factor of conscientiousness included items addressed to order and motivation for achievement and school performance.

Table 7.1 Items and varimax factor structure of the inventory on cognitive abilities

Items

Social thought
I understand easily the intentions of others before they express them.
I understand easily what others are thinking before they express their thoughts.
I understand easily the feelings of others before they express them.
I manage well in my relations with other people.

Quantitative thought
I like solving mathematical problems.
I can easily apply the mathematical rules I have been taught to new problems.
I immediately solve everyday problems involving numbers.
*I avoid problems that require mathematical knowledge.

Hypercognition
I can monitor what is going inside me.
I can monitor my thoughts.
I can monitor my emotions.
I can monitor the condition of my body.
I am aware of my strong and my weak points.
I can easily sort out what is relevant to a subject.
After taking an action, I evaluate whether I did the right thing.
*I have a hard time figuring out what has to be done in each occasion.
When doing something, I often stop to check if I am doing it right.
*I am rather insensitive to what is going inside me.
I can easily change the way I think if I discover that my initial approach is not correct.
I often think about myself.
I want to know what others think about me.

Verbal ability
I enjoy talking.
*I often have difficulty to express what I think.
I am very good in speaking.
I like learning new words.

Drawing
I like drawing.
I can draw a person very accurately.
I can imagine new things and paint them so that everyone understands how I imagined it to be.
*I can hardly draw a single line when I have to draw something.

Causal thought
When I hear one interpretation of an event, I always think that it may not be the real one.
I always think that things may not be as they seem.
When someone says something, I frequently wonder what else he/she means.
I like experimenting on topics that interest me.

Spatial-imaginal thought
When I bring to mind something I have read, I have a picture of the page in my mind.
*I can't retain a very clear picture of things.
Even if I meet someone once, I never forget the face.
I am a visualiser.

Factors					
Social thought	Quantitative thought	Hypercognition	Verbal ability	Drawing	Causal thought
.826					
.812					
.777					
			.753		
	.891				
	.862				
	.837				
	.791				
		.757			
		.755			
		.751			
		.664			
		.306			
		.759			
		.589			
		.551			
		.362			
			.871		
			.835		
			.752		
			.664		
				.761	
				.656	
				.624	

Table 7.1 (continued)

Items

Processing System

I am very fast in finding solutions to problems.

I can easily understand what others explain to me.

*I need time to find the solution to a problem.

I am fast in making decisions.

I can easily remember large parts from the texts that I read.

I can easily remember telephone numbers, even the ones I hear only once.

I can easily remember the names of persons from the first time I meet them.

Learning and reasoning

When need be, I can immediately remember things I learnt a long time ago.

I learn easily.

*I am not bothered when hearing unreasonable things.

I like drawing logical conclusions, which can be justified by the data I have.

When I present arguments about some subject, I use all the information I have on the subject.

In discussions with others, I often examine whether what they are saying fits the reality.

Categorical thought

I can easily detect the relations among seemingly irrelevant things.

I can easily detect the differences among seemingly similar things.

I can easily detect the latent relations among things.

Notes

1 The Cronbach's α was tested separately for each set of items primary loading on a factor. The α for each of these factors was as follows: Social thought: $\alpha = .869$; Quantitative thought: $\alpha = .870$; Hypercognition = .815; Verbal ability: $\alpha = .700$; Drawing: $\alpha = .819$; Causal thought: $\alpha = .717$.

2 Items marked with an asterisk were inversely recoded for the purposes of this analysis.

3 Items were presented in randomized order.

The factor of openness to experience (or culture) included items addressed to intellect and openness to experience. The factor of agreeableness included items addressed to altruism, emotional sensitivity, and compliance. Finally, the factor of extraversion included items addressed to sociability, extraversion, and introversion.

RESULTS

To specify the dimensions involved in the three inventories, four exploratory factor analyses were run. That is, each of the three inventories was first analysed separately in order to test if the dimensions used to build these

Factors					
Social thought	Quantitative thought	Hypercognition	Verbal ability	Drawing	Causal thought
	.530				
	.406		.344		
	.355				
			.319		
					.346
			.484		
					.631
.568					
.554					
.709					

inventories were present in the responses of the participants. A fourth common analysis was applied on all three inventories in order to specify the most important dimensions running through the three inventories and obtain a first comprehensive picture of their interrelationships.

The cognitive self-image battery

Fourteen factors with an eigen value bigger than 1 were extracted by this analysis. These factors accounted for 63.5% of the total variance. Based on the scree test, only six of these factors, accounting for 43.5% of the variance, are discussed below (see Table 7.1).

The first factor represents *social thought*. This factor is also associated with

Table 7.2 Items and varimax factor structure of the inventory on thinking styles

Items

Ideal self and social desirability
I like being the centre of attention.
I want everyone to ask my opinion.
I like being the one with the best ideas about something.
*I don't mind failing.

Systematicity
I deal with each matter as much as necessary when necessary.
I organise my actions and I proceed systematically in order to achieve what I want.
I like everything to be settled properly.
*I can stand untidiness.

Impulsivity
I like acting fast without much thought.
I do not sit and think what I have to do.
*I prefer to be careful, even if it takes time.
When I have many things I must do, I do not stop to think which is the most important.

Legislative style
I like working on problems for which there are no pre-prepared solutions.
*I prefer applying ready-made solutions.
When I think about a problem, I often try to find solutions others have not thought of.
I often find problems where everybody thinks things are going well.

Executive style
I believe people should go by the rules.
I think that those who break a rule should be penalised.
I like working where there are pre-defined rules of operation.
*I believe that people are entitled to break the rules with which they disagree.

Judicial style
I often evaluate others on whether they are doing their work well.
I like deciding what is right and what isn't.
I frequently want to know whether people follow the rules by which they should do something.
*It is not my business to judge other people.

Notes
1   The Cronbach's α was tested separately for each set of items primary loading on a factor. The α for each of these factors was as follows: Ideal self-Social desirability: $\alpha = .791$; Executive style-Systematicity: $\alpha = .689$; Impulsivity: $\alpha = .518$; Legislative style-Systematicity: $\alpha = .436$.
2   Items marked with an asterisk were inversely recoded for the purposes of this analysis.
3   Items were presented in randomized order.

Factors			
Ideal self-Social desirability	Executive style-Systematicity	Impulsivity	Legislative style-Systematicity
.816			
.779			
.768			
		−.522	
	.497		.468
	.458	−.378	.302
	.335	−.316	
		−.304	
		.696	
		.625	
	−.398	.535	
		.403	
			.768
	−.421		.649
.587			.393
	.722		
	.659		
	.612		
	.313		
.593			
.387	.338		
	.642		

Table 7.3 Items and varimax factor structure of the personality inventory

Items

Emotional reactivity (manageability/neuroticism)
I talk back to my parents.
I eat only what I like.
I insist on my opinion, even if it is wrong.
I want always to be the leader.
I am spiteful.
I am selfish.
I complain all the time.
I am egoist.
I am stubborn.
I would rather take more than give.
I like to get things my own way.
I am jealous.
I demand excessively.
I get angry easily.

Emotional reactivity (emotional instability)
I fight, argue with others.
I am aggressive.
My mood changes easily.
I am vivid/active.
I have ups and downs.
I have unpredictable reactions.
I am nervous.
I overreact when scolded.
I am reactionary.

Conscientiousness (order, will to achieve)
I am perfectionist.
I stick to my obligations, I am consistent.
I am orderly.
*I am untidy/disorderly.
I want to get better.
I am careful.
I am organized.
Once I start something, I want to finish it.
I am responsible.
*I am absent-minded.
I am mature for my age.
I get easily anxious.

Conscientiousness (school performance)
I am diligent.
I am studious/hard-working.
*I am not interested in my studies.
*I need pressure to do my homework.
*I am lazy.
*I am negligent.
I like studying.

Factors

Agreeableness	Extraversion	Conscientiousness	Openness to experience	Neuroticism	Emotional instability
				.315	.420
				.517	
			.465	.337	
				.539	
				.660	
				.455	
				.760	
				.701	
				.553	
				.707	
				.415	
				.510	
				.399	.635
				.300	.703
					.820
	.494		.387		
				.291	
					.485
				.343	.357
				.313	.487
		.457			
		.736			
		.773			
		.628			
.358		.335	.353		
		.607			
		.789			
		.530			
.386		.697			
.387			.310		
		.745			
		.516			
		.314			
		.299			
		.441			
		.619			

Table 7.3 (continued)

Items

Openness to experience (intellect)

I am clever/intelligent.
I am good observer.
My mind is critical/analytical.
I have my own opinion on issues.
I am imaginative.
I learn quickly/easily.
I have good memory.
I am interested in new things.
I like to discuss on various subjects.
I have quick perception.

Openness to experience

I have a strong character/personality.
I am inventive.
I have many interests/hobbies.
I take strong stands.
I am creative.
I take initiative.
I am independent.
I am self-confident.

Agreeableness (altruism)

I am lovable.
I am emotional/sentimental.
I am friendly.
I am willing to offer my help.
I am good-hearted.
I am affectionate/caring.
I share other people's suffering/I am compassionate.
I am sensitive.
I am concerned/care about other people's problems.
I am zealous of my honour/pride.

Agreeableness (emotional sensitivity)

I cry easily.
I get frustrated if scolded.
I get hurt on the slightest criticism.
I like to cuddle.

Agreeableness (compliance)

I am manageable.
I listen to others' advice.
I am understanding.
I am honest.
I am polite/kind.
I respect the elderly.
I am ready to compromise.
I am protective with others.

Factors					
Agreeableness	Extraversion	Conscientiousness	Openness to experience	Neuroticism	Emotional instability
			.431		
.340			.579		
			.756		
.317					
			.303		
			.595		
.317			.493		
	.334		.616		
			.305		
	.498				
	.331		.686		
			.335		
	.295		.621		
			.462		
		.309	.403		
	.554				
.446	.536				
.650					
.652					
.674					
.675					
.376					
.744					
.689					
.372					
.362				−.301	
.626					
.670					
.600					
.415					
.490			.359		

Table 7.3 (continued)

Items		

Extraversion-Introversion (sociability)
I adjusts myself easily in new environment.
I am happy.
I am expressive/outgoing.
I am spontaneous, impulsive.
I am sociable.
I am open/expressive/extravert.

Extraversion-Introversion (extraversion)
I have a lot of friends.
I like having people around.
I like to go out.
I like to go out with people of my age.
I like to be always on the move.
I prefer not to stay alone.
I am interested in relations with opposite sex.

Extraversion-Introversion (introversion)
*I am lonely.
*I prefer to stay at home.
*I shut myself off.
*I am difficult in making friends.

Notes
1   The Cronbach's α was tested separately for each set of items primary loading on a factor. The α for each of these factors was as follows: Agreeableness: α = .897; Extraversion: α = .882; Conscientiousness: α = .889; Openness to experience: α = .886; Neuroticism: α = .855; Emotional instability: α = .755.
2   Items marked with an asterisk were inversely recoded for the purposes of this analysis.
3   Items were presented in randomized order.

processes underlying relational thought. Thus, it seems that social understanding is considered to involve an ability to use inductive reasoning in order to decipher hidden or non-apparent relations.

The second factor stands clearly for *quantitative thought*. Interestingly, this factor also loaded on three of the speed of processing items. Therefore, in the mind of the thinker, quantitative thought is directly related to fundamental aspects of the processing system. Probably this connection is caused by the fact that mathematical though is demanding enough to require effortful processing. Thus, it generates the experiences which are conducive to awareness of processing such.

The third factor stands clearly for the *hypercognitive system*. It can be seen that this factor loaded highly on all of the self-monitoring items. Interestingly, learning is also related to this factor.

Factors					
Agreeableness	*Extraversion*	*Conscientiousness*	*Openness to experience*	*Neuroticism*	*Emotional instability*
	.516				
	.632				
	.431				
	.415		.297		
	.735				
	.714				
	.760				
	.460				
	.381				
	.494		.311		
	.577				
	.292				
	.643				
	.708				

The fourth factor stands for *verbal ability*. This factor also loaded on the item representing social skills and, secondarily, on speed of understanding, learning and reasoning.

The fifth factor stands clearly for *drawing* as it loaded on the four respective items. It is notable that this factor did not load on any other item, indicating that drawing is very distinct from other abilities in the mind of the thinkers.

The sixth factor stands for *causal thought* as it loaded highly on three of the four suppositional thought items. Expectedly this factor also loaded on items representing inferential thought applied on social problems.

It is worth noting that of the remaining non-discussed factors three were interpretable. Specifically, one of them loaded on the reasoning items and one loaded on working and long-term memory items suggesting that reasoning and memory are recognised as distinct processes in one's own mind.

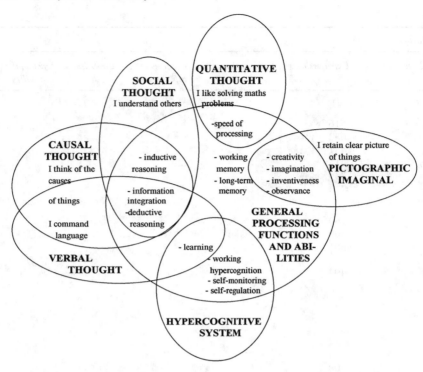

Figure 7.1 General and domain-specific factors abstracted from self-reports of abilities in the cognitive image inventory

Interestingly enough, there was also a factor that might be regarded as equivalent to psychometric general intelligence. This factor loaded on speed of processing, causal thought, self monitoring, and learning items .

Three general conclusions are suggested by this analysis. First, most environment-oriented systems are very powerful dimensions of cognitive self-representation. At the same time, however, the various systems, although distinct, are thought by the thinker to be interrelated. Figure 7.1 was prepared to illustrate how the various systems are interrelated according to the thinkers themselves.

Second, of the two general systems, the hypercognitive system proved to be very powerfully present in the thinker's self-image, indicating that persons are aware of their self-awareness mechanisms and processes. Of course it is recognized here that the composition of the sample of this study may be related to this finding. That is, highly intelligent university students during their studies may be more prone than adolescents or older persons to take notice of the functioning of their mind. This is consistent with similar findings by Demetriou (1990) which showed that students are more self-aware than middle age secondary school teachers.

Third, the processing system seems not to be recorded directly as an autonomous system. Rather, it seems to be recorded in its relationships to the domain-specific systems it supports. That is, the more the functioning of an SCS is effortful the more this SCS is taken to require the various functions of the processing system, such as speed of processing. The quantitative system is a particularly strong example of these privileged relationships. This is of course fully consistent with our findings presented earlier about the relationships between general cognitive abilities with the other systems of abilities and self-representations. Moreover, it is also consistent with modern views which claim that the processing system is an "empty system" (Bickhard, 1999; Demetriou and Raftopoulos, 1999; Demetriou, Raftopoulos, and Kargopoulos, 1999; Jensen, 1998) that is continuously occupied by the other systems and that it is thus coloured by these other systems.

The thinking styles inventory

The analysis applied on this inventory abstracted six factors with an eigen value bigger than 1. These factors accounted for 53.9% of the total variance. Based on the scree test, only four of these factors, accounting for 43.1% of the variance, are discussed below (see Table 7.2).

Specifically, the first factor loaded primarily on three of the four items addressed to the *ideal self* and *social desirability*. This factor also loaded on two of the items addressed to the judicial style and on one of the items addressed to originality. Thus, it seems that for the young students involved in this study, social desirability and the ambition to excel involves a component of social dominance and control.

Factor 2 loaded primarily on three of the *executive style* items and three of the *systematicity* items. Therefore, to be systematic and to operate under well-defined conditions are closely related in the mind of the young students who participated in this study.

Factor 3 is clearly the *impulsivity factor* as it loaded highly on three of the four items addressed to this dimension. Moreover this factor was secondarily and negatively related to three of the systematicity items. This is very reasonable in its implication that impulsivity is incompatible with systematicity.

Factor 4 stands for the *legislative style* as it loaded on three of the four respective items. This factor also loaded secondarily on two of the systematicity items indicating that, for these students, originality involves a component of *systematicity*. The last two factors were not interpretable because each of them loaded on items representing three of the constructs involved in this inventory.

In conclusion, the findings of this analysis are only partially consistent with the finding of the first study. Specifically, three of the six factors did stand up clearly. That is, the ideal self/social desirability factor does seem to be a pivotal construct in the system of self-representations about style and personality. It is also notable that impulsity and originally did stand up as autonomous constructs. However, systematicity and the executive style were integrated into a single construct in this study. This finding may not be surprising in its implication that these dimensions may be the two sides of the same coin. That is, they may represent a single overarching construct which is defined by a tendency to be systematic and thus have a readiness to follow rules (the executive style) which, in turn, provide a framework that is conducive for the actualization of this tendency. Finally, the judicial style vanished here, being absorbed mainly by ideal self.

The personality inventory

The analysis applied on this inventory abstracted 23 factors accounting for 70.91% of the total variance. The scree test suggested that six of these factors, accounting for 45.90% of the total variance, would have to be retained. Inspection of Table 7.3 suggests that all Big Five factors were clearly identified.

It can be seen that the first factor stands for *agreeableness*. This factor loaded highly on items representing two of the three facets included in this construct, that is altruism and compliance. The second factor stands for *extraversion*. This factor loaded on items representing all three facets of this dimension, that is extraversion, introversion, and sociability. The third factor stands for *conscientiousness* and it loaded on items representing both facets, that is, order and motivation for achievement and academic performance. The fourth factor stands for *openness to experience*. Also, this factor loaded on items representing both facets included in the test, that is intellect and openness. The fifth factor loaded on items representing both of the facets of *neuroticism* or *emotional reactivity*, that is manageability and emotional instability. Finally, the sixth factor loaded on items representing the facet of *emotional instability* of neuroticism. Therefore, it can be concluded that all of the personality dimensions represented in this inventory were clearly identified. The analysis below will show how the different types of dimensions are interrelated.

The common factor analysis

Finally, the common factor analysis applied on all three inventories yielded 44 factors with an eigen value bigger than 1. These factors accounted for 72.7% of the total variance. Following the scree test, 15 of these factors were retained, which accounted for 49.8% of the total variance. These factors are shown in Table 7.4.

It can be seen that the first factor loaded primary on items addressed to *extraversion*. Moreover, there were secondary loadings on many items addressed to openness to experience. Interestingly, social skills and verbal ability from the cognitive self-image inventory also loaded on this factor. It seems, therefore, that extraversion, openness to experience, social skill, and verbal ability are intertwined. The second factor clearly represents *conscientiousness*. Moreover, three of the four items addressed to systematicity in the thinking styles inventory also loaded on this factor. Therefore, systematicity may be seen as an aspect of conscientiousness, because this construct is specified in the literature about the Big Five. The third and the fourth factor stand clearly for *agreeableness* and *emotional reactivity*, respectively. It can be seen that these factors loaded primarily on the respective items.

The fifth factor represents an interesting combination between the *ideal self/social desirability* factor tapped by the thinking styles inventory and the facet of *neuroticism* of the factor of emotional reactivity. Moreover, in agreement with the analysis applied on the thinking styles inventory, this factor also loaded on one of the items addressed to originality and one item addressed to the judicial style. It seems, therefore, that this dimension is very strong and distinct from the other personality dimensions captured by the first four factors.

Factors 6, 7, 9, 10, and 11 are identical to the factors standing for *quantitative thought*, *social thought*, the *hypercognitive system*, *drawing*, and *openness to experience*. Factor 12 captured *verbal and discourse ability*. Factor 13 captured *emotional sensitivity*. Factor 14 captured the *executive style*. Factor 15 clearly stands for *memory*.

Special attention is drawn to factor 8. This factor stands primarily for the ability to learn and understand quickly and efficiently and retain the results of learning. Thus, it is similar to the learning factor identified by the first study. However, in the context of present study, this factor is wider because it loaded on items addressing speed of understanding and apprehension, self-monitoring, and working memory. Therefore, this factor might be taken to represent the thinker's awareness of what is called *fluid intelligence* in the classical psychometric theory of intelligence (Cattell, 1971; Gustafsson and Undheim, 1996).

In conclusion, this analysis suggests that the various dimensions of personality are distinct from the dimensions of mind and thinking style in one's self-system. At the same time, however, these dimension seem to be variously related. The analysis to be presented below aims to uncover in more depth the relationships underlying the various types of dimensions.

Table 7.4 Items and varimax factor structure of the inventory on cognitive abilities, thinking styles, and personality

Items	Factors														
	Extraversion	Conscientiousness	Agreeableness	Emotional reactivity	Ideal self-Neuroticism	Quantitative thought	Social thought	Fluid intelligence	Hypercognition	Drawing	Openness to experience	Verbal ability	Emotional sensitivity	Executive style	Memory
	1	2	3	4	5	6	7	8	9	10	11	12	13	14	15
COGNITIVE ABILITIES															
Social thought															
I understand easily the intentions of others before they express them.							.783								
I understand easily what others are thinking before they express their thoughts.							.810								
I understand easily the feelings of others before they express them.							.793								
I manage well in my relations with other people.	.767														
Quantitative thought															
I like solving mathematical problems.						.893									
I can easily apply the mathematical rules I have been taught to new problems.						.856									
I immediately solve everyday problems involving numbers.						.824									
*I avoid problems that require mathematical knowledge.						.772									

Hypercognition

Item					
I can monitor what is going inside me.				.746	
I can monitor my thoughts.				.716	
I can monitor my emotions.				.761	
I can monitor the condition of my body.				.666	
I am aware of my strong and my weak points.				.319	
I can easily sort out what is relevant to a subject.			.352		
After taking an action, I evaluate whether I did the right thing.					
*I have a hard time figuring out what has to be done in each occasion.					
When doing something, I often stop to check if I am doing it right.					
*I am rather insensitive to what is going inside me.					
I can easily change the way I think if I discover that my initial approach is not correct.					
I often think about myself.		.308			
I want to know what others think about me.		.407			

Verbal ability

Item					
I enjoy talking.	.528				
*I often have difficulty to express what I think.	.362				
I am very good in speaking.					.365
I like learning new words.					

Table 7.4 (continued)

Items	Factors														
	Extraversion	Conscientiousness	Agreeableness	Emotional reactivity	Ideal self-Neuroticism	Quantitative thought	Social thought	Fluid intelligence	Hypercognition	Drawing	Openness to experience	Verbal ability	Emotional sensitivity	Executive style	Memory
	1	2	3	4	5	6	7	8	9	10	11	12	13	14	15
Drawing															
I like drawing.										.836					
I can draw a person very accurately.										.817					
I can imagine new things and paint them so that everyone understands how I imagined it to be.										.735					
*I can hardly draw a single line when I have to draw something.										.682					
Causal thought															
When I hear one interpretation of an event, I always think that it may not be the real one.					.330										
I always think that things may not be as they seem.															
When someone says something, I frequently wonder what else he/she means.															
I like experimenting on topics that interest me.											.664				

Spatial-imaginal thought

Processing System

Learning and reasoning

Item				
Spatial-imaginal thought				
When I bring to mind something I have read, I have a picture of the page in my mind.				
*I can't retain a very clear picture of things.				
Even if I meet someone once, I never forget the face.				
I am a visualiser.	.327			
Processing System				
I am very fast in finding solutions to problems.				.476
I can easily understand what others explain to me.			.341	.321
*I need time to find the solution to a problem.			.530	.330
I am fast in making decisions.			.312	
I can easily remember large parts from the texts that I read.				
I can easily remember telephone numbers, even the ones I hear only once.	.692			
I can easily remember the names of persons from the first time I meet them.	.649			
Learning and reasoning				
When need be, I can immediately remember things I learnt a long time ago.	.343		.307	
I learn easily.			.738	
*I am not bothered when hearing unreasonable things.	.351			
I like drawing logical conclusions, which can be justified by the data I have.		.330		
When I present arguments about some subject, I use all the information I have on the subject.		.330		
In discussions with others, I often examine whether what they are saying fits the reality.				

Table 7.4 (continued)

Items	Factors														
	1	2	3	4	5	6	7	8	9	10	11	12	13	14	15
	Extraversion	Conscientiousness	Agreeableness	Emotional reactivity	Ideal self-Neuroticism	Quantitative thought	Social thought	Fluid intelligence	Hypercognition	Drawing	Openness to experience	Verbal ability	Emotional sensitivity	Executive style	Memory
Categorical thought															
I can easily detect the relations among seemingly irrelevant things.							.335								
I can easily detect the differences among seemingly similar things.							.340								
I can easily detect the latent relations among things.							.528								
THINKING STYLES															
Ideal self and social desirability															
I like being the centre of attention.					.722										
I want everyone to ask my opinion.					.721										
I like being the one with the best ideas about something.					.679										
*I don't mind failing.															

Systematicity

Item	1	2	3	4
I deal with each matter as much as necessary when necessary.	.607			
I organise my actions and I proceed systematically in order to achieve what I want.	.692			
I like everything to be settled properly.	.524			
*I can stand untidiness.				

Impulsivity

Item	1	2	3	4
I like acting fast without much thought.				
I do not sit and think what I have to do.				
*I prefer to be careful, even if it takes time.				
When I have many things I must do, I do not stop to think which is the most important.		.313		

Legislative style

Item	1	2	3	4
I like working on problems for which there are no pre-prepared solutions.			.476	
*I prefer applying ready-made solutions.				
When I think about a problem, I often try to find solutions others have not thought of.			.524	
I often find problems where everybody thinks things are going well.				

Executive style

Item	1	2	3	4
I believe people should go by the rules.				.720
I think that those who break a rule should be penalised.				.775
I like working where there are pre-defined rules of operation.				.346
*I believe that people are entitled to break the rules with which they disagree.				.481

Table 7.4 (continued)

Items	Factors														
	Extraversion	Conscientiousness	Agreeableness	Emotional reactivity	Ideal self-Neuroticism	Quantitative thought	Social thought	Fluid intelligence	Hypercognition	Drawing	Openness to experience	Verbal ability	Emotional sensitivity	Executive style	Memory
	1	2	3	4	5	6	7	8	9	10	11	12	13	14	15

Judicial style

Item	1	2	3	4	5	6	7	8	9	10	11	12	13	14	15
I often evaluate others on whether they are doing their work well.					.392										
I like deciding what is right and what isn't.															
I frequently want to know whether people follow the rules by which they should do something.														.398	
*It is not my business to judge other people.															

PERSONALITY

Emotional reactivity (manageability/neuroticism)

Item	1	2	3	4	5	6	7	8	9	10	11	12	13	14	15
I talk back to my parents.				.531											
I eat only what I like.				.334	.504										
I insist on my opinion, even if it is wrong.					.664										
I want always to be the leader.				.480											
I am spiteful.															
I am selfish.				.409											
I complain all the time.															

Item				
I am egoist.			.486	.388
I am stubborn.			.566	.441
I would rather take more than give.				.312
I like to get things my own way.			.412	.618
I am jealous.			.319	
I demand excessively.			.312	.334
I get angry easily.			.784	
Emotional reactivity (emotional instability)				
I fight, argue with others.			.659	
I am aggressive.			.787	
My mood changes easily.			.316	
I am vivid/active.	.598			
I have ups and downs.			.349	
I have unpredictable reactions.		−.313	.323	
I am nervous.			.584	
I overreact when scolded.			.526	
I am reactionary.			.639	
Conscientiousness (order, will to achieve)				
I am perfectionist.		.441		
I stick to my obligations, I am consistent.		.709		
I am orderly.		.798		
*I am untidy/disorderly.		.677		
I want to get better.		.333	.309	
I am careful.		.575		
I am organized.		.779		
Once I start something, I want to finish it.		.489		
I am responsible.		.663	.361	
*I am absent-minded.			.338	
I am mature for my age.				.324
I get easily anxious.				

Table 7.4 (continued)

Items	Factors														
	Extraversion	Conscientiousness	Agreeableness	Emotional reactivity	Ideal self-Neuroticism	Quantitative thought	Social thought	Fluid intelligence	Hypercognition	Drawing	Openness to experience	Verbal ability	Emotional sensitivity	Executive style	Memory
	1	2	3	4	5	6	7	8	9	10	11	12	13	14	15
Conscientiousness (school performance)															
I am diligent.		.740													
I am studious/hard-working.		.528													
*I am not interested in my studies.		.338													
*I need pressure to do my homework.		.324													
*I am lazy.		.487													
*I am negligent.		.634													
I like studying.															
Openness to experience (intellect)															
I am clever/intelligent.								.472							.369
I am good observer.	.303														
My mind is critical/analytical.					.311							.381			
I have my own opinion on issues.												.639			
I am imaginative.										.365					
I learn quickly/easily.								.698							
I have good memory.								.390							.573
I am interested in new things.											.529				
I like to discuss on various subjects.	.392											.483			
I have quick perception.							.307	.394							

Openness to experience

Item					
I have a strong character/personality.	.424				
I am inventive.	.492	.509			
I have many interests/hobbies.	.450	.364			
I take strong stands.			.442		
I am creative.	.377	.510		.318	
I take initiative.					
I am independent.	.312				.384
I am self-confident.	.300			.344	

Agreeableness (altruism)

Item	Loading	Emotional sensitivity
I am lovable.	.499	
I am emotional/sentimental.		.808
I am friendly.	.517	.442
I am willing to offer my help.	.669	
I am good-hearted.	.635	
I am affectionate/caring.	.667	
I share other people's suffering/I am compassionate.	.726	
I am sensitive.	.339	.752
I am concerned/care about other people's problems.	.773	
I am zealous of my honour/pride.	.613	

Agreeableness (emotional sensitivity)

Item	Loading
I cry easily.	.631
I get frustrated if scolded.	
I get hurt on the slightest criticism.	.300
I like to cuddle.	

Agreeableness (compliance)

Item	Loading	Emotional sensitivity
I am manageable.	.339	
I listen to others' advice.	.379	
I am understanding.	.663	
I am honest.	.596	
I am polite/kind.	.580	
I respect the elderly.	.369	
I am ready to compromise.		
I am protective with others.	.533	.314

Table 7.4 (continued)

Items	Factors														
	Extraversion	Conscientiousness	Agreeableness	Emotional reactivity	Ideal self-Neuroticism	Quantitative thought	Social thought	Fluid intelligence	Hypercognition	Drawing	Openness to experience	Verbal ability	Emotional sensitivity	Executive style	Memory
	1	2	3	4	5	6	7	8	9	10	11	12	13	14	15
Extraversion-Introversion (sociability)															
I adjusts myself easily in new environment.	.508														
I am happy.	.628														
I am expressive/outgoing.	.554														
I am spontaneous, impulsive.	.533														
I am sociable.	.782														
I am open/expressive/extravert.	.817														
Extraversion-Introversion (extraversion)															
I have a lot of friends.	.677														
I like having people around.	.523														
I like to go out.	.436														
I like to go out with people of my age.												.301			
I like to be always on the move.	.546														
I prefer not to stay alone.															
I am interested in relations with opposite sex.															
Extraversion-Introversion (introversion)															
*I am lonely.	.625														
*I prefer to stay at home.	.342														
*I shut myself off.	.722														
*I am difficult in making friends.	.719														

Notes

1 The Cronbach's α was tested separately for each set of items primary loading on a factor. The α for each of these factors was as follows: Extraversion: α = .941; Conscientiousness: α = .907; Agreeableness: α = .894; Emotional reactivity: α = .841; Ideal self-Neuroticism: α = .841; Quantitative thought: α = .844; Social thought: α = .887; Fluid intelligence: α = .830; Hypercognition: α = .815; Drawing: α = .819; Openness to experience: α = .751; Verbal ability: α = .754; Emotional sensitivity: α = .776; Executive style: α = .632; Memory: α = .657.

2 Items marked with an asterisk were inversely recoded for the purposes of this analysis.

The intertwining of cognitive self-representations, personality, and thinking styles

To specify the interrelationships between the various dimensions of cognitive self-representation, personality, and thinking styles, structural equations modelling was employed. Specifically, in line with the strategy that we followed in dealing with the results of the previous studies, a series of mean scores were created for each of the dimensions involved in the three inventories. Specifically, we created half-scores for the following dimensions of cognitive self-image: speed of processing, memory, reasoning, hypercognition, drawing, imaginal, social, verbal, quantitative, and causal thought. Moreover, we created two half-scores for each of the six factors represented in the thinking styles inventory; that is, for the factors of ideal self, systematicity, impulsivity, and the legislative, the executive, and the judicial style. Concerning personality, a mean score was created for each of the facets involved in each of the factors. The dimensions involved in this analysis are shown in Figure 7.2. The reader is reminded that most of these dimensions were identified as distinct factors by the three separate factor analyses applied on the three inventories. It was decided to let the few dimensions that did not show up as separate factors in the previous analyses (that is, basically the executive and the judicial style) to appear here as distinct factors. This manipulation allows one to compare directly the present model with the models tested in the previous studies.

The best fitting model is shown in Figure 7.2, $\chi^2(859) = 926.525$, p = .054, CFI = .981, GFI = .819, AGFI = .763, RMSEA = .023. Specifically, at the lower end of the figure one can see the various cognitive factors. It can be seen that these factors are organized as expected. That is, the six domain-specific factors are organized into three second-order factors that stand for visual creativity (drawing and imaginal thought), analytical inferential thought processes applied to the physical world quantitative and causal thought), and interpersonal thought (social and verbal thought). At the right part of the figure one can see that the four first-order factors that stand for general processes (speed of processing, memory, reasoning, and self-monitoring) relate to a second-order factor. Therefore, it is suggested that there is a single construct which reflects the individual's self-representation of general cognitive efficiency, and a number of constructs which reflect his self-representations of the domain-specific systems of thought. Moreover, in line with the assumptions about the relationship between general processing potentials and global self-worth, the self-representation of general cognitive efficiency is directly connected to both the processing and the domain-specific systems. Obviously, this part of the model is very close to similar models tested in the previous studies.

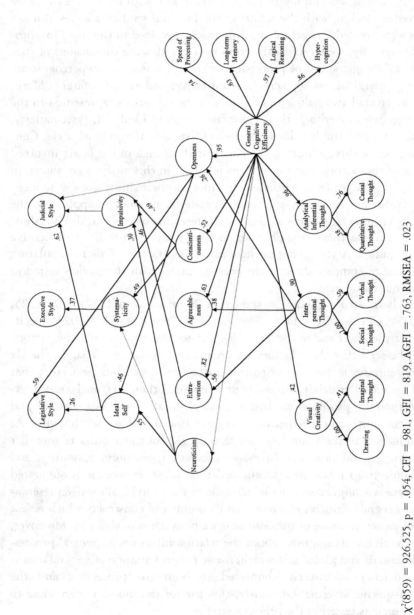

$\chi^2(859) = 926.525$, p = .054, CFI = 981, GFI = 819, AGFI = .763, RMSEA = .023

Figure 7.2 The model of the relations between cognitive self-image factors, personality factors, and thinking styles factors

At the middle of the model we see the Big Five factors of personality. It is highly interesting to note that excepting the factor of emotional reactivity, all were highly related to the self-representation of general cognitive efficiency. Thus, all dimensions of personality but the dimension of emotional reactivity involve a component of cognitive efficiency. The fact that the relationship between openness to experience and the general cognitive efficiency factor was almost unity, requires special mention. In our view, this relation suggests that the persons who think of themselves as cognitively strong are also open to experience because they feel that they have the capacity to cope with the new. Moreover, it needs to be noted that three of the five personality factors were related to self-perceived social thinking.

In line with the findings of the first study and the results of common exploratory factor analysis applied here, the constructs reflecting self-representations of thinking styles are derived from the factors of personality. Specifically, it can be seen that the more general dimensions of Sternberg's styles (that is, systematicity and impulsivity) and ideal self are here shown to occupy a more fundamental level than more specialized styles (such as the legislative, the executive and the judicial style). One can also see that the more fundamental thinking styles were highly predictable from the various personality constructs. For instance, the ideal self factor was closely related to neuroticism and openness to experience; systematicity to conscientiousness; and impulsivity to neuroticism, extraversion, and conscientiousness. Finally, the legislative style was found to be related to ideal self and openness, the executive style to systematicity, and the judicial style to ideal self.

CONCLUSIONS

The findings of the common factor analysis applied on all three inventories are highly interesting in their implications about what is included in the map of the person's representations of personality and the mind. That is, these findings suggest that both personality and the mind stand out as distinct realms in this map. Specifically four of the Big Five Factors (i.e. extraversion, conscientiousness, agreeableness, and emotional reactivity) are very powerful dimensions in the realm of the map concerned with personality. Openness to experience, together with verbal ability and social skill are absorbed by extraversion, indicating that this factor represents one's readiness to interact with the world in general, the social world in particular. An addition to the list is the ideal self/social desirability factor. This factor involves cognitive, social, and emotional components and it represents one's ambition to excel and become recognized in all three dimensions.

In as far as the cognitive realm is concerned, practically all of the levels and systems specified by our theory were identified. That is, the person is self-represented in reference to a number of general cognitive functions (that is, learning and reasoning, memory and self-monitoring and self-regulation) and the various domain-specific systems described by the theory (that is, social, quantitative, causal, imaginal, verbal thought, and drawing). Some of these processes are more clearly represented than others.

Finally, it is noteworthy that most of the thinking styles identified by our previous studies proved to be rather weak by the present study. This indicates that these styles are derivatives of the more fundamental dimensions involved in the realms of personality and cognition. In a sense, this finding is in line with Sternberg's conception of thinking styles as the interface between personality, intelligence, and actual performance. The price of this status is that once one specifies the condition of the fundamental dimensions underlying thinking styles one can live without them because these can be derived from the dimensions themselves.

The structural analyses applied on the various factors presented a more clear picture of the relationships interconnecting the various dimensions. Specifically, four of the five dimensions of personality were found to intervene, in various combinations with each other, between the cognitive realm and thinking styles. It was found, for instance, that individuals who have a strong sense of cognitive efficiency are also open to experience. These individuals, if they are also emotionally stable, tend to think highly of themselves, as suggested by the rather strong relationships between these two personality dimensions with the ideal self factor. In turn, thinking highly of oneself together with being open to experience orients one to activities which require originality. Those who think highly of themselves but they are not open to experience tend to have a judicial style of thought, which orients them to activities requiring evaluation. Interestingly, a combination of emotional reactivity with extraversion seems to lead to impulsivity; impulsivity itself is negatively related to conscientiousness, which is, however, related to systematicity. In turn, systematic personalities tend to have an executive style, which leads them to activities with predefined rules. We believe that these findings are a first step in the direction of integrating the psychology of the mind with the psychology of personality. We will elaborate more on this integration in the concluding chapter.

8　General discussion

The emerging self: the convergence of mind, personality, and self

The studies presented in this book have focused on self-evaluation and self-representation with particular emphasis on specifying the dimensions encompassed in self-concept, and highlighting both their organization and their relationships with processes and abilities in other levels of the architecture of the mind and the self. These studies were directed by a series of hypotheses derived from our theory about the organization and development of the mind and from other theories of self, personality, and thinking styles. These hypotheses are concerned with the architecture and development of the mind and the self, the place of dimensions of personality and thinking style in this architecture, and social influences on this system. The discussion below will involve three sections, one for each set of hypotheses. Moreover, there will be a section on the relationships between our theories and other theories of the mind and the self. Our aim here is to summarize the main findings of the studies presented in this book and raise questions and issues worthy for future research and theorizing.

The architecture and development of the mind and the self

Briefly, our theory postulates that the mind is a three-level hierarchical universe. Two of the levels in this universe involve knowing systems, one environment-oriented and the other self-oriented, and the third level involves general-purpose potentials which are activated as required by any system at the other levels. Furthermore, the environment-oriented level structures are constructionally, functionally, and developmentally distinct. The self-oriented level or, in our terms, the hypercognitive system, comprises maps of the environment-oriented systems, which are by and large accurate in their depiction of the organization and the relationships among environment oriented systems. These maps reflect the differential experiences generated by the activation of the various SCSs and are available whenever decisions related to course of action, covert or overt, must be made. The processing system is seen as a dynamic field that is always occupied by elements from the other two hierarchical levels, in proportions which vary from moment to moment. Specifically, the input to this system is environment-relevant information, skills, and processes, pertaining to an SCS (or something equivalent), and management and evaluation processes, pertaining to the hypercognitive system. These latter processes serve to orchestrate the processing of the former and evaluate the outcome of processing in relation to its goal. At the same time, however, orchestration and evaluation of processing is guided by both the dynamics underlying the organization of the environment-oriented systems and the already available hypercognitive maps of this organization. Moreover, the potentialities of the processing system constrain what problems can be solved, how they can be solved, and how they can be recorded.

The results presented throughout this book validated and extended this picture of the mind. They also suggested a number of interesting questions that, if answered, might further expand our knowledge of the mind. Specifically, the various structural analyses applied to the data generated by the first study suggested clearly that the causal, quantitative, and spatial SCSs are structurally autonomous, which is consistent with our earlier research on these SCSs (Demetriou and Efklides, 1985, 1989; Demetriou et al., 1993a). The present study suggested that drawing and social thought are also SCSs equivalent to those previously identified. The reader is reminded that performance on the respective tasks clearly represented independent dimensions in all structural analyses presented in the first study, concurring with recent research by Case (1992; Case et al., 1996). Case's research has also suggested that social thought and drawing can be considered central conceptual structures (CCSs). According to Case, CCSs constitute mental organizations which are semantically, representationally, and, to a certain extent, developmentally distinct.

The results of the first study suggested some further conclusions regarding the organization of cognitive abilities. Specifically, it was found that the SCSs are organized into higher-order families of SCSs, differentiated on the basis of their orientation to reality and problem solving. The causal, quantitative, and social SCS are primarily inferential in character and, under our test conditions, were directed to problems for which there was only one correct solution. In contrast, drawing and the ideational fluency tasks involve primarily visual representation, and are thereby primarily holistic and intuitive in their generation of goal-relevant ideas. Moreover, they were directed to open problems for which more than one correct solution may be given. Validating the autonomy of the SCSs confirms hypothesis 2.1 (see Introduction), and identifying two new SCSs and specifying SCS-families extends our theory in new directions. Of course, this requires further research that would clarify the composition of these SCSs and specify their dynamic interrelationships.

The results on the organization of difficulty/success evaluation, and our findings related to self-attribution of cognitive abilities (in terms of tasks used in the study) confirmed hypotheses 2.2 and 2.3, respectively. Specifically, difficulty and success were clearly differentiated in the evaluations produced by the participants; all SCSs were found to preserve their identity in both evaluations; each type of evaluation was influenced by general cognitive ability, general self-representation, and the condition of the domain-specific system evaluated; finally, both types of evaluations were found to be sensitive to experience. In self-representations of cognitive processes and abilities, SCS-specific and family-specific constellations of cognitive processes and characteristics were identical to those at the level of actual performance. These findings substantiate our assumptions that working hypercognition involves distinct evaluation processes which spare the particularities of the SCSs (hypothesis 2.2). As a result, the mental maps constructed on the basis of the interactions with the world reflect the organizational forces underlying actual cognitive abilities (hypothesis 2.3).

We recognize, of course, that the human mind is much more complex than simply cognitive abilities and processes, and their representation. As posited in hypothesis 2.4, more dynamic dimensions, such as ambition and impulsivity, form the self-image as much as do the cognitive dimensions. These two types of dimensions (i.e. cognitive and personality dimensions) interact to shape the individual's preferred style of activities, which in turn can influence the choice of activities one would like to engage in.

One of the most interesting findings of the studies presented in this book relates to the dynamic organization of the self-image. The reader is reminded that all hierarchical models, as described in the first study, strongly indicated a unifying force pertaining to both the self-evaluation system and the self-attribution of abilities and characteristics system. In fact, we identified a kind of "personal constant", which moderates and adapts both on-line feedback generated at person-task encounters and also more general self-representations. Identification of this force lends support to hypothesis 2.5, which posited (based on the work of important other scholars, e.g. Erikson, 1963; Freud, 1923; James, 1982; Harter, 1999) that the human mind involves strong integrative functions which may underlie identity. An interesting conclusion is therefore suggested by the findings of the studies presented here. Specifically, the co-presence of this force with the domain-specific dimensions suggests that the mind is simultaneously both a modular and a transmodular system in both the cognitive and the social/personality systems. We propose that this picture suggests that the two strong but separate traditions in psychology, namely the cognitivist and the more socially and dynamically related traditions, can be integrated into an overarching system.

The mind is modular in two different respects. First, it is modular at the level of the environment-oriented systems. In fact, modularity at this level may take one of several forms. There is modularity of the core functions included in the various systems. This kind of modularity may reflect the constructional peculiarities of the hardware systems underlying the various SCSs, such as the perceptual systems or the motor systems. Examples here might be the perception of causality for the causal system, the perception of small numbers (that is known as subitization) for the quantitative system, or the perception of depth for the spatial system. This kind of modularity may bear some of the basic properties of modularity as initially introduced by Fodor (1983). That is, it refers to processes which may to a large extent be informationally encapsulated; this kind of processes, once activated by domain-relevant information, impose a particular kind of interpretation of the stimuli present which is not affected by other surrounding information. Modern research in neuroscience suggests that this type of modularity may even reflect the fact that different cognitive processes are supported by different neural networks in the brain (Elman, Bates, Johnson, Karmiloff-Smith, Parisi, and Plunket, 1996).

However, there is also operational or preferential modularity. Operational modularity refers to the peculiarities and specificities which characterize the mental operations involved in the various SCSs, such as isolation of variables in the causal system, arithmetic operations in the quantitative system, or mental rotation in the spatial system. Our earlier studies have shown that there are operations of this type in each SCS which are logically irreducible to each other and thus require different logics to be satisfactorily modelled (Kargopoulos and Demetriou, 1998). Moreover, we have also shown in terms of connectionist modelling (Demetriou and Raftopoulos, 1999; Demetriou, Raftopoulos, and Kargopoulos, 1999) that these operations are computationally different. It is noted, however, that this type of modularity is "softer", so to speak, than the type of modularity discussed above. That is, operational modularity does not necessarily entail encapsulation. In fact, operations from different SCSs may be integrated or combined for the sake of understanding concepts that bridge different domains of relationships in the environment. We have recently elaborated in some depth how operational integration may occur across different SCSs (Demetriou and Raftopoulos, 1999; Demetriou *et al.*, 1999).

Finally, there is preferential modularity. This is a kind of soft modularity, which may stem from the individual's differential involvement and ensuing facility in operating a specific SCS. Needless to say, these three types of modularity are not mutually exclusive and, in fact, it is very reasonable to assume that one may lead to the other. That is, the modularity of core functions sets the constraints for operational modularity and this, in turn, paves the way for the development of individual preferences and talents.

However, it is not only at the level of the environment-oriented systems that the mind is modular; modularity is also evident at the level of environment-oriented SCS representation. That is, different SCSs not only involve different hardware and/or operational systems which are functionally autonomous in their interactions with the domains of the environment concerned; this is also felt or known by the mind to a considerable degree.

The mind is transmodular in at least three respects. One the one hand, the very ability to oversee, record, and differentiate the modules is by definition a transmodular function because it transcends the modules. On the other hand, the personal constant identified here is a transmodular mechanism because it operates on all modules. In this capacity, the personal constant causes implicit or explicit adjustments at two different levels: objective adjustments in performance across modules which bring about a certain similarity in performance variations; and subjective adjustments which render different aspects of performance or the self similar to the individual even when they are not. The reader may recall here how the subjective evaluations of the performance attained on the tasks covaried with the various dimensions of self-image. Therefore, the personal constant is a unifying force rather than simply a transmodular overviewer.

It is interesting that these transmodular functions are geared to a limited number of dimensions in the self-image, which represent general rather than specialized cognitive or social and personality characteristics. These dimensions, which were found to primarily represent reasoning and learning power (in terms of cognitive functions) and ambition and impulsivity (in regard to social and personality characteristics), are used as the basis for more domain-specific self-descriptions and orientations, when needed. In so doing, they can actually influence the decisions an individual makes in regard to different styles of activities, and by implication, they may affect the individual's actual course of development. We note here that the way in which individuals conceive themselves in regard to these dimensions also influences their choice of occupation (Demetriou, Kazi, Sirmali, and Tsiouri, in preparation).

These dimensions are formed in relation to the individual's processing and reasoning power. In line with hypothesis 2.5 of the first study, the third of the studies presented in this book clearly suggested that these general dimensions of self-representation (logicality in particular) depend on both processing speed, which defines the efficiency of the processing system, and the reasoning processes involved in analogical thought and propositional reasoning. We believe that this finding substantiates our assumption that the hypercognitive system relates directly to both the processing system and the processes involved in the environment-oriented SCSs. The conclusion is clear: the image that the mind constructs of itself as a system which represents and reasons about the world, itself, and other minds, is to a large extent affected by those parameters defining the lower level systems of the mental architecture. That is, it emerges in reference to systems which although very efficient in their functioning, have been traditionally considered to operate subconsiously. At the same time, however, the current status of self-image influences the functioning of these lower level systems by regulating both on-line functioning and long-term choices.

These findings clearly support our assumption that working hypercognition is the active part of the hypercognitive system interconnecting the environment-oriented level of the mind with the mind's self-representations. Moreover, our research indicates that working hypercognition operates under the constraints of the processing system in two different respects. First, the various self-monitoring and self-control processes are themselves constrained by the current processing potentials of the mind, such that no observation, recording, selection, or modification processes can be implemented if they require more speed or storage than is currently possible. Second, working hypercognition processes are applied to environment-oriented processes which are also constrained by current potentials. Thus, working hypercognition competes for processing resources with the environment-oriented module on which it is applied (Case, 1985). This state of affairs creates an interesting paradox: the more demanding a task is (due to complexity or novelty) the more processing resources, monitoring and regulation it requires. However, increased monitoring and regulation require resources that might otherwise be used to represent the dimensions defining the problem itself. In other words, there seems to be a conflict of interest between the demands of the environment-oriented modules and the demands of working hypercognition. This conflict must underlie the experience of mental effort and, of course, the more efficiently the conflict is resolved the more efficient the problem solving must be. This must also underlie an individual's sense of general efficiency. This is then translated into feelings of general self-worth and it is projected at both the level of an individual's self construct (e.g. "I learn quickly", "I am competent in reasoning", etc.) and others' representations of this individual (e.g. "He learns quickly", "He is competent in reasoning", etc.).

Thus, working hypercognition plays a privileged role within the self-system because it reflects the operating constraints of the mind, the mind's flexibility to overcome these constraints, and the registration of the respective experiences. Our findings reveal that the various dimensions defining the functioning of the processing system, namely speed of processing and storage, together with self-representations of self-monitoring and self-regulation, form a general self-representation complex which directly influences the individual's self-representations about the environment-oriented cognitive systems and the various dimensions of personality. Therefore, it is clear that this compound of actual cognitive potentials and their self-representations occupies a very central position in an individual's self-system and influences his style and general orientation. Moreover, it becomes a pivotal factor in the formation of interpersonal and reflected appraisals (see Demetriou, 2000).

The findings related to development highlighted this dynamic relationship between the different levels of the mental architecture. Two points require special mention in this regard. First, self-evaluation accuracy never dropped below a minimum, which was always high, across all age, gender, and SES groups in our study. Throughout the age span studied, variations in self-evaluation of performance tended to reflect changes in performance itself, such that improved performance was associated with an initial and temporary decrease in self-evaluation accuracy.

Second, there was a major structural change in the relationship between the hypercognitive and the other levels of the mental architecture. This change begins at the age 11–12 years, when the personal constant begins to be transformed or re-scaled to accommodate the changes occurring in the various systems, and it continues until middle adolescence. This change results in increasing communication between the environment-oriented and the self-oriented level of the mind. As a side-effect of this increasing communication, self-attribution of abilities and characteristics tended to become stricter with either age or improvement in cognitive performance, as anticipated by hypothesis 2.6. Attention is drawn here to the fact that, on the one hand, self-evaluation (as studied here) reflects experiences generated by on-line functioning, which experiences need not be explicit. On the other hand, self-attribution of abilities and characteristics requires explicit self-representations in this regard. These differences between the two functions of the hypercognitive system may help explain both the differences in their developmental pattern, their reciprocal effects, and their effects on the development of the environment-oriented systems. When implicit metacognitive experiences generated by working hypercognition during on-line functioning are encoded, stabilized, and reflected upon, they ultimately shape the dimensions of long-term hypercognition. Therefore, we see that developmental cycles alternate between changes in self-evaluation of cognitive performance, which represents working hypercognition, and self-representation, which stands for long-term hypercognition.

Of course it is to be noted that our longitudinal findings suggested that changes in self-evaluation as a result of cognitive development vary from person to person, depending upon each person's general attitude to self-evaluation and self-representation. That is, changes in self-evaluation and self-representation tended to follow the changes in cognitive performance more in persons who are accurate in their self-representation than in persons who are not accurate.

The place of personality in the self-system

The mind is tightly intertwined with personality. Our studies on the place of the dimensions of personality and the self-system in the organization of the person indicated clearly that the various dimensions of cognition, personality, and self interact in complex ways thereby producing different profiles of ability and action. Let us then summarize and try to further understand these interactions.

First, the reader is reminded that self-representations of the Big Five dimensions of personality intervene between both self-representations of cognitive abilities, and thinking styles and activity preferences. In fact, it was found that four of the Big Five dimensions of personality have a very strong (reflected) cognitive component. This is a combination of the individual's self-representation of cognitive efficiency (i.e. processing and reasoning), person-oriented thought process (i.e. social and verbal thought), and self-monitoring/self-regulation strategies and characteristics. The combination of these three dimensions almost fully accounts for variation in the dimensions of extraversion and openness to experience. In fact, the relationship between self-representation of cognitive efficiency and openness is so close that one might say that the more cognitively efficient one feels the more open to experience one may be. It is also notable that the dimension of neuroticism stands alone in that it is not related to any of the dimensions of cognitive self-representation. Thus, emotional stability is independent of intellectual functioning.

Another aspect of this relationship is equally interesting: four of the five dimensions of personality intervene, in various combinations with each other, in the formation of thinking styles. Specifically, individuals who are open to experience and neurotic think highly of themselves, as suggested by the rather strong relationships between these two personality dimensions with the factor standing for ambition. In turn, thinking highly of oneself together with being open to experience orients one to activities which require originality. Those who think highly of themselves but they are not open to experience tend to have a judicial style of thought, which orients them to activities requiring evaluation. Interestingly, a combination of neuroticism with extraversion seems to lead to impulsivity; impulsivity itself is negatively related to conscientiousness, which is, however, positively related to systematicity. In turn, systematic personalities tend to have an executive style, which leads them to activities with predefined rules.

This pattern of relations is interesting and potentially useful because it opens the way for understanding how intellectual and personality processes and characteristics merge into activity styles and preferences. It needs to be noted, however, that very little is known about the underlying mechanisms that interconnect the functions of mind, personality, and self in everyday functioning and channel development into different courses and paths. A series of studies conducted by Kochanska and colleagues seem relevant (Kochanska, 1995, 1997; Kochanska, Coy, Tjebkes and Husarek, 1997). These studies suggest, "that early differences in inhibitory control forecast future personality development, and especially adult differences in conscientiousness or constraint, one of the Big Five" (Kochanska *et al.*, 1997, p. 274).

These findings are in line with an earlier longitudinal study conducted by Mischel and colleagues in the context of the delay of gratification paradigm. In a delay of gratification study, children are usually given two choices: a small reward that is immediately available or a large reward that requires a period of waiting. Waiting for the large reward is considered to indicate an ability to inhibit impulses and thus to signify self-control. In this study, parents of children involved in a delay of gratification study were asked in a follow-up study (10 years later) about the competencies and shortcomings of their children. The findings were very clear: children who were unable to delay gratification in the initial study were characterized as impatient adolescents, unable to postpone gratification. In contrast, those children able to delay gratification were characterized as adolescents who were academically more competent, more socially skilled, better able to cope with stress, more confident and self-reliant. Moreover, these children obtained higher scores on the scholastic aptitude test (Mischel, Shoda, and Peake, 1988). These findings on the relationships between the development of self-control and personality fully concur with the model proposed here, which posits direct links between the processing system, self-representation of cognitive efficiency, and personality. Can then these links be specified?

Rothbart's theory of temperamental control (Rothbart and Bates, 1998) suggests how self-control may be related to the development of processing capacity. According to this theory, the ability to monitor and inhibit inappropriate impulses and tendencies depends on the development of attentional networks, as these enable the individual to co-represent internal tendencies and external stimuli. This is so because to resist a temptation requires awareness and simultaneous representation of the two competing objects (the temptation, such as an immediately available and a more distant but more valued reward), the emotional-motivational consequences of each choice, and the mental or actual operations that can be used to direct attention and action

from the lesser to the more important goal. Self-regulation will not be possible in these situations in as far as this complex of representations can not be
held simultaneously in an active state. This occurs at the age of five years,
that is at the age at which delay of gratification was found to be possible.
Therefore, the development of self-regulation seems to follow the development of both processing potentials and working hypercognition.

It needs to be noted that self-awareness itself is also directly involved in
the formation of activity patterns associated with the functioning of personality. This is obvious in the relationships between the development of self-
understanding and self-regulation. The reader is reminded that preschool
children cannot clearly recognize different mental processes and they do not
comprehend that they can use one process in order to affect the functioning
of another. Naturally, then, they do not use these processes as a means of
self-regulation. With development in the understanding of the nature and
functioning of these processes and in self-representation in regards to each of
them, self-regulation of behaviour and thought becomes increasingly more
efficient (Demetriou, 2000).

The mechanisms involved in the development of the ability to delay gratification may be invoked as an example. The studies which investigated the
development of this ability revealed that *distraction* is the primary means by
which children attempt to delay gratification. Children will try to divert
their attention with overt or mental actions that will transform or conceal
the temptation. Some children cover their eyes so that they cannot see the
tempting stimuli, others sing so that they are otherwise engaged during the
waiting period, and others transform the incentive mentally so that they
represent it as being unappealing rather than attractive.

The use of distraction as a means to delay gratification develops
systematically in a way which is consistent with the pattern of development
outlined above. Preschoolers do not know that distraction can help them
resist temptations; as a result, they do not use it even when instructed to do
so or taught self-instructional strategies. Instead, they continue to focus
attention on the desirable properties of the incentives, which leads them to
succumb to rather than resist the temptation. Efficient use of distraction
appears at about the age of 6–8 years, when children begin to employ simple
strategies, such as covering their eyes or the object itself. Cognitive distrac-
tions that result in the transformation of the incentives do not appear until
early adolescence. Kuhl (1992) posits that while early school age children are
capable of attention control, only later can they use motivation control as a
means of self-regulation. Thus, the development of the hypercognitive
system, which produces self-awareness, becomes a crucial factor in the development and establishment of behaviours associated with the organization
and functioning of personality.

However, it needs to be noted that the integration of temperamental qualities with the processes involved in the processing system, such as speed of processing and inhibition may escape awareness. Kagan's (1994b) research is relevant in this regard. Kagan used a Stroop-like experimental design and found that inhibited individuals take longer time to read fearful words (e.g. drown, kill, shy, poison) as compared to words with a pleasant connotation (e.g. love, fond, friend); uninhibited individuals were not affected. This finding implies that personality dispositions are directly involved in how information is initially registered and interpreted by the individual.

One might go as far as to assume that Freud's (1923) psychodynamic mechanisms of ego defense represent this interleaving of personality dispositions with the processing system. The reader is reminded that, according to Freud, several mechanisms, such as repression, rejection, or rationalization, filter or transform information or representations in particular ways with the aim to protect an individual's identity, self-regard, and psychological well-being. Therefore, these mechanisms may be taken as tokens of the direct and dynamic interaction between cognitive and personality functioning. Of course, the crucial questions about these dynamics are still unanswered. When does this interaction begin and how does it change with development? How does it affect subsequent self-regulatory actions in persons of different temperaments and styles? We may suppose that some mechanisms are stronger in some individuals rather than others. For instance, inhibited individuals may tend to use repression more than other mechanisms; extraverts may use rationalization more than repression. Likewise, we still do not know how initial differences in the parameters of processing efficiency, such as speed and inhibition, are transformed into feelings of cognitive self-efficacy which may make a person open to experience.

Moreover, many questions about self-awareness itself still remain unanswered. For example, why some individuals are more self-aware and reflective than others from the beginning? According to the model proposed here, this is to be expected because self-awareness is an autonomous component of the mental architecture; thus, it is a dimension of individual differences in itself. The stability of individual differences suggested by the fact that our four combinations of cognitive ability and self-evaluation persisted over time provides support to this assumption. Moreover, different types of interaction between persons may contribute to differences in reflectivity and self-awareness. However, there is no research on how these initial differences interact with differences in the other levels and systems of the mental architecture and the temperamental dispositions to generate different types or styles of self-representation and self-regulation. Moreover, we still do not understand how initial differences in the functioning of the various domain-specific systems of thought, such as mathematical, causal, or social thought, shape particular attitudes to problem solving which are then formulated into personal strategies, orientations, and choices.

Towards an overarching model of mind, personality, and self

The above analysis suggests that we can move in the direction of an overarching model that would capture the integrated functioning of the mind, personality and the self. The model shown in Figure 8.1 is an approximation to this ideal. It can be seen that we propose that the hierarchical levels of personality and the self-system correspond to the three hierarchical levels of mind depicted by our theory of the cognitive architecture. The model posits that the Big Five factors of personality (that is, Graziano's level I) correspond to the domain-specific systems that reside at the environment-oriented level of knowing. That is, the domain-specific systems of understanding channel the functioning of the mind and the Big Five factors channel patterns of action and relationships with the social and cultural environment (see level I of the model shown in Figure 8.1). In a similar vein, temperament is considered as the dynamic aspect of processing potentials. Thus, the processing potentials constrain the complexity and type of information that can be understood at a given age and temperament constrains how information is to initially be received and reacted to (see level II of the model shown in Figure 8.1). These constructs are controlled by the active processes of self-knowing implicated in James' I-self or Markus' working self-concept or by the monitoring and control processes involved in working hyper-cognition (see level III of the model shown in Figure 8.1). The functioning of these control processes generate feelings and representations of general cognitive efficiency or global self-worth and general self-esteem (see level IV of the model shown in Figure 8.1). In parallel to these general self-representations we have the more localized or specialized self-systems (that is, Graziano's level II, James' Me-self, and Markus collection of self-representations). These correspond to the various self-representations which reside in the long-term hypercognitive maps of the organization of the mind (see level V of the model shown in Figure 8.1). Thus, the constructs at this level reflect how individuals register and represent themselves in regard to the various dimensions of understanding the world and the various dispositions of interacting with the world. Finally, Sternberg's thinking styles (see level VI of the model shown in Figure 8.1) and Graziano's level III (see level VII of the model shown in Figure 8.1) stand on their own as frames that shape perceived or actual adaptations to particular tasks or contexts.

As an integrated representation of the thinking and acting individual, this model captures both the dynamic (that is, the motivational and emotional) and the meaning making (that is, the representational) components

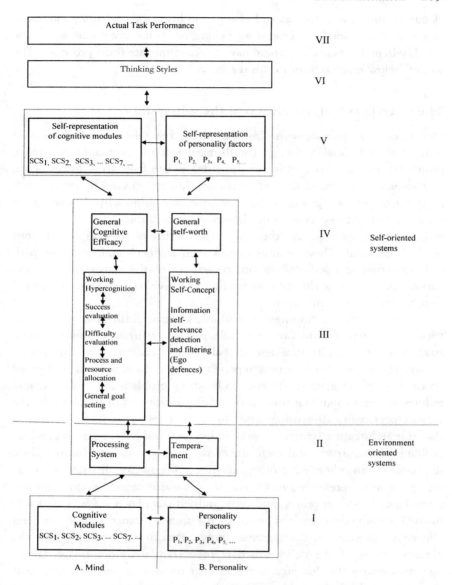

Figure 8.1 The general model of the mind and personality

Note
SCS stands for specialised capacity systems. P stands for personality factor.

of understanding, experience, and action. However, persons do not live alone. They live with other persons in groups and societies. Individuals exert influences on one another as they interact and negotiate their views about the world and one another. Moreover, individuals are parts of the processes of our evolution as a species and also of the historical, cultural, and social processes that shaped the groups we belong to. Thus, any model about the mind, self, and personality, would have to accommodate these processes. The section below is an attempt in this direction.

The inter-personal dimension of the self-system

Our studies do provide some insights about the relative contribution of individual and social factors in the formation of the particular self-image profiles that characterize different individuals. We have seen, for instance, that some dimensions of the self-image are directly affected by factors such as speed of processing which, by definition, are minimally dependent on social factors. At the same time, however, these dimensions are somehow visible to other persons and they shape these other persons' representations of the individual. These representations then feedback and, together with self-evaluation and self-observation, contribute to the construction of the various dimensions of the self-concept by the individual, which are projected to other individuals, and so on.

In conclusion, our findings on children's actual abilities in relation to their self-representations, and to their parents' representations of them, suggest that the architecture described above is intersubjective as much as it is intrasubjective. That is, others' representations of an individual are formed on the basis of her general efficiency in handling problems, her successes and failures in the various domains, and her dispositions and tendencies in the various personality dimensions and thinking styles. This finding suggests that this architecture frames both the individuals' subjective experiences and ensuing self-constructs and each others' descriptions and attributions. In a sense, we see in others what others see in us because we all share the same system of self-representation. Of course, some dimensions occupy a more pivotal position than others, and some individuals play a more central role in the intersubjective space. The reader is reminded that the child's general efficiency, together with domains transparent to awareness, shape the parents' image of the child which is then translated into images about opaque domains. In this process the mother occupies a central role in that she influences both the child and the father.

A general model of this dynamic system is shown in Figure 8.2. Each of the four systems in this model stands for an individual and the four of them together constitute a system. Each individual is defined in terms of the following types of constructs: (1) abilities and characteristics (that is, the components of levels I and II in Figure 8.1); (2) self-representations and self-esteem (that is, the components of levels III and IV in Figure 8.1); (3) life-choices and activities (that is, the components of levels VI and VII in Figure

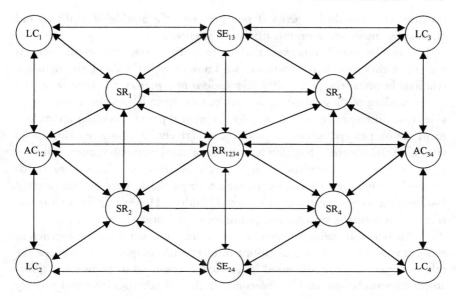

Figure 8.2 Model of the interrelationships between abilities and characteristics (AC), self-representations (SR), reciprocal representations (RR), self-esteem (SE), and life-choices (LC) within and between persons (the numbers 1, 2, 3, 4 stand for four interrelated persons

8.1); and (4) mutual representations, that is the representations that individuals hold about each other.

Attention is drawn to three aspects of this model. First, self-representations are allocated a central position within each individual to indicate that they function as an interface between the various other constructs that define an individual. Second, mutual representations are placed in the centre of the system. This indicates that individuals function within a collective space that lies between them. This derives from each individual who at one and the same time projects onto others both her own identity and her representations about their identities and also becomes the recipient of similar projections all other individuals participating in a network. Third, it is also indicated that each of the constructs is dynamically related with institutional constructs, actual or virtual, that frame what the individuals can or must do. For instance, cognitive abilities interact with the educational possibilities, priorities, and resources of a family and a given society at large. Personality characteristics interact with social norms and priorities that define what is acceptable or preferable within various social or cultural formations. Life choices necessarily take place within the context of alternative pathways and possibilities provided by the culture and the social group. For instance, to follow the career of the scientist, one must live in a society that provides this possibility, even if one possesses the profile of abilities and talents that make one a promising future scientist.

It must be noted, however, that there is little research on the various aspects of this model. For instance, we know very little about the dynamic relations between the personality dispositions of a person, the parents' actual understanding of these dispositions, and parenting style. Recent research suggests that different dispositions require different types of parenting if development is to proceed smoothly and constructively. Specifically, Kochanska (1995, 1997) showed that different types of temperament require different types of parental discipline if high levels of conscientiousness are to be attained. That is, gentle discipline, which keeps the level of anxious arousal low, promotes conscientiousness in fearful children. However, positive motivation and security of attachment promotes conscientiousness in fearless children. To our knowledge, there is no evidence suggesting how the different types of parenting style and discipline interact with temperament to shape the other personality types discussed here, such as openness to experience, agreeableness, neuroticism, and extraversion, or the various cognitive and activity styles, such as the judicial or the executive style.

The rising of the mind, self, and personality in the evolution of the human species

How then did mind, personality, and self arise during our evolution as a species?

> Human beings have evolved to be able to know themselves (their own and each other's mind). A species capable of self-understanding has an important comparative advantage relative to species lacking this capability: it can make use of its own history in order to cope with the continuous change in the external world. Practically, this implies an ability to model one's own skills, knowledge, talents, and tendencies vis-à-vis the surrounding world (physical, social, psychological, and symbolic) so as to make choices for the necessary or preferable course of action. Subsequently, once individuals are aware of their own and others' minds and dispositions, they need to have a sense of personal identity or a self-construct. This enables each person to differentiate himself or herself from others as a means of both protecting his or her own personal view of the world and/or negotiating it with others. Thus, self and identity emerge and become established gradually as individuals become more accurate in monitoring, representing, evaluating, and regulating themselves and others in their problem solving and behaviour and in the abilities and dispositions, cognitive and other, which underlie problem solving and behaviour.
>
> (Demetriou *et al.*, 1999a, p. 403)

From an evolutionary point of view, the environment-oriented problem solving systems and processes came long before self-monitoring, self-recording, and self-regulation. According to Donald (1991), the human mind evolved along four stages, namely the episodic, the mimetic, the mythic, and the theoretical. At the first of these stages there were very elaborated environment-oriented systems but no awareness of one's own or the others' mind. This awareness increased gradually so that it first enabled humans to imitate each other and then reflect on the world and each other. Finally, self-awareness became elaborate enough to enable the formalization of reflections in terms of personal or scientific theories. Mithen (1996) and Wesson (1991) have recently advanced similar theories about the evolution of the human mind.

In fact, this sequence in the construction of the two levels of knowing is reflected in the evolution of the brain itself. The frontal lobe, which appears to specialize in monitoring and control of behaviour, is the most recent development of the human brain, thus subsequent to those areas of the brain which host the various environment-oriented systems and processes. Moreover, the frontal lobe is the last to reach its mature state during individual development as well (van der Molen and Ridderinkhof, 1998). Thus, the ontogeny of the brain recapitulates its phylogeny in this regard.

This direction in human evolution suggests that the mind became possible because humans acquired systems and processes at a higher order of organization which could register and represent the "lower" order processes. In other words, in evolution, mindfulness emerged as a result of humans first observing and manipulating each other and then as a result of self-observation, self-evaluation, and self-mapping. This is equivalent to saying that *the mind is the processes, functioning, and products of this self-oriented level of knowing. The self is the personalized aspect of this level* and it may refer to cognitive systems and processes (e.g. I am good in reasoning, learning, mathematics, drawing, social interaction, etc.) or to personality traits or dispositions (e.g. I enjoy being with people; I am stable; I am irritable, etc.).

These traits and dispositions set the tone of each person's idiosyncratic functioning. In other words, the sense of identity that each human has is a reflection, at the level of self-awareness, of one out of many possible variations of intellectual and temperamental-personality profiles that were shaped during our evolution as a species. Thus, the struggle of each person to preserve his or her identity and make it acceptable by and possibly impose it on others may be seen as the projection, at the level of self-awareness, of the main force of evolution. That is, it reflects the forces of survival and spread of one's own characteristics.

Unfortunately, there is no study on the emergence of these traits during the evolution of the human species. That is, although theorizing about personality goes back to classical Greeks (see Kagan, 1994b), there is no valid information and theorizing about the emergence of different types of personality during our evolution as a species and their possible interrelationships with the emergence of mind. This is to be contrasted to the recent proliferation of research and theorizing about the evolution of the mind (Donald, 1991; Mithen 1996; Wesson, 1993). It would be interesting, however, to study modal differences in personality between different species which are in existence today and try to see if these differences are related to differences in the kind of self-awareness they are capable of. This would provide evidence about the evolutionary mechanisms that contributed to the intertwining of the mind and the self. Based on the assumptions advanced here, we can predict that personality differentiation in the members of different species must be a function of the species' position on a scale of self-awareness. That is, the more the members of a species are self-aware of their own body and their problem-solving capacities and their dispositions the more differentiated personalities they would have to have. The evidence recently reviewed by Rogers (1997) about awareness in animals is congruent with this assumption. In Rogers' words:

> No two animals are exactly the same, but individuality in brain function and behaviour must have become increasingly elaborate during evolution.
>   Physical and mental uniqueness of individuals might be a precursor to self-awareness because the self must be distinguishable from others. Social behaviour also relies on individuals being different. Each individual must be recognised by its appearance and behaviour.
>
>   (Rogers, 1997, p. 182)

In humans everything is of course embedded in a social and cultural context where minds, selves, and personalities interpret and interact with each other under the influence of forces pertinent to both the individuals involved and their social, cultural, and historical environment. Thus, in humans, the games of evolution take place at one and the same time at the level of the animal, the self-aware person, and the reflective society and culture. Future research would have to disentangle the dynamic interactions that take place between the forces residing at each of these levels.

Relationships with other theories

We have already discussed the relationships between various aspects of our theory and other theories of intelligence, cognitive development, and personality (Demetriou, 1998a, 1998b; Demetriou and Georgiou, 1999;

Demetriou, Kazi, and Georgiou, 1999a; Demetriou and Raftopoulos, 1999; Demetriou *et al.*, 1993a; Demetriou, Raftopoulos, and Kargopoulos 1999b; Kargopoulos and Demetriou, 1998a, 1998b; see also critiques of this theory by Asendorpf, 1999; Bickhard, 1998, 1999; Campbell, 1993; Engel, 1998; Hair and Graziano, 1999; Marton, 1999; Pascual-Leone, 1998; Smith, 1998; Sternberg, 1999; van Lieshout, 1999). The emphasis here will be on the relationships with theories, classical or modern, which are concerned with the architecture of the mind and the self.

Admittedly, slices of the architecture and developmental dynamics discussed in this book have been with us for many years. The distinction between an environment-oriented and a self-oriented level is implied in the ancient Greek commandment "know thyself" (that is, there is a level of knowing that can be known by a different set of processes) and in Descartes' "cogito ergo sum" (that is, human's realization of existence comes through reflection on knowing processes and because of it). In fact, our model is impressively close to the Kantian conception of the mind. Specifically, most of our environment-oriented systems are close to Kant's categories of reason. According to Kant, the categories of reason are as follows: quantity (that is, the number of things); quality (that is, the reality or the identifying characteristics of things); relation (that is, the interaction between things that defines their cause-effect relations); and modality (which refers to the possibility-impossibility of events and their necessary versus contingent relations). Time and space refer to the frames or the envelopes in which things are located, events are happening, and changes occur. The similarity between Kant's categories of reason and our SCSs is obvious.

It is noteworthy that Piaget's programme of research aimed to highlight how the development of logical reasoning underlies changes in the understanding of each of these categories of reason to lead to their complete mastery. In fact, most of Piaget's tasks were designed as instanstiations of these categories at different levels of complexity and abstraction. However, Piaget's passion to identify the kind of mental structure underlying these categories led him to underestimate their role in actual psychological functioning and development. Thus, our methods enabled us to restore the psychological significance of Kant's ideas which was wrongly underestimated in Piaget's theory.

Moreover, Kant's "I think" requires special attention because it is directly related to the concept of transmodularity as discussed above and some modern views about intelligence to be discussed below. According to Kant (see Cassam, 1997), the "I think" bears the following characteristics. First, it defines the person's identity because it underlies all consciousness. Second, it is universal, because it accompanies all thought; thus it applies to all thinking subjects. Third, it is empty, in that it is not an intuition or a concept but an abstraction that transcends all thought activity, which defines each person's identity. Fourth, it is formal in that it is attached to all representations, thereby making the person conscious of them. Finally, it is non-determinative because it is not an intuition of the self. We will see below that Kant's "I think" is close to modern conceptions of intelligence as well.

In psychology, the two-level knowing architecture is also clearly indicated in James' differentiation between the I-self and the Me-self, and it is elaborated in modern models of cognitive development, such as Campbell and Bickhard's (1986) knowing levels model, in modern models of the self, (e.g. Markus and Wurf, 1987), and in modern models of personality, (e.g. Graziano *et al.*, 1997). On the other hand, information processing theorists in cognitive (Baddeley, 1991) and cognitive developmental psychology (Case, 1992; Halford, 1993; Pascual-Leone, 1988) have attempted to model the levels of the processing and the environment-oriented systems and specify how the condition of the first constrains the condition and development of the second. Moreover, the hierarchical conception of the mind and self postulated by our theory and substantiated by the studies described here is also espoused by a number of modern models of the self-concept (Hattie, 1992; Shavelson and Marsh, 1986).

It is notable that that this hierarchical conception prevails in modern psychometric theories of intelligence (Gustafsson, 1994; Gustaffson and Undheim, 1996; Jensen, 1998). These theories define intelligence as a three-level hierarchy, which involves g or general intelligence, a number of very general dimensions, such as fluid and crystallized intelligence, and a number of domain-specific abilities, such as number, spatial, and verbal abilities. The reader is reminded that this is exactly the architecture found by the studies presented in this book. In fact, our studies provide crucial evidence that bears direct implications to long lasting and currently heated discussions about the nature of intelligence and the mind.

Specifically, Jensen (1998) has recently maintained that the g factor cannot be specified psychologically. In Jensen's words:

> It is wrong to regard g as a cognitive process, or as an operating principle of the mind, or as a design feature of the brain's neural circuitry. At the level of psychometrics, ideally, g may be thought of as a distillate of the common source of individual differences in all mental tests, completely stripped of their distinctive features of information content, skill, strategy, and the like. In this sense, g can be roughly likened to a computer's central processing unit. (p. 74, emphasis in original)
>
> Unlike any of the primary, or first-order, psychometric factors revealed by factor analysis, g cannot be described in terms of knowledge content of mental test items, or in terms of skills, or even in terms of

theoretical cognitive processes. It is not fundamentally a psychological or behavioural variable, but a biological one.

(Jensen, 1998, p. 578)

First of all, attention is drawn here to the fact that Jensen's definition of *g* as a contentless construct that defines an individual's general potentials is very similar to Kant's definition of "I think" as an empty construct that defines a person's identity. How are these constructs related to the model and studies presented here?

On the one hand, it is clear that our processing system is close to the *g* factor of psychometric theory. In fact, the fourth of the studies presented in this book did show that the processing system is an "empty system" even in the thinker's self-representations. This supports our position that the processing system is not a knowing level but an interface between the two knowing levels (Demetriou and Raftopoulos, 1999; Demetriou, Raftopoulos, and Kargopoulos, 1999) and is in agreement with Jensen's position that *g* itself cannot be defined psychologically.

However, this is the half of the story. That is, *g* cannot be specified psychologically if by this we mean actual computational or operating processes. These seem to be associated with the various SCSs. However, *g* does acquire psychological and subjective meaning once and to the degree that it is recorded by the hypercognitive system and comes under the control of it through working hypercognition. In other words, the projection of processing power into one's self-image of cognitive efficiency and its coupling with one's personal constant affects general self-esteem (Coopersmith, 1967) and also decisions about what tasks one is to work on and how. In turn, this engrafting influences general strategies and styles, which characterize a person's understanding, problem solving, and action. This is obviously a psychological marking of *g* by any definition.

On the other hand, working hypercognition, at a general level, is empty and formal because it refers to processes applied on all mental activities. As such, it reminds one of the emptiness and formality of Kant's "I think". As it functions, working hypercognition surpasses the temporary character and variations of domain-specific experiences thereby ensuring the unity of the self. At the same time, it generates memories and maps of these experiences, which constitute our long-term hypercognition. Long-term hypercognition reflects the individual's strengths and weaknesses and dispositions and characteristics vis-à-vis himself, the environment, and other individuals. One's differentiated self-image is actually commensurate to these memories and maps. The universality of the "I think" is ensured by the fact that hypercognition is inter-subjective as much as it is intra-subjective. As a result, the hypercognitive maps have a collective dimension. This may actually set the frame in which individual *gs* and personalities function, thereby continuously changing the possibilities available to the individuals in culture and time.

What does then our theory add to this long tradition of scholarship? We would propose that the main contribution is rather simple. This is the combination of the principle of domain-specificity of the environment-oriented mental structures and dispositions with the principle of self-mapping underlying the operation of the hypercognitive system. This combination lays the ground for integrating the study of intelligence and cognitive functioning with the study of personality and self. According to this combination, there are environment-oriented systems which are modular by construction and there is a self-oriented system which, once it was formed during evolution, observes, evaluates, and maps these modules. In doing so it produces self-concepts and self-definitions that reflect the differential condition of these modules and it thus underlies one's sense of personality and self. In other words, our theory specifies the building blocks of intellectual ability, personality, and style of acting, which are brought to bear on the environment and it postulates that these blocks are also used in the incessant (re)construction of self-awareness. Self-awareness itself is of course always the orienting force that directs the persons in their interactions with themselves, each other, and the world.

Appendices

Table A4.1 Mean performance (and standard deviations) for cognitive tasks across subject groups and SCSs

Age	SES	Gender	Ability				
			Quantitative-relational	Causal-experimental	Social	Spatial-imaginal	Drawing
10.5	LOW	F	.267 (.211)	.086 (.131)	.382 (.279)	.929 (.440)	.757 (.520)
		M	.302 (.302)	.071 (.131)	.405 (.348)	.869 (.443)	.714 (.457)
	MIDDLE	F	.417 (.373)	.040 (.105)	.594 (.295)	.950 (.154)	.975 (.499)
		M	.333 (.298)	.031 (.093)	.433 (.323)	.885 (.294)	1.019 (.479)
	UPPER-	F	.500 (.298)	.188 (.186)	.633 (.276)	.656 (.437)	1.000 (.483)
	MIDDLE	M	.467 (.352)	.213 (.233)	.550 (.226)	.933 (.495)	.900 (.541)
11.5	LOW	F	.542 (.357)	.219 (.280)	.695 (.321)	1.047 (.265)	1.062 (.453)
		M	.459 (.253)	.081 (.145)	.449 (.337)	.959 (.341)	.770 (.435)
	MIDDLE	F	.514 (.326)	.233 (.305)	.703 (.361)	.771 (.329)	1.437 (.496)
		M	.536 (.447)	.261 (.237)	.370 (.276)	.935 (.229)	.913 (.358)
	UPPER-	F	.795 (.501)	.431 (.390)	.721 (.495)	.923 (.534)	1.038 (.320)
	MIDDLE	M	.792 (.419)	.413 (.305)	.703 (.292)	1.250 (.258)	.938 (.479)
12.5	LOW	F	.578 (.288)	.142 (.184)	.586 (.328)	1.033 (.197)	.578 (.511)
		M	.390 (.336)	.077 (.180)	.465 (.342)	.926 (.417)	.479 (.541)
	MIDDLE	F	.895 (.352)	.189 (.216)	.816 (.290)	.921 (.507)	1.395 (.427)
		M	1.048 (.590)	.362 (.367)	.667 (.336)	1.143 (.359)	1.119 (.631)
	UPPER-	F	.667 (.444)	.000 (.000)	.837 (.334)	1.000 (.527)	1.050 (.369)
	MIDDLE	M	.500 (.285)	.029 (.107)	.536 (.279)	.786 (.378)	.786 (.545)
13.5	LOW	F	.582 (.364)	.302 (.345)	.485 (.250)	.951 (.350)	.971 (.441)
		M	.549 (.415)	.217 (.371)	.461 (.339)	.969 (.418)	.708 (.471)
	MIDDLE	F	1.000 (.471)	.200 (.283)	.861 (.296)	.944 (.167)	1.278 (.667)
		M	.833 (.266)	.567 (.350)	.833 (.334)	1.083 (.289)	1.042 (.498)
	UPPER-	F	1.185 (.526)	.496 (.409)	.829 (.340)	.870 (.451)	.833 (.620)
	MIDDLE	M	1.120 (.383)	.576 (.401)	.725 (.327)	.940 (.333)	.880 (.506)
14.5	LOW	F	.667 (.321)	.382 (.342)	.639 (.353)	.909 (.407)	.875 (.507)
		M	.829 (.374)	.377 (.347)	.642 (.352)	.953 (.285)	.640 (.630)
	MIDDLE	F	1.119 (.361)	.557 (.394)	.830 (.412)	1.107 (.525)	1.179 (.421)
		M	1.051 (.267)	.492 (.240)	.837 (.373)	.923 (.449)	1.000 (.500)
	UPPER-	F	1.028 (.404)	.783 (.437)	.740 (.258)	.937 (.450)	1.229 (.625)
	MIDDLE	M	.877 (.569)	.463 (.411)	.586 (.339)	1.211 (.481)	.816 (.606)

Note
Figure 4.1 is based on this table.

Table A4.2 Means (and standard deviations) for hypercognitive accuracy indexes (HAIs) across age, SES, gender, type of self-evaluation, time, and SCS

Age	SES	Gender	Success Pre-performance					Post-performance		
			QR	CE	SO	ROT	DR	QR	CE	SO
10.5	LOW	F	.400	−.343	−.314	−.143	−.314	.457	−.429	−.171
			(.976)	(1.056)	(1.451)	(1.332)	(1.451)	(1.197)	(.850)	(1.224)
		M	.000	−.310	.262	−.143	−.452	.048	−.500	−.190
			(1.036)	(1.199)	(1.795)	(1.555)	(1.253)	(1.188)	(1.042)	(1.366)
	MIDDLE	F	.150	−.250	.050	.050	.000	.650	.200	.700
			(.988)	(1.164)	(1.356)	(1.356)	(1.298)	(1.137)	(.834)	(1.174)
		M	.346	−.692	−.615	.154	.500	.846	−.192	−.346
			(1.164)	(1.087)	(1.627)	(1.190)	(1.304)	(1.255)	(1.059)	(1.696)
	UPPER-MIDDLE	F	.187	.000	.125	−.750	−.250	.563	−.750	−.188
			(1.047)	(.966)	(1.258)	(1.653)	(1.528)	(.964)	(1.065)	(1.377)
		M	−.067	.000	−.533	−.067	−.200	.067	−.733	−.267
			(.594)	(1.512)	(1.727)	(1.831)	(1.146)	(1.163)	(.961)	(1.033)
11.5	LOW	F	.063	−.125	.531	.469	.344	.250	−.406	.219
			(.948)	(1.070)	(1.586)	(1.164)	(1.066)	(.916)	(.798)	(1.070)
		M	.108	−.378	−.324	.486	−.081	.216	−.514	−.351
			(1.173)	(1.299)	(1.492)	(1.465)	(1.164)	(1.031)	(1.239)	(1.160)
	MIDDLE	F	.542	.583	.375	.250	1.500	.417	.500	.500
			(.884)	(1.381)	(1.279)	(1.539)	(1.285)	(1.139)	(.834)	(1.063)
		M	.000	.261	−.087	.348	.522	−.348	−.174	−.087
			(1.044)	(1.453)	(1.621)	(1.152)	(.994)	(1.027)	(1.723)	(1.411)
	UPPER-MIDDLE	F	.615	.077	−.154	−.308	.769	.769	.538	.000
			(.870)	(1.801)	(1.519)	(1.974)	(1.166)	(1.301)	(1.330)	(.913)
		M	.000	.063	.438	1.000	−.188	−.125	.000	.187
			(.816)	(1.731)	(1.031)	(1.155)	(1.276)	(.719)	(1.265)	(1.109)
12.5	LOW	F	.422	−.289	−.067	.578	−.200	.267	−.400	.444
			(1.033)	(.991)	(1.421)	(1.215)	(1.198)	(.837)	(.780)	(1.198)
		M	.000	−.106	.277	.277	−.702	−.191	−.596	.000
			(1.043)	(.890)	(1.263)	(1.625)	(1.267)	(1.296)	(1.116)	(1.022)
	MIDDLE	F	.316	−.579	.053	−.526	.842	.316	−.526	.211
			(.946)	(1.216)	(1.026)	(1.504)	(.898)	(.946)	(1.073)	(.855)
		M	.286	−.095	.381	.524	.619	.381	−.238	.190
			(.845)	(1.300)	(1.857)	(1.365)	(1.161)	(1.244)	(1.044)	(1.365)
	UPPER-MIDDLE	F	.100	−.300	.400	−.600	−.300	.500	−.200	.700
			(1.287)	(.949)	(.966)	(1.265)	(.823)	(.707)	(1.229)	(.949)
		M	.000	−.429	.571	.286	−.500	.214	−.357	−.286
			(1.038)	(.852)	(1.505)	(1.383)	(1.345)	(.975)	(.842)	(1.139)
13.5	LOW	F	.020	−.588	−.353	.059	.196	.059	−.353	−.255
			(.948)	(1.080)	(1.623)	(1.348)	(1.249)	(.925)	(.820)	(1.197)
		M	.188	−.063	.250	.375	−.125	−.125	−.563	.000
			(1.161)	(1.040)	(1.451)	(1.378)	(1.393)	(.981)	(1.270)	(1.185)
	MIDDLE	F	−.444	−1.222	−.222	−.778	.333	−.222	.000	−.111
			(.726)	(1.202)	(1.093)	(1.093)	(1.118)	(.972)	(.866)	(1.167)
		M	−.333	.083	.083	.250	.167	−.250	−.583	−.167
			(1.231)	(1.379)	(1.676)	(.965)	(.937)	(.754)	(1.379)	(1.193)
	UPPER-MIDDLE	F	.704	−.407	.111	−.556	−.037	.852	.407	1.000
			(.993)	(1.575)	(1.396)	(1.188)	(1.126)	(1.134)	(1.248)	(1.144)
		M	.120	−.040	−.040	.080	.080	.040	−.160	.080
			(1.333)	(1.645)	(1.428)	(1.382)	(1.470)	(.935)	(1.519)	(1.115)
14.5	LOW	F	.432	−.114	−.273	.500	.136	.159	−.182	.205
			(1.149)	(1.185)	(1.420)	(1.886)	(1.374)	(.888)	(1.018)	(1.153)
		M	.349	.000	.163	.512	−.256	.209	−.349	.047
			(1.066)	(1.345)	(1.326)	(1.437)	(1.049)	(.861)	(1.325)	(1.379)
	MIDDLE	F	.286	−.071	−.071	.071	.714	.429	−.143	.286
			(.914)	(1.817)	(1.328)	(1.639)	(1.590)	(.646)	(1.231)	(.914)
		M	−.077	−.231	.154	−.231	1.077	−.077	−.615	.000
			(.862)	(1.013)	(1.345)	(1.739)	(.954)	(.954)	(.870)	(.913)
	UPPER-MIDDLE	F	.208	.917	.417	−.292	1.042	.250	.792	.250
			(1.021)	(1.586)	(1.213)	(1.756)	(1.197)	(.897)	(1.615)	(.737)
		M	.316	.632	.105	.842	.316	.474	.053	−.158
			(1.250)	(1.342)	(1.560)	(1.259)	(1.600)	(1.172)	(1.393)	(1.608)

Note
Figure 4.2 is based on this table.

	Difficulty Pre-performance					Post-performance					
OT	DR	QR	CE	SO	ROT	DR	QR	CE	SO	ROT	DR
.057	−.714	.400	−.429	−.514	.143	−.257	.543	−.400	−.229	.371	−.629
830)	(1.487)	(.881)	(.917)	(1.502)	(1.309)	(1.421)	(1.146)	(1.090)	(1.457)	(1.497)	(1.767)
.238	−.738	.310	−.310	.214	.286	−.286	.262	−.381	−.119	.095	−.738
764)	(1.191)	(.841)	(.869)	(1.474)	(1.627)	(1.195)	(1.014)	(1.058)	(1.501)	(1.543)	(1.398)
.300	.100	.100	−.400	−.050	−.150	−.050	.500	.250	.400	.650	.250
081)	(1.447)	(1.252)	(1.095)	(1.146)	(1.226)	(1.701)	(1.235)	(1.118)	(1.095)	(1.226)	(1.713)
.038	.192	.500	−.615	−.423	.615	.500	1.077	−.077	−.231	.538	.346
455)	(1.327)	(1.175)	(.983)	(1.748)	(1.329)	(1.241)	(1.197)	(1.197)	(1.608)	(1.392)	(1.198)
.625	.062	.000	−.250	.750	−.812	−.312	.813	−.438	−.250	−.313	.000
204)	(1.063)	(1.155)	(.856)	(1.528)	(1.721)	(1.401)	(1.167)	(1.263)	(1.065)	(1.537)	(1.592)
.067	−.467	.400	−.600	−.667	−.333	.133	−.067	−.333	−.467	.000	−.867
668)	(.834)	(.737)	(.828)	(1.291)	(1.633)	(1.246)	(.961)	(1.175)	(1.125)	(1.464)	(1.125)
.094	.125	.406	−.219	.688	.156	.188	.250	−.500	.250	.500	.094
304)	(1.100)	(1.043)	(1.008)	(1.355)	(1.051)	(1.203)	(.950)	(.950)	(1.016)	(1.016)	(1.174)
.297	−.622	.135	−.297	.081	.432	−.378	.432	−.297	−.324	.189	−.784
199)	(.828)	(1.159)	(1.127)	(1.320)	(1.405)	(1.139)	(1.042)	(1.450)	(1.248)	(1.050)	(.917)
.167	1.167	.458	.458	.500	−.125	1.000	.625	.708	.542	.208	1.000
523)	(.868)	(.884)	(1.285)	(1.383)	(1.727)	(1.142)	(1.013)	(1.083)	(1.021)	(1.250)	(1.251)
.087	.565	−.043	−.043	−.217	.174	.522	−.087	−.478	.000	.565	.478
083)	(.896)	(.878)	(1.364)	(1.594)	(1.230)	(1.238)	(.996)	(1.806)	(1.314)	(1.161)	(1.123)
.692	.538	.615	−.462	−.077	−.231	.462	.692	.077	−.077	.846	.231
750)	(1.127)	(.870)	(1.854)	(1.382)	(2.127)	(.967)	(1.316)	(1.188)	(1.038)	(1.463)	(1.301)
.000	.063	.250	.063	.250	.625	−.187	.125	.625	.313	1.750	.063
966)	(1.436)	(1.000)	(1.289)	(1.065)	(1.310)	(1.223)	(.806)	(1.147)	(.946)	(1.065)	(1.237)
.311	−.244	.511	−.378	−.289	.667	−.311	.244	−.556	.178	.511	−.444
411)	(1.090)	(.843)	(.936)	(1.199)	(1.044)	(1.276)	(.908)	(1.013)	(1.248)	(.991)	(1.271)
.319	−.894	.149	−.277	.255	.574	−.617	−.170	−.319	.149	.085	−.723
603)	(1.238)	(1.197)	(.826)	(1.390)	(1.557)	(1.278)	(1.222)	(1.045)	(1.215)	(1.316)	(1.280)
.526	1.158	.579	−.526	.158	−.211	.789	.316	−.316	−.158	.737	.842
219)	(.898)	(.769)	(.964)	(1.068)	(1.182)	(.855)	(1.108)	(1.336)	(.958)	(1.240)	(1.068)
.000	.619	.571	.048	.143	.238	.048	.619	.048	.143	.762	.048
225)	(1.322)	(1.248)	(1.203)	(1.352)	(1.091)	(1.071)	(1.244)	(1.284)	(1.236)	(1.044)	(1.284)
.300	.400	.200	−.600	.700	−.500	−.500	.400	−.200	.700	.900	.100
703)	(.699)	(1.229)	(.966)	(.949)	(1.581)	(.707)	(.699)	(.632)	(.949)	(1.524)	(.876)
.000	−.071	−.214	−.714	.000	−.429	−.500	.214	−.714	−.143	.071	−.286
359)	(1.207)	(1.051)	(.825)	(1.359)	(1.342)	(1.345)	(1.188)	(.994)	(1.167)	(1.685)	(1.139)
.137	.353	.235	−.569	−.196	−.137	.255	.098	−.549	−.471	.176	−.118
265)	(1.278)	(.907)	(.985)	(1.637)	(1.200)	(1.146)	(1.082)	(.986)	(1.255)	(.974)	(1.125)
.104	−.167	.375	.021	.333	.521	.063	−.125	−.583	−.229	.375	−.458
372)	(1.191)	(1.024)	(1.000)	(1.209)	(1.516)	(1.245)	(1.003)	(1.350)	(1.387)	(1.393)	(1.288)
.111	1.222	−.444	−1.000	−.222	−1.000	−.111	−.333	−.444	.000	.222	.889
167)	(2.108)	(.726)	(1.225)	(.667)	(.866)	(1.054)	(.866)	(1.014)	(1.118)	(.972)	(1.616)
.000	.333	.417	.333	.000	.417	.000	.083	−.583	−.417	.667	.250
739)	(1.155)	(1.240)	(1.614)	(1.537)	(1.165)	(.953)	(.793)	(1.782)	(1.379)	(.651)	(.965)
.481	.519	.407	−.481	.148	−.185	−.296	.667	.111	.741	.296	.111
695)	(1.451)	(1.152)	(1.252)	(1.460)	(1.861)	(1.489)	(1.177)	(1.311)	(1.259)	(1.463)	(1.311)
.480	−.040	.280	−.080	.080	−.400	.040	.200	.080	.080	.200	.040
085)	(1.207)	(1.061)	(1.470)	(1.441)	(1.354)	(1.369)	(1.041)	(1.656)	(1.187)	(.913)	(1.274)
.250	−.068	.364	−.205	−.068	−.023	−.114	.136	−.205	.091	.295	.182
512)	(1.108)	(1.014)	(1.047)	(1.301)	(1.705)	(1.166)	(.878)	(1.193)	(1.254)	(1.340)	(1.225)
.116	−.163	.279	−.163	.256	.302	−.488	.349	−.419	.163	.395	.163
313)	(1.252)	(1.260)	(1.252)	(1.329)	(1.206)	(1.099)	(1.021)	(1.636)	(1.214)	(.955)	(1.132)
.000	1.071	.357	.071	.000	−.143	.643	.500	−.286	.286	.929	.643
664)	(1.141)	(.842)	(1.141)	(1.414)	(1.512)	(1.151)	(.760)	(1.267)	(1.204)	(1.774)	(.929)
.154	.308	−.154	.000	.154	−.077	.538	.077	−.615	.077	.308	.154
519)	(1.032)	(.899)	(.707)	(1.519)	(1.553)	(1.127)	(.862)	(1.044)	(1.382)	(1.437)	(1.214)
.542	1.042	.333	.583	.375	.000	1.000	.375	.875	.208	.333	1.000
615)	(1.398)	(1.049)	(1.692)	(1.245)	(1.414)	(1.216)	(.924)	(1.569)	(.721)	(1.404)	(1.383)
.579	.263	.526	.421	.053	.789	.000	−.053	−.053	−.421	.947	−.474
387)	(1.327)	(1.219)	(1.170)	(1.747)	(1.512)	(1.491)	(1.353)	(1.433)	(1.427)	(1.353)	(1.611)

Table A4.3 Means (and standard deviations) for cognitive performance scores and self-evaluation across age, SES, and person category

Age	SES	Person category							
		LA		LI		HI		HA	
		Cognitive	Self-evaluation	Cognitive	Self-evaluation	Cognitive	Self-evaluation	Cognitive	Self-evaluation
10.5	LOW	.800 (.447)	22.400 (.894)	.800 (.447)	31.200 (1.304)	3.000 (.000)	25.400 (1.517)	3.600 (.548)	32.600 (2.302)
	MIDDLE	.800 (.447)	19.600 (2.074)	.600 (.548)	27.200 (1.304)	4.200 (.447)	23.400 (1.949)	4.400 (.894)	29.200 (2.558)
	UPPER-MIDDLE	1.200 (.837)	22.200 (2.168)	1.600 (.894)	31.800 (2.049)	3.600 (.548)	24.000 (2.550)	3.600 (.548)	33.400 (.894)
11.5	LOW	1.600 (.548)	21.400 (3.130)	1.600 (.548)	32.800 (1.483)	4.200 (.447)	25.800 (1.095)	4.800 (.837)	34.000 (1.225)
	MIDDLE	1.200 (.837)	23.000 (1.000)	2.200 (.837)	32.800 (1.924)	5.200 (1.643)	23.600 (1.140)	5.600 (1.517)	32.000 (1.225)
	UPPER-MIDDLE	2.000 (1.000)	22.800 (2.775)	2.200 (.837)	30.200 (1.643)	4.400 (.548)	25.600 (.894)	6.000 (2.236)	31.400 (2.608)
12.5	LOW	.600 (.548)	21.400 (1.140)	1.200 (1.095)	33.600 (1.517)	3.400 (.548)	24.600 (.548)	4.600 (.548)	33.000 (.707)
	MIDDLE	2.400 (1.517)	24.600 (2.074)	2.800 (.447)	33.400 (1.517)	5.400 (.548)	24.800 (1.789)	7.000 (1.581)	33.400 (.894)
	UPPER-MIDDLE	1.800 (.837)	23.200 (1.304)	2.600 (.548)	31.400 (1.342)	4.250 (.500)	24.250 (1.258)	5.250 (.500)	30.500 (2.380)
13.5	LOW	1.800 (.837)	22.400 (2.702)	1.200 (.447)	33.000 (1.414)	4.200 (.447)	24.400 (1.517)	6.400 (1.140)	31.800 (1.304)
	MIDDLE	2.800 (1.643)	27.800 (2.775)	3.400 (.548)	33.400 (1.517)	6.000 (.816)	27.750 (2.872)	6.400 (1.140)	32.800 (1.924)
	UPPER-MIDDLE	2.200 (.837)	23.600 (2.608)	3.200 (.447)	32.400 (1.517)	6.600 (.548)	25.400 (1.140)	7.000 (1.000)	33.600 (1.817)
14.5	LOW	1.800 (.837)	22.000 (2.000)	2.800 (.447)	34.600 (.894)	5.200 (1.095)	23.800 (2.683)	5.800 (.837)	34.000 (1.225)
	MIDDLE	3.000 (1.000)	25.200 (2.490)	3.000 (.707)	3.100 (1.414)	5.400 (.548)	26.000 (1.581)	6.400 (.894)	33.000 (1.581)
	UPPER-MIDDLE	3.000 (.000)	23.600 (2.510)	3.000 (1.225)	31.800 (1.304)	5.800 (.837)	26.000 (1.000)	7.600 (1.140)	34.400 (1.342)
15.5	UPPER-MIDDLE	3.200 (1.304)	27.400 (3.209)	5.000 (.707)	34.200 (1.304)	7.200 (.447)	27.800 (1.643)	9.400 (1.140)	35.000 (.707)

Table A4.4 Means (and standard deviations) for self-attribution of ability across age, gender, person category, and ability

Age	Gender	Person category	Ability				
			Quantitative-relational	Causal-experimental	Social	Spatial-imaginal	Drawing
10.5	F	LA	4.917	5.141	4.547	5.781	4.266
			(1.575)	(1.111)	(1.067)	(1.257)	(1.556)
		LI	5.060	5.643	5.696	6.179	4.946
			(1.407)	(.861)	(.773)	(.494)	(.935)
		HI	5.119	5.250	4.643	5.571	4.500
			(1.159)	(.966)	(1.520)	(1.179)	(1.599)
		HA	6.167	5.797	5.734	6.125	5.844
			(.668)	(1.108)	(.841)	(.756)	(1.191)
	M	LA	5.387	5.804	5.500	5.500	4.982
			(1.370)	(.989)	(1.000)	(1.362)	(.977)
		LI	5.630	5.734	5.594	5.938	5.672
			(.848)	(1.298)	(.809)	(1.308)	(1.262)
		HI	4.833	5.422	4.594	4.594	4.594
			(.373)	(.874)	(.637)	(.990)	(1.032)
		HA	5.607	5.786	5.446	5.429	4.464
			(1.007)	(.589)	(.472)	(1.344)	(1.566)
11.5	F	LA	3.526	4.797	4.500	5.031	4.141
			(1.688)	(1.389)	(1.046)	(1.081)	(1.087)
		LI	4.764	5.125	4.604	5.333	4.500
			(1.231)	(.912)	(1.150)	(.847)	(.766)
		HI	4.620	5.266	5.266	5.688	4.516
			(1.210)	(1.053)	(1.220)	(1.075)	(1.472)
		HA	4.702	6.179	5.732	6.179	5.054
			(2.056)	(.787)	(.956)	(.932)	(1.638)
	M	LA	4.518	4.393	4.000	3.929	4.751
			(.845)	(1.004)	(1.445)	(1.018)	(1.401)
		LI	5.319	5.097	4.944	5.750	4.319
			(1.117)	(1.203)	(1.039)	(1.008)	(1.276)
		HI	4.250	4.714	4.268	4.679	3.786
			(1.194)	(.957)	(.795)	(1.498)	(.585)
		HA	4.818	5.219	4.696	5.438	5.313
			(.789)	(.812)	(.956)	(.943)	(.971)
12.5	F	LA	3.562	5.396	5.167	4.458	4.563
			(1.767)	(1.023)	(1.269)	(2.244)	(1.506)
		LI	5.854	5.469	5.438	6.000	5.188
			(.520)	(1.252)	(1.139)	(.707)	(1.201)
		HI	4.464	4.953	4.859	4.750	3.375
			(1.108)	(.691)	(.934)	(.720)	(1.116)
		HA	4.681	4.938	5.792	5.375	5.146
			(1.330)	(1.211)	(1.086)	(1.232)	(.986)
	M	LA	5.185	4.972	4.736	5.028	4.472
			(.854)	(.924)	(1.052)	(1.349)	(.863)
		LI	5.489	5.477	5.670	5.455	4.682
			(1.312)	(1.109)	(.891)	(1.177)	(1.779)
		HI	4.778	5.563	4.500	5.167	2.979
			(.874)	(.596)	(1.049)	(1.538)	(.992)

Age	Gender	Person category	Ability				
			Quantitative-relational	Causal-experimental	Social	Spatial-imaginal	Drawing
		HA	5.115	5.625	5.469	5.875	3.828
			(.804)	(.675)	(.901)	(.612)	(1.420)
13.5	F	LA	4.099	5.094	5.281	5.406	3.609
			(1.819)	(.746)	(.604)	(.834)	(1.759)
		LI	4.781	5.281	6.063	4.813	5.125
			(1.128)	(.832)	(.484)	(1.663)	(.907)
		HI	4.446	5.413	5.363	5.550	4.288
			(1.575)	(1.082)	(1.483)	(1.129)	(2.407)
		HA	5.089	5.696	5.857	5.429	5.125
			(.839)	(.590)	(.579)	(1.321)	(1.560)
	M	LA	4.571	5.196	4.982	4.964	4.054
			(1.339)	(.918)	(.873)	(1.194)	(1.449)
		LI	5.030	4.852	4.511	5.727	4.125
			(1.384)	(.833)	(.958)	(.467)	(1.055)
		HI	3.667	4.313	4.531	4.063	3.313
			(.983)	(.599)	(.524)	(.473)	(1.546)
		HA	5.563	5.359	5.203	5.156	4.234
			(1.287)	(.708)	(.889)	(.865)	(1.125)
14.5	F	LA	3.267	4.350	4.750	4.250	3.500
			(.646)	(.773)	(.612)	(.637)	(.791)
		LI	4.764	5.958	5.688	6.375	5.292
			(1.418)	(.270)	(.377)	(.627)	(1.190)
		HI	3.303	5.136	5.443	5.682	3.477
			(1.255)	(1.102)	(.485)	(.783)	(1.021)
		HA	4.083	5.889	5.583	5.972	4.681
			(1.414)	(.674)	(.827)	(1.019)	(1.242)
	M	LA	3.943	3.891	3.953	4.375	4.453
			(1.023)	(1.097)	(.738)	(.886)	(.779)
		LI	3.807	5.031	4.297	4.156	3.203
			(1.783)	(1.253)	(.788)	(1.558)	(1.295)
		HI	3.969	4.813	4.063	4.188	2.844
			(.309)	(.916)	(.260)	(.851)	(1.243)
		HA	4.278	5.521	5.813	6.250	5.104
			(1.989)	(.682)	(.492)	(.570)	(1.105)

Note
Figure 4.3 is based on this table.

Table A4.5 Means (and standard deviations) for self-attribution of personal strategies and characteristics across age, gender, person category, and type of strategy or characteristics.

Age	Gender	Person category	Personal strategies/characteristics				
			Ambition to excel	Impulsivity	Learning	Planning	Logicality
10.5	F	LA	5.729 (.992)	3.906 (1.339)	4.604 (.963)	5.750 (.838)	3.792 (.659)
		LI	5.690 (.790)	4.339 (1.089)	4.905 (.962)	6.214 (.868)	3.714 (1.304)
		HI	4.286 (1.216)	2.607 (1.243)	4.714 (.744)	6.024 (.701)	4.167 (.577)
		HA	6.188 (.726)	3.781 (1.215)	4.917 (.636)	6.474 (.614)	4.229 (.549)
	M	LA	5.714 (1.141)	3.268 (.849)	4.857 (.766)	5.601 (1.262)	3.810 (.656)
		LI	5.042 (1.318)	4.313 (1.369)	4.938 (.604)	5.745 (1.352)	3.729 (1.137)
		HI	4.958 (1.408)	3.531 (.873)	4.854 (.580)	5.693 (.991)	3.979 (.500)
		HA	5.429 (.892)	3.679 (1.043)	4.738 (.849)	6.262 (.466)	4.071 (.317)
11.5	F	LA	4.146 (1.857)	4.297 (1.431)	3.604 (.972)	5.667 (1.193)	3.292 (1.057)
		LI	4.611 (1.381)	2.938 (1.169)	4.833 (.596)	5.306 (.869)	3.528 (1.280)
		HI	5.083 (1.569)	3.672 (1.015)	4.167 (1.043)	5.896 (.662)	4.062 (.718)
		HA	5.857 (1.422)	3.625 (1.418)	4.929 (.673)	6.173 (.465)	4.119 (.798)
	M	LA	4.714 (.393)	4.286 (.717)	4.190 (1.458)	4.857 (.902)	2.500 (.861)
		LI	5.500 (1.339)	3.472 (1.609)	4.667 (.878)	6.130 (.583)	4.056 (1.054)
		HI	4.595 (.897)	3.214 (.825)	4.310 (.959)	4.964 (1.624)	3.405 (.932)
		HA	6.229 (.672)	3.641 (1.115)	4.625 (.749)	5.766 (.678)	3.917 (.642)
12.5	F	LA	5.861 (1.435)	4.000 (1.285)	4.417 (.705)	5.771 (.846)	3.833 (.760)
		LI	4.708 (2.458)	3.406 (.832)	4.792 (.832)	6.167 (.561)	3.792 (1.013)
		HI	4.854 (1.481)	3.109 (1.249)	4.229 (1.120)	5.969 (1.004)	4.187 (.491)
		HA	5.944 (1.109)	3.521 (1.519)	4.194 (1.176)	5.236 (1.330)	5.528 (1.222)
	M	LA	5.130 (1.083)	4.097 (1.114)	4.630 (.611)	5.375 (1.031)	3.852 (.562)
		LI	5.909 (1.221)	3.864 (1.406)	4.864 (.756)	5.939 (.791)	4.015 (.608)
		HI	3.917 (1.433)	2.875 (1.543)	4.167 (.471)	5.549 (.887)	4.028 (.386)

Age	Gender	Person category	Personal strategies/characteristics				
			Ambition to excel	Impulsivity	Learning	Planning	Logicality
		HA	5.458	4.219	4.625	5.625	3.833
			(.975)	(.593)	(.406)	(.648)	(.792)
13.5	F	LA	5.042	3.609	4.729	5.500	3.792
			(1.469)	(.797)	(.938)	(.962)	(.647)
		LI	6.333	3.094	5.167	6.323	4.458
			(.828)	(1.280)	(.527)	(.719)	(.250)
		HI	4.917	3.275	3.983	5.517	3.900
			(1.318)	(1.437)	(1.126)	(1.252)	(.721)
		HA	6.095	2.911	4.905	5.554	4.262
			(.623)	(.567)	(.798)	(.646)	(.407)
	M	LA	4.738	3.339	4.357	5.583	3.714
			(1.092)	(.886)	(.495)	(.850)	(.768)
		LI	5.121	4.011	4.303	5.485	3.348
			(1.232)	(1.128)	(.836)	(.898)	(1.045)
		HI	5.792	3.313	4.667	4.917	3.500
			(.865)	(.916)	(.593)	(.506)	(.609)
		HA	5.271	2.578	4.854	5.776	4.229
			(1.383)	(1.239)	(.580)	(.950)	(.427)
14.5	F	LA	4.694	4.500	3.778	4.778	3.528
			(.980)	(1.252)	(1.078)	(1.356)	(.356)
		LI	6.361	4.417	4.750	5.556	4.056
			(.609)	(1.232)	(.697)	(.743)	(.430)
		HI	5.258	3.068	3.895	5.754	4.015
			(1.156)	(.933)	(.747)	(.720)	(.508)
		HA	5.500	2.639	4.741	5.519	4.241
			(1.339)	(.847)	(.713)	(1.234)	(.584)
	M	LA	5.019	3.403	3.667	4.625	3.537
			(1.234)	(.939)	(1.000)	(.631)	(.666)
		LI	4.685	3.514	4.648	5.282	3.500
			(1.226)	(1.473)	(.930)	(.812)	(.745)
		HI	4.583	3.313	4.167	4.729	3.542
			(.967)	(.439)	(.653)	(1.161)	(.417)
		HA	5.806	3.292	4.639	5.521	4.111
			(1.051)	(.797)	(.636)	(1.388)	(.491)

Note
Figure 4.4 is based on this table.

Table A4.6 Means (and standard deviations) for self-attribution of professional preferences across age, gender, person category, and job type

Age	Gender	Person category	Professional preferences			
			Professional responsibility	Rule abiding	Originality	Evaluating professions
10.5	F	LA	6.000 (.964)	5.844 (.865)	5.094 (.844)	5.188 (1.551)
		LI	5.893 (1.088)	5.857 (.988)	5.679 (.997)	4.964 (1.851)
		HI	6.179 (.494)	5.821 (1.134)	5.429 (1.491)	4.536 (1.510)
		HA	6.406 (.755)	6.188 (1.059)	5.500 (1.316)	5.406 (1.362)
	M	LA	6.393 (.802)	5.393 (2.096)	5.393 (1.533)	4.571 (1.018)
		LI	5.656 (1.603)	5.938 (1.163)	5.656 (1.043)	5.313 (1.487)
		HI	5.500 (.756)	5.594 (.896)	5.719 (.949)	4.594 (1.085)
		HA	6.393 (.405)	6.500 (.629)	5.750 (.354)	5.107 (1.144)
11.5	F	LA	5.938 (.691)	5.844 (1.093)	4.438 (1.624)	5.563 (.691)
		LI	5.667 (1.103)	5.833 (.876)	4.625 (1.579)	4.250 (.866)
		HI	5.719 (.920)	4.906 (1.871)	5.375 (.824)	4.938 (1.301)
		HA	6.000 (1.061)	5.821 (.607)	5.107 (.775)	5.000 (1.041)
	M	LA	5.143 (.318)	5.036 (1.302)	4.571 (1.125)	4.714 (.895)
		LI	6.167 (.829)	5.861 (.772)	4.917 (1.329)	4.194 (2.102)
		HI	5.250 (1.369)	5.250 (.559)	4.643 (.815)	4.393 (1.574)
		HA	5.938 (.741)	5.625 (.845)	5.469 (.619)	4.813 (1.163)
12.5	F	LA	5.542 (1.005)	6.292 (.697)	4.708 (1.853)	4.958 (1.654)
		LI	5.750 (1.137)	5.750 (2.179)	4.125 (1.876)	4.313 (1.344)
		HI	6.000 (.802)	5.531 (1.780)	4.969 (1.339)	4.656 (1.851)
		HA	6.125 (.771)	4.917 (1.522)	5.708 (.993)	4.792 (.886)
	M	LA	5.556 (1.059)	5.556 (.846)	4.833 (.848)	4.528 (1.086)
		LI	5.909 (.839)	6.159 (.853)	5.091 (1.271)	5.205 (.967)
		HI	5.500 (.837)	5.083 (1.033)	4.542 (1.418)	3.958 (1.453)

Table A4.6 (continued)

Age	Gender	Person category	Professional preferences			
			Professional responsibility	*Rule abiding*	*Originality*	*Evaluating professions*
		HA	5.875	5.813	5.219	4.906
			(.802)	(.665)	(1.191)	(.844)
13.5	F	LA	6.156	4.438	5.625	4.719
			(.865)	(.741)	(.598)	(1.221)
		LI	5.688	5.875	5.438	5.875
			(1.329)	(1.010)	(.966)	(1.051)
		HI	6.200	4.875	5.175	4.475
			(.963)	(1.497)	(1.807)	(1.579)
		HA	6.000	5.143	5.214	5.143
			(.577)	(.748)	(.699)	(.430)
	M	LA	5.250	5.464	4.607	4.393
			(1.109)	(.393)	(1.282)	(1.198)
		LI	5.409	5.205	5.227	3.955
			(1.251)	(.828)	(1.092)	(1.288)
		HI	5.313	5.000	4.938	3.688
			(.375)	(1.173)	(.473)	(1.313)
		HA	6.094	5.750	5.375	5.063
			(1.069)	(.768)	(.856)	(1.487)
14.5	F	LA	5.792	4.958	4.792	4.583
			(.579)	(1.042)	(.579)	(1.506)
		LI	6.208	5.708	5.917	6.000
			(.900)	(1.042)	(.719)	(.652)
		HI	5.705	5.250	5.205	4.841
			(.980)	(1.146)	(1.373)	(.931)
		HA	6.250	5.056	5.444	4.056
			(1.000)	(1.402)	(1.440)	(1.292)
	M	LA	4.889	4.361	4.194	3.611
			(.830)	(.961)	(1.151)	(.741)
		LI	5.333	5.278	5.111	6.639
			(.839)	(.341)	(.985)	(1.376)
		HI	5.125	4.813	3.875	4.563
			(.777)	(1.231)	(.595)	(1.344)
		HA	5.875	5.167	5.667	4.958
			(1.555)	(.785)	(.665)	(1.346)

Note
Figure 4.5 is based on this table.

Table A4.7 Means (and standard deviations) for cognitive performance scores across age, person category, and SCS at the three testing waves

SCS	Person category	1st wave					2nd wave					3rd wave				
		10.5	11.5	12.5	13.5	14.5	11.5	12.5	13.5	14.5	15.5	12.5	13.5	14.5	15.5	16.5
Quantitative-relational	LA	.306 (.223)	.333 (.318)	.407 (.222)	.778 (.373)	.625 (.278)	.667 (.318)	.639 (.437)	.926 (.494)	1.148 (.475)	1.417 (.496)	.722 (.343)	.944 (.446)	.889 (.471)	1.074 (.641)	1.250 (.463)
	LI	.190 (.215)	.436 (.285)	.576 (.336)	.694 (.361)	.767 (.417)	.833 (.485)	.795 (.462)	.909 (.262)	.944 (.239)	1.300 (.292)	.905 (.442)	1.000 (.451)	1.182 (.524)	1.222 (.478)	1.267 (.378)
	HI	.548 (.281)	.939 (.327)	.786 (.384)	1.303 (.547)	1.083 (.289)	.714 (.342)	.909 (.336)	.738 (.396)	1.364 (.277)	1.472 (.460)	.952 (.450)	.970 (.379)	1.143 (.447)	1.182 (.405)	1.472 (.413)
	HA	.667 (.318)	.949 (.468)	1.074 (.572)	1.485 (.345)	1.359 (.440)	.861 (.388)	1.103 (.516)	.926 (.434)	1.515 (.405)	1.641 (.372)	1.083 (.452)	1.026 (.440)	1.296 (.351)	1.636 (.407)	1.436 (.344)
Causal-experimental	LA	0 (0)	.042 (.144)	0 (0)	0 (0)	0 (0)	.458 (.498)	.083 (.289)	.222 (.441)	.611 (.486)	.375 (.518)	.500 (.640)	.208 (.334)	.389 (.486)	.389 (.601)	.500 (.463)
	LI	0 (0)	.115 (.300)	.045 (.151)	.083 (.289)	.050 (.158)	.036 (.134)	.423 (.494)	.273 (.467)	.458 (.498)	.300 (.483)	.571 (.584)	.654 (.625)	.682 (.462)	.667 (.615)	.500 (.471)
	HI	0 (0)	.273 (.410)	.071 (.182)	.091 (.302)	.250 (.452)	.464 (.499)	.364 (.674)	.393 (.446)	.500 (.671)	.583 (.469)	.714 (.671)	.591 (.664)	.357 (.457)	.727 (.647)	.542 (.334)
	HA	.042 (.144)	.423 (.449)	.222 (.441)	.773 (.684)	.308 (.480)	.375 (.483)	.538 (.628)	.167 (.354)	1.227 (.518)	.962 (.660)	.417 (.669)	.731 (.599)	.889 (.546)	1.364 (.505)	.962 (.660)
Social	LA	.583 (.469)	.750 (.500)	.944 (.527)	.667 (.500)	.625 (.582)	1.000 (.674)	1.125 (.711)	.778 (.870)	1.389 (.651)	.875 (.694)	1.125 (.569)	1.208 (.620)	.944 (.726)	.778 (.507)	1.188 (.594)
	LI	.643 (.535)	.846 (.376)	.727 (.564)	.708 (.782)	.500 (.577)	1.214 (.469)	1.346 (.516)	.955 (.611)	1.292 (.542)	1.050 (.685)	1.107 (.594)	1.192 (.805)	1.409 (.491)	1.167 (.685)	1.100 (.459)
	HI	1.464 (.603)	1.318 (.717)	1.536 (.499)	1.273 (.647)	1.375 (.644)	1.607 (.446)	1.409 (.491)	1.500 (.555)	1.500 (.500)	1.292 (.689)	1.500 (.480)	1.273 (.607)	1.393 (.684)	1.455 (.650)	1.375 (.483)
	HA	1.333 (.492)	1.577 (.494)	1.722 (.441)	1.364 (.809)	1.654 (.555)	1.625 (.433)	1.308 (.630)	1.833 (.250)	1.091 (.735)	1.538 (.594)	1.792 (.396)	1.269 (.563)	1.500 (.354)	1.136 (.710)	1.385 (.583)
Spatial-imaginal	LA	.625 (.483)	.833 (.537)	.944 (.464)	.778 (.363)	.688 (.458)	1.333 (.326)	1.125 (.483)	1.167 (.500)	1.444 (.464)	1.188 (.259)	1.292 (.334)	1.375 (.226)	1.333 (.250)	1.444 (.464)	1.313 (.259)

Table A4.7 (continued)

SCS	Person category	1st wave					2nd wave					3rd wave				
		10.5	11.5	12.5	13.5	14.5	11.5	12.5	13.5	14.5	15.5	12.5	13.5	14.5	15.5	16.5
	LI	.679	.923	1.045	1.000	.850	1.357	1.269	1.182	1.333	1.400	1.357	1.154	1.318	1.375	1.200
		(.464)	(.400)	(.151)	(.369)	(.530)	(.306)	(.330)	(.603)	(.246)	(.316)	(.306)	(.427)	(.337)	(.226)	(.587)
	HI	.964	1.091	1.107	1.000	1.167	1.357	1.364	1.321	1.545	1.500	1.393	1.455	1.464	1.409	1.500
		(.365)	(.202)	(.289)	(0)	(.326)	(.413)	(.234)	(.421)	(.350)	(.302)	(.350)	(.270)	(.237)	(.584)	(.213)
	HA	1.000	1.077	1.167	1.091	1.269	1.375	1.269	1.500	1.591	1.385	1.375	1.346	1.500	1.500	1.577
		(.369)	(.277)	(.250)	(.302)	(.439)	(.311)	(.439)	(0)	(.302)	(.300)	(.377)	(.376)	(.250)	(.447)	(.277)
Drawing	LA	.833	.792	.722	.611	.750	.958	.833	.611	1.056	.688	.875	.625	.611	.778	.813
		(.389)	(.450)	(.441)	(.601)	(.463)	(.144)	(.444)	(.333)	(.527)	(.259)	(.377)	(.433)	(.486)	(.441)	(.259)
	LI	.821	.808	1.000	.833	.750	.857	.769	.773	.875	.800	.893	.615	.818	.750	.750
		(.464)	(.253)	(.224)	(.389)	(.635)	(.306)	(.388)	(.261)	(.311)	(.483)	(.289)	(.463)	(.337)	(.337)	(.425)
	HI	1.107	1.136	.929	1.136	1.125	1.071	1.000	1.036	1.182	.833	1.143	.864	.929	.955	.958
		(.656)	(.452)	(.475)	(.745)	(.678)	(.514)	(.447)	(.237)	(.405)	(.389)	(.497)	(.234)	(.331)	(.522)	(.396)
	HA	1.125	1.462	1.278	1.273	1.346	.833	1.038	1.167	1.091	1.000	1.083	1.115	.944	1.091	1.192
		(.644)	(.477)	(.618)	(.410)	(.376)	(.246)	(.320)	(.354)	(.375)	(.408)	(.557)	(.363)	(.464)	(.539)	(.325)

Note
Figure 4.7 is based on this table.

Table A4.8 Means (and standard deviations) for self-evaluation across age, person category, and SCS at the three testing waves

SCS	Person category	1st wave					2nd wave					3rd wave				
		10.5	11.5	12.5	13.5	14.5	11.5	12.5	13.5	14.5	15.5	12.5	13.5	14.5	15.5	16.5
Quantitative-relational	LA	2.417	3.097	3.056	4.296	3.417	4.153	4.431	5.148	6.370	5.354	4.583	4.917	5.778	6.019	5.583
		(1.222)	(1.292)	(.624)	(1.142)	(1.225)	(1.282)	(1.357)	(1.506)	(.767)	(.897)	(1.300)	(1.678)	(1.629)	(1.538)	(.807)
	LI	4.690	5.205	5.636	5.903	5.633	5.000	5.910	5.742	5.806	6.233	5.619	5.346	6.394	6.153	5.933
		(1.257)	(1.085)	(1.048)	(.773)	(1.274)	(1.629)	(.804)	(.938)	(1.103)	(.851)	(1.277)	(1.420)	(.410)	(.922)	(1.233)
	HI	3.095	4.121	3.976	5.303	4.917	4.798	4.833	4.976	6.303	5.875	5.417	5.924	5.702	5.788	5.792
		(1.214)	(.879)	(.821)	(.819)	(.920)	(1.206)	(.994)	(1.310)	(.812)	(1.023)	(1.267)	(.929)	(1.268)	(1.633)	(1.108)
	HA	5.375	5.769	5.815	6.652	6.705	5.514	5.756	5.630	6.515	6.641	5.958	5.821	6.315	6.697	6.295
		(1.108)	(.682)	(1.251)	(.438)	(.420)	(1.009)	(1.086)	(1.511)	(.497)	(.659)	(1.194)	(.899)	(.733)	(.433)	(.646)
Causal-experimental	LA	2.750	2.583	2.444	3.833	2.625	3.458	3.917	4.778	5.222	4.500	4.708	4.708	4.222	5.222	4.438
		(1.390)	(1.276)	(1.236)	(1.173)	(1.275)	(1.422)	(1.203)	(1.822)	(1.302)	(1.604)	(1.936)	(2.083)	(1.716)	(1.439)	(1.050)
	LI	4.643	4.962	4.455	5.167	5.350	4.286	4.808	4.636	5.167	5.150	4.821	5.038	5.318	5.292	3.950
		(1.099)	(1.464)	(.850)	(1.285)	(1.334)	(1.565)	(1.494)	(1.247)	(1.482)	(1.415)	(1.793)	(1.726)	(1.309)	(1.588)	(1.462)
	HI	2.786	3.091	2.571	3.182	2.250	4.964	3.818	3.857	4.682	4.333	4.786	5.045	4.607	4.591	4.000
		(.893)	(.831)	(.805)	(.982)	(.839)	(1.770)	(1.722)	(1.669)	(1.290)	(1.788)	(1.626)	(1.604)	(1.483)	(2.047)	(1.537)
	HA	4.875	5.346	4.833	5.091	4.846	4.667	4.731	5.167	5.773	6.038	5.333	5.308	5.778	6.500	5.192
		(1.494)	(1.345)	(1.620)	(1.393)	(1.125)	(1.387)	(1.727)	(1.323)	(1.148)	(.691)	(1.320)	(1.548)	(1.460)	(.548)	(1.843)
Social	LA	3.792	4.708	5.722	4.444	4.625	5.292	5.375	6.000	6.111	5.500	5.917	5.625	6.056	6.056	5.000
		(1.097)	(.656)	(1.372)	(2.007)	(.694)	(1.514)	(1.189)	(1.146)	(.546)	(.926)	(.973)	(1.785)	(.808)	(.726)	(1.535)
	LI	6.143	6.654	6.045	6.250	6.150	6.000	6.385	6.136	6.292	6.500	5.750	6.346	6.318	6.333	5.800
		(1.200)	(.427)	(.723)	(.989)	(.784)	(1.144)	(.820)	(1.002)	(.782)	(.816)	(1.070)	(.851)	(.681)	(.718)	(1.358)
	HI	5.000	4.636	4.643	4.227	4.833	5.429	5.000	5.464	5.909	6.208	5.464	5.909	5.964	6.045	6.208
		(1.240)	(1.286)	(.908)	(1.385)	(.961)	(1.869)	(1.628)	(1.308)	(1.044)	(.582)	(1.216)	(.944)	(1.117)	(.934)	(.582)
	HA	6.500	6.000	6.500	5.682	6.192	6.083	5.846	6.389	5.455	6.462	6.292	5.654	6.389	5.955	6.269
		(.769)	(.890)	(.707)	(1.290)	(.693)	(.634)	(1.028)	(.651)	(1.508)	(.721)	(.940)	(1.688)	(.601)	(.789)	(.832)
Spatial-imaginal	LA	4.917	4.458	5.333	5.167	5.000	5.542	5.625	6.056	6.444	5.438	6.042	6.542	6.111	6.500	5.000
		(1.145)	(1.157)	(1.118)	(1.225)	(1.512)	(1.529)	(.932)	(.982)	(.682)	(1.116)	(1.499)	(.865)	(1.167)	(.433)	(1.711)

Table A4.8 (continued)

SCS	Person category	1st wave					2nd wave					3rd wave				
		10.5	11.5	12.5	13.5	14.5	11.5	12.5	13.5	14.5	15.5	12.5	13.5	14.5	15.5	16.5
	LI	6.036	6.231	6.500	6.583	6.150	6.036	6.308	6.455	6.375	6.250	6.357	6.269	6.455	6.417	6.300
		(1.100)	(.525)	(.707)	(.515)	(1.156)	(1.337)	(.925)	(.650)	(.908)	(1.087)	(.864)	(.753)	(1.036)	(.848)	(.632)
	HI	5.214	5.000	5.179	5.000	5.417	6.107	5.182	5.821	5.773	6.125	6.000	6.318	6.393	6.636	6.583
		(1.204)	(1.118)	(1.234)	(1.204)	(1.041)	(1.228)	(1.347)	(1.310)	(1.034)	(1.110)	(1.160)	(.681)	(.738)	(.505)	(.417)
	HA	6.333	6.538	6.167	6.455	6.500	5.750	5.962	6.833	6.591	6.500	6.250	6.154	6.667	6.773	6.654
		(.913)	(.558)	(1.199)	(.611)	(.612)	(1.077)	(1.181)	(.354)	(.539)	(.577)	(1.034)	(1.049)	(.354)	(.344)	(.315)
Drawing	LA	3.875	4.708	4.167	4.667	4.125	4.917	4.875	5.278	5.333	4.875	5.292	5.375	5.667	4.889	4.438
		(1.479)	(.689)	(1.090)	(1.732)	(1.482)	(1.649)	(1.680)	(1.394)	(1.677)	(1.188)	(1.815)	(1.798)	(.968)	(2.012)	(1.425)
	LI	6.179	5.962	6.500	6.042	5.800	5.214	5.385	5.318	5.042	5.350	5.964	5.231	5.273	5.250	4.000
		(1.049)	(.749)	(.592)	(.620)	(.949)	(1.424)	(1.557)	(1.505)	(1.616)	(1.684)	(.950)	(1.975)	(1.808)	(1.588)	(1.810)
	HI	5.143	4.409	4.250	3.455	3.458	5.321	4.000	5.214	4.182	4.125	4.714	4.364	4.821	3.182	4.417
		(1.336)	(1.546)	(1.205)	(.986)	(1.252)	(2.015)	(1.517)	(1.236)	(2.016)	(1.990)	(1.451)	(2.099)	(1.449)	(2.065)	(1.756)
	HA	6.333	6.269	5.833	5.864	6.308	5.542	5.462	5.833	5.864	5.654	5.417	6.000	5.944	5.727	5.769
		(.778)	(.949)	(.829)	(.977)	(.522)	(1.010)	(1.198)	(1.146)	(.839)	(1.028)	(1.857)	(1.225)	(.950)	(1.403)	(.949)

Note
Figure 4.8 is based on this table.

Table A4.9 Means (and standard deviations) for self-attribution of personal characteristics across person category at the three testing waves

Personal characteristics	Person category	1st wave	2nd wave	3rd wave
Learning ability	LA	5.124	5.056	4.944
		(1.253)	(1.134)	(1.073)
	LI	5.710	5.657	5.230
		(.956)	(.832)	(1.044)
	HI	5.148	4.906	4.977
		(.989)	(1.166)	(1.063)
	HA	5.672	5.214	5.010
		(.924)	(1.153)	(1.171)
Impulsivity	LA	3.905	3.510	3.523
		(1.127)	(1.020)	(1.139)
	LI	3.660	3.412	3.483
		(1.311)	(1.267)	(.987)
	HI	3.131	3.046	3.179
		(1.076)	(.935)	(.868)
	HA	3.291	3.237	3.009
		(1.164)	(1.162)	(.961)

Note
Figure 4.9 is based on this table.

Table A5.1 Means (and standard deviations) for mothers' attributions of ability across person category and SCS

Person category	Ability				
	Quantitative-relational	Causal-experimental	Social	Spatial-imaginal	Drawing
LA	4.414	5.000	5.692	5.275	4.583
	(1.072)	(.820)	(.753)	(.821)	(1.518)
LI	4.685	4.905	5.431	5.534	3.845
	(1.160)	(1.156)	(.759)	(.716)	(1.626)
HI	4.793	4.975	5.350	5.481	4.644
	(1.205)	(1.132)	(.980)	(.852)	(1.507)
HA	5.114	5.225	5.506	5.463	4.731
	(1.220)	(.949)	(.777)	(.880)	(1.496)

Note
Figure 5.7 is based on this table.

Table A5.2 Means (and standard deviations) for self-attribution and mothers' attribution of personal characteristics across person category at the second testing wave

Personal characteristics	Person category	Children	Mothers
Learning ability	LA	5.207	5.460
		(1.076)	(.941)
	LI	5.814	6.083
		(.858)	(1.021)
	HI	5.015	6.005
		(1.027)	(.839)
	HA	5.315	6.130
		(1.253)	(.749)
Impulsivity	LA	3.738	3.725
		(.893)	(.959)
	LI	3.409	3.608
		(1.387)	(1.124)
	HI	3.284	3.613
		(.949)	(.959)
	HA	3.284	3.278
		(1.161)	(1.085)

Note
Figure 5.8 is based on this table.

Table A6.1 The task addressed to verbal short-term memory

Difficulty level	Items
2	χτένα βροχή
	λάμπας ρυζιού
3	ράφια φούρνοι λίμνες
	μύγα δάσος τοίχος
4	ήλιοι κότες πόδια ρόδες
	γλάρο ψωμιού πέτρας κήπους
5	μύτη πάρκο ψάρι γάλα φωτιά
	γάτας πόλης ναών καπνού νησιού
6	καρποί γυαλιά δρόμοι βαφές σταύλοι κλαδιά
	στόμα άμμος σκάλα δίχτυ σκεύος χαρτί
7	βιολί αγρός πανί γλάστρα νερό στολή βυθός
	πλοία άνθη κρασιά τάξεις λαιμοί ρίζες μάσκες

Table A6.2 The task addressed to numerical short-term memory

Difficulty level	Items
2	32 57
	60 40
3	22 55 88
	73 48 64
4	50 80 20 60
	58 23 52 79
5	49 67 34 72 93
	80 20 50 40 70
6	66 88 33 99 55 77
	75 29 43 85 63 46
7	50 80 30 70 40 20 90
	28 36 59 83 45 94 68

Table A6.3 Mean performance (and standard deviations) for the speed of processing and the verbal analogies tasks attained by the subjects who were selected to participate in the four person categories involved in Study 2

Age	Person category							
	Slow-Low		Slow-High		Fast-Low		Fast-High	
	Speed	Verbal analogies	Speed	Verbal analogies	Speed	Verbal analogies	Speed	Verbal analogies
11	.957	.083	.894	.583	.687	.167	.718	.750
	(.041)	(.144)	(.084)	(.144)	(.078)	(.144)	(.065)	(.250)
13	.895	.500	.815	.750	.639	.333	.607	.833
	(.024)	(.000)	(.033)	(.000)	(.054)	(.144)	(.107)	(.144)
15	.754	.333	.811	.917	.536	.500	.577	.833
	(.026)	(.144)	(.105)	(.144)	(.056)	(.000)	(.072)	(.144)

Bibliography

Adekoya, J. A. (1994). *Metacognitive awareness of the structure and processing complexity of cognitive abilities in adolescence: A cross-cultural study in Greece and Nigeria.* Unpublished doctoral thesis. Department of Psychology, Aristotle University of Thessaloniki.

Allport, G. W. (1937). *Personality: A psychological interpretation.* New York: Holt, Rinehart, and Winston.

Asendorpf, J. B. (1999). Commentary on the emerging self by Demetriou *et al. Developmental Science, 2,* 416–417.

Asendorph, J. B., and van Aken, M. A. G. (1998). *When predictive power increases over time: A type approach to personality development.* Unpublished manuscript.

Baddeley, A. (1991). *Working memory.* Oxford: Oxford University Press.

Baldwin, J. M. (1968). *The development of the child and of the race.* New York: Augustus M. Kelley. (Original work published 1894.)

Bandura, A. (1989). Regulation of cognitive processes through perceived self-efficacy. *Developmental Psychology, 25,* 729–735.

Bandura, A. (1990). "Conclusion: Reflections on non-ability determinants of competence." In R. J. Sternberg and J. Kolligian, Jr. (eds.), *Competence considered* (pp. 315–362). New Haven: Yale University Press.

Bentler, P. M. (1989). *EQS: Structural equations program manual.* Los Angeles, CA: BMDP Statistical Software.

Berndt, T. J. (in press). "The social self-concept." In B. A. Bracken (ed.), *Handbook of self-concept.* New York: Wiley.

Besevegis, E., Pavlopoulos, V., and Mourousaki, S. (1996). Children's personality characteristics as assessed by parents in natural language. *Psychology: The Journal of the Hellenic Psychological Society, 3 (2),* 46–57.

Bickhard, M. (1998). Constraints on the architecture of mind: Comments on "Logical and psychological partitioning of mind: Depicting the same map?" by Philip V. Kargopoulos and Andreas Demetriou. *New Ideas in Psychology, 16,* 97–106.

Bickhard, M. (1999). On the cognition of cognitive development. *Developmental Review, 19,* 369–388.

Boekaerts, M. (1997). Self-regulated learning: A new concept embraced by researchers, policy makers, educators, teachers, and students. *Learning and Instruction: The Journal of the European Association for Research on Learning and Instruction, 7,* 161–186.

Bonoti, F. (1998). Structure and development of drawing from infancy to childhood. Thessaloniki: University of Thessaloniki. (Unpublished doctoral dissertation.)

Bracken, B. (1996). "Clinical applications of a context-dependent multi-dimensional model of self-concept." In B. A. Bracken (ed.), *Handbook of self-concept.* New York: Wiley.

Brown, A. (1987). "Metacognition, executive control, self-regulation, and other mysterious mechanisms." In F. Weinert and R. Kluwe (eds.), *Metacognition, motivation, and understanding* (pp. 65–116). Hillsdale, NJ: Erlbaum.

Brown, J. D. (1998). *The self.* Boston: McGraw Hill.

Byrne, B. M. (1995). "Academic self-concept: Its structure, measurement, and relation with academic achievement." In B. A. Bracken (ed.), *Handbook of self-concept.* New York: Wiley.

Campbell, R. L. (1993). Epistemological problems for neo-Piagetians. *Monographs of the Society for Research in Child Development, 58* (5, Serial No. 234), 168–191.

Campbell, R. L., and Bickhard, M. H. (1986). *Knowing levels and developmental stages.* Basel: Karger.

Carey, S. (1985). *Conceptual change in childhood. Cambridge,* MA: MIT Press.

Carpendale, J. I., and Chandler, M. J. (1996). On the distinction between false belief understanding and subscribing to an interpretive theory of mind. *Child Development, 67,* 1686–1706.

Case, R. (1985). *Intellectual development: Birth to adulthood.* New York: Academic Press.

Case, R. (1991). Stages in the development of the young child's first sense of self. *Developmental Review, 11,* 210–230.

Case, R. (1992). *The mind's staircase.* Hillsdale, NJ: Erlbaum.

Case, R., Okamoto, Y., Griffin, S., McKeough, A., Bleiker, C., Henderson, B., and Stephenson, K. M. (1996). The role of central conceptual structures in the development of children's thought. *Monographs of the Society for Research in Child Development, 61* (1–2, Serial No. 246).

Caspi, A. (1998). "Personality development across the life course." In N. Eisenberg (ed.), W. Damon (series ed.), *Handbook of Child Psychology (5th ed.): Vol. 3: Social, Emotional, and Personality Development* (pp. 177–235). New York: Wiley.

Cassam, Q. (1997). *Self and world.* Oxford: Oxford University Press.

Cattell, R. B. (1930). *The subjective character of cognition.* Cambridge: Cambridge University Press.

Cattell, R. B. (1971). *Abilities: Their structure, growth, and action.* Boston: Houghton Mifflin.

Chandler, M., Boyes, M., and Ball, L. (1990). Relativism and stations of epistemic doubt. *Journal of Experimental Child Psychology, 50,* 370–395.

Cooley, C. H. (1964). *Human nature and the social order.* New York: Schocken Books. (Original work published 1902).

Coopersmith, S. (1967). *The antecedents of self-esteem.* San Francisco: Freeman.

Costa, P. T., Jr., and McCrae, R. R. (1997). "Longitudinal stability of adult personality." In R. Hogan, J. Johnson and S. Briggs (eds.), *Handbook of Personality Psychology* (pp. 269–290). San Diego: Academic Press.

Costanzo, P. R. (1991). "Morals, mothers, and memories: The social context of developing social cognition." In R. Cohen and R. Siegel (eds.), *Context and development* (pp. 91–132). Hillsdale, NJ: Erlbaum.

Damon, W., and Hart, D. (1986). Stability and change in children's self-understanding. *Social Cognition, 4,* 102–118.

Demetriou, A. (1990). "Structural and developmental relations between formal and post-formal capacities: Towards a comprehensive theory of adolescent and adult cognitive development." In M. Commons, F. Richards, C. Armon and J. Sinnot (eds.), *Beyond formal operations 2: The development of adolescent thought and perception,* 147–173. New York: Praeger (Adult Development Series).

Demetriou, A. (1993). On the quest of the functional architecture of developing mind. *Educational Psychology Review, 5,* 1–18.

Demetriou, A. (1998a). Nooplasis: 10 + 1 Postulates about the formation of mind. *Learning and Instruction: The Journal of the European Association for Research on Learning and Instruction,* 8, 271–287.

Demetriou, A. (1998b). "Cognitive development." In A. Demetriou, W. Doise, K. F. M. van Lieshout (eds.), *Life-span developmental psychology* (pp. 179–269). London: Wiley.

Demetriou, A. (2000). "Organization and development of self-understanding and self-regulation." In M. Boekaerts, P. R. Pintrich, and M. Zeidner (eds.), *Handbook of self-regulation* (pp. 209–251). New York: Academic Press.

Demetriou, A. and Efklides, A. (1985). Structure and sequence of formal and postformal thought: General patterns and individual differences. *Child Development,* 56, 1062–1091.

Demetriou A., and Efklides, A. (1989). The person's conception of the structures of developing intellect: Early adolescence to middle age. *Genetic, Social, and General Psychology Monographs,* 115, 371–423.

Demetriou, A., and Efklides, A. (1994). "Structure, development, and dynamics of mind: A meta-Piagetian theory." In A. Demetriou and A. Efklides (eds.), *Mind, intelligence, and reasoning: Structure and development* (pp. 75–109). Amsterdam: Elsevier.

Demetriou, A., Efklides, A., and Platsidou, M. (1993a) The architecture and dynamics of developing mind: Experiential structuralism as a frame for unifying cognitive developmental theories. *Monographs of the Society for Research in Child Development,* 58 (5, Serial No. 234).

Demetriou, A., Efklides, A., Papadaki, M., Papantoniou, A., and Economou, A. (1993b). The structure and development of causal-experimental thought. *Developmental Psychology,* 29, 480–497.

Demetriou, A., and Georgiou, S. (1999). Striving for the "grant theory": response to the commentators. *Developmental Science,* 2:4, 418–422.

Demetriou, A., Gustafsson, J. E., Efklides, A., and Platsidou, M. (1992). "Structural systems in developing cognition, science, and education." In A. Demetriou, M. Shayer, and A. Efklides (eds.), *The neo-Piagetian theories of cognitive development go to school: Implications and applications for education* (pp. 79–103). London: Routledge.

Demetriou, A., Kazi, S., and Georgiou, S. (1999). The emerging self: The convergence of mind, personality, and thinking styles, *Developmental Science,* 2:4, 387–422.

Demetriou, A., Kazi, S., Sirmali, K., and Tsiouri, I. (in preparation). *Personality, thinking styles, and job selection.*

Demetriou, A., and Kargopoulos, D. (in preparation). Logical reasoning across different domains.

Demetriou, A., Pachaury, A., Metallidou, Y., and Kazi. S. (1996). Universals and specificities in the structure and development of quantitative-relational thought: A cross-cultural study in Greece and India. *International Journal of Behavioral Development,* 19, 255–290 .

Demetriou, A., Platsidou, M., and Sirmali, K. (in preparation). The structure and development of processing capacity from 9 to 17 years of age: A longitudinal study.

Demetriou, A., Platsidou, M., Efklides A., Metallidou, Y., and Shayer, M. (1991). Structure and sequence of the quantitative-relational abilities and processing potential from childhood and adolescence. *Learning and Instruction: The Journal of the European Association for Research on Learning and Instruction,* 1, 19–44.

Demetriou, A., and Raftopoulos, A. (1999). Modeling the developing mind: From structure to change. *Developmental Review,* 19, 319–368.

Demetriou, A., Raftopoulos, A., and Kargopoulos, P. (1999). Interactions, computations, and experience: Interleaved Springboards of Cognitive Emergence, *Developmental Review,* 19, 389–414.

Demetriou, A., and Valanides, N. (1998). "A three level of theory of the developing mind: Basic principles and implications for instruction and assessment." In R. J. Sternberg and W. M. Williams (eds.), *Intelligence, instruction, and assessment* (pp. 149–199). Hillsdale, NJ: Lawrence Erlbaum.

Dempster, F. N., and Brainerd, C. (1995) (eds.). *Interference and inhibition in cognition.* New York: Academic Press.

Donald, M. (1991). *Origins of the modern mind:* Cambridge, MA: Harvard University Press.

Dunn, G., Everitt, B., and Picckles, A. (1993). *Modelling covariance structures and latent variables using EQS.* London: Chapman and Hall.

Eccles, J. S., Wigfield, A., Harold, R. D., and Blumenfeld, P. (1993). Age and gender differences in children's self- and task perception during elementary school. *Child Development,* 64, 830–847.

Efklides, A., Demetriou, A., and Metallidou, Y. (1994). "The structure and development of propositional reasoning ability: Cognitive and metacognitive aspects." In A. Demetriou and A. Efklides (eds.), *Intelligence, mind, and reasoning: Structure and development* (pp. 151–172). Amsterdam: North-Holland.

Ekstrom, R. B., French, J. W., and Harman, H. H. (1976). *Kit of factor referenced cognitive tests.* Princeton, NJ: Educational Testing Service.

Elman, J. L., Bates, E, Johnson, M. H., Karmiloff-Smith, A., Parisi, D., Plunket, K. (1996). *Rethinking innateness: A connectionist perspective on development.* Cambridge, MA: MIT Press, 1996.

Emmons, R. A. (1995). Levels and domains in personality: An introduction. *Journal of Personality,* 63, 341–364.

Engel, P. (1998). Comments on "Logical and psychological partitioning of mind: Depicting the same map?" *New Ideas in Psychology, 16,* 107–114.

Epstein, S. (1973). The self-concept revisited or a theory of a theory. *American Psychologist, 28,* 404–416.

Epstein, S. (1991). "Cognitive-experiential self-theory: Implications for developmental psychology." In M. R. Gunnar and L. A. Sroufe (eds.), *Self processes and development: The Minnesota Symposium on Child Development* (Vol. 23, pp. 111–137). Hillsdale, NJ: Erlbaum.

Erikson, E. H. (1963). *Childhood and society.* New York: Norton.

Fabricius, W. V., and Schwanenflugel, P. J. (1994). "The older child's theory of mind." In A. Demetriou and A. Efklides (eds.), *Intelligence, mind, and reasoning: Structure and development* (pp. 111–132). Amsterdam: North-Holland.

Felson, R. B. (1993). "The (somewhat) social self: How others affect self-appraisals." In J. Suls (ed.), *Psychological perspectives on the self* (Vol. 4, pp. 1–26). Hillsdale, NJ: Erlbaum.

Ferrari, M., and Sternberg, R. J. (1998). "The development of mental abilities and styles." In D. Kuhn and R. Siegler (eds.), W. Damon (series ed.), *Handbook of Child Psychology (5th ed.): Vol. 2: Cognition, Perception and Language* (pp. 899–946). New York: Wiley.

Fischer, K. W. (1980). A theory of cognitive development: The control and construction of hierarchies of skills. *Psychological Review, 87,* 477–531.

Fischer, K. W., and Aboud, C. (1993). "Affective splitting and dissociation in normal and maltreated children: Developmental pathways for self in relationships." In D. Cicchetti and V. Carlson (eds.), *Child maltreatment: theory and research on the cause and consequences of child abuse and neglect.* New York: Cambridge University Press.

Fischer, K. W. and Pipp, S. L. (1984). "Development of the structures of unconscious thought." In K. Bowers and D. Meichenbaum (eds.), *The unconscious reconsidered* (pp. 88–148). New York: Wiley.

Flavell, J. (1979). Metacognition and cognitive monitoring: A new area of cognitive developmental inquiry. *American Psychologist, 34,* 906–911.

Flavell, J. H. (1988). "The development of children's knowledge about the mind: From cognitive connections to mental representations." In J. W. Astington, P. L. Harris, and D. R. Olson (eds.), *Developing theories of mind* (pp. 244–267). Cambridge: Cambridge University Press.

Flavell, J. H., Green, F. L., and Flavell, E. R. (1995). Young children's knowledge about thinking. *Monographs of the Society for Research in Child Development, 60* (1, Serial No. 243).

Flavell, J. H., Green, F. L., Flavell, E. R., and Grossman, J. B. (1997). The development of children's knowledge about inner speech. *Child Development, 68*, 39–47.

Fodor, J. A. (1983). *The modularity of mind*. Cambridge, MA: MIT Press.

Freud, S. (1923). "The ego and the id." In *Standard edition* (Vol. 19, pp. 12–66).

Gallistel, C. R. (1993). *The organization of learning*. Cambridge: MIT Press.

Gardner, H. (1983). *Frames of mind: The theory of multiple intelligences*. New York: Basic Books.

Globerson, T. (1985). Field dependence/independence and mental capacity: A developmental Approach. *Developmental Review, 5*, 261–273.

Graziano, W. G., and Waschull, S. B. (1995). "Social development and self-monitoring." In N. Eisenberg (ed.), *Social development: Review of personality and social psychology* (Vol. 15, pp. 233–260). London: Sage.

Graziano, W. G., Jensen-Campbell, L. A., and Finch, J. F. (1997). The self as a mediator between personality and adjustment. *Journal of Personality and Social Psychology, 73 (2)*, 392–404.

Graziano, W., Jensen-Campbell, L. A., and Sullivan, G. (in press). Temperament, activity and expectations for later personality development. *Journal of Personality and Social Psychology*.

Grigorenko, E., and Sternberg, R. J. (1995). "Thinking styles." In D. H. Saklofske and M. Zeidner (eds.), *International handbook of personality and intelligence* (pp. 205–229). New York: Plenum Press.

Gustafsson, J. E. (1988). "Hierarchical models of individual differences in cognitive abilities." In R. J. Sternberg (ed.), *Advances in the psychology of intelligence* (Vol. 4, pp. 35–71). Hillsdale, NJ: Erlbaum.

Gustafsson, J. E. (1988). "Broad and narrow abilities in research on learning and instruction." In R. Kanfer, P. L. Ackerman, and R. Cudeck (eds.), *Abilities, motivation, and methodology: The Minnesota symposium on learning and individual differences* (pp. 203–237). Hillsdale, NJ: Lawrence Erlbaum.

Gustafsson. J.-E. (1994). "Hierarchical models of intelligence and educational achievement." In A. Demetriou and A. Efklides (eds.), *Intelligence, mind, and reasoning: Structure and development* (pp. 75–110). Amsterdam: North-Holland.

Gustafsson, J.-E., and Undheim, J. O. (1996). "Individual differences in cognitive functions." In D. C. Berliner, and Calfee, R. C. (eds.), *Handbook of educational psychology* (pp. 186–242). New York: Simon and Schuster Macmillan.

Hair, E. C., and Graziano, W. G. (1999). What are the developmental origins of the emerging self? *Developmental Science, 2*, 415–416.

Halford, G. (1993). *Children's Understanding: The development of mental models*. New York: Erlbaum.

Harter, S. (1985). "Competence as a dimension of self-evaluation: Toward a comprehensive model of self-worth." In R. L. Leahy (ed.), *The development of the self* (pp. 55–121). Orlando, Florida: Academic Press, Inc.

Harter, S. (1990). "Causes, correlates, and the functional role of global self-worth: A life-span perspective." In R. J. Sternberg and J. Kolligian, Jr. (eds.), *Competence considered* (pp. 67–97). New Haven: Yale University Press.

Harter, S. (1998). "The development of self-representations." In N. Eisenberg (ed.), W. Damon (series ed.), *Handbook of Child Psychology (5th ed.): Vol. 3: Social, Emotional, and Personality Development* (pp. 553–617). New York: Wiley.

Harter, S. (1999). *The construction of the self.* New York: The Guilford Press.

Hartup, W. W., and van Lieshout, C. F. M. (1995). Personality development in social context. *Annual Review of Psychology,* 1995, 46, 655–687

Hattie, J. (1992). *Self-concept.* Hillsdale, NJ: Erlbaum.

Higgins, E. T. (1987). Self-discrepancy: A theory relating self and affect. *Psychological Review,* 94, 319–340.

Higgins, E. T. (1991). "Development of self-regulatory and self-evaluative processes: Costs, benefits, and tradeoffs." In M. R. Gunnar and L. A. Sroufe (eds.), *Self processes and development: The Minnesota Symposia on Child Development* (Vol. 23, pp. 125–166). Hillsdale, NJ: Erlbaum.

Houghton, G., and Tipper, S. P. "A model of inhibitory mechanisms in selective attention." In D. Dagenbach, D. and T. H. Carr (eds.), *Inhibitory processes in attention, memory, and language* (pp. 53–112). New York: Academic Press.

Inhelder, B., and Piaget, J. (1958). *The growth of logical thinking from childhood to adolescence.* London: Routledge and Kegan Paul.

James, W. (1890). *Principles of psychology.* Chicago: Encyclopedia Britannica.

James, W. (1892). *Psychology: The briefer course.* New York: Henry Holt.

Jensen, A. R. (1998). *The g factor: The science of mental ability.* New York: Praeger.

Jensen, A. R. and Rohwer, W. D. (1966). The Stroop color-word test: A review. *Acta psychologica,* 25, 36–93.

Kagan, J. (1965). "Impulsive and reflective children: Significance of conceptual tempo." In J. D. Krumboltz (ed.), *Learning and the educational process.* Chicago: Rand McNally.

Kagan, J. (1991). The theoretical utility of constructs for self. *Developmental Review, 11,* 244–250.

Kagan, J. (1994a). On the nature of emotion. *Monographs of the Society for Research in Child Development, 59,* 7–24 (2–3, Serial No. 240).

Kagan, J. (1994b). *Galen's prophesy: Temperament in human nature.* London: Free Association Books.

Kail, R. (1988). Developmental functions for speeds of cognitive processes. *Journal of Experimental Child Psychology, 45,* 339–364.

Kargopoulos, P., and Demetriou, A. (1998a). Logical and psychological partitioning of mind. Depicting the same map? *New Ideas in Psychology, 16,* 61–87.

Kargopoulos, P., and Demetriou, A. (1998b). What, why, and whence logic? A response to the commentators. *New Ideas in Psychology, 16,* 125–139.

Kazi, S., and Makris, N. (1992). Laymen's implicit theories about the intelligence of children and adults. *Psychology: The Journal of the Hellenic Psychological Society, 1,* 52–70.

Kenny, D. A., and DePaulo, B. M. (1993). Do people know how others view them? An empirical and theoretical account. *Psychological Bulletin, 114,* 145–161.

Kochanska, G. (1995). Children's temperament, mothers' discipline, and security attachment: Multiple pathways to emerging internalization. *Child Development, 66,* 597–615.

Kochanska, G. (1997). Multiple pathways to conscience for children with different temperaments: From toddlerhood to age 5. *Developmental Psychology, 33,* 228–240.

Kochanska, G., Coy, K., Tjebkes, T. L., and Husarek, S. J. (1997). Individual differences in emotionality in infancy. *Child Development, 69,* 375–390.

Kohnstamm, G. A., and Mervielde, I. (1998). "Personality development." In A. Demetriou, W. Doise, and K. F. M. van Lieshout (eds.), *Life-span developmental psychology* (pp. 399–445). London: Wiley.

Kohnstamm, G. A., Mervielde, I., Besevegis, E., and Halverson, C. F. Jr. (1995). Tracing the Big Five in parents' free descriptions of their children. *European Journal of Personality, 9,* 283–304.

Kolb, D. A. (1977). *Learning style inventory: A self-description of preferred learning modes.* Boston: McBer.

Kougioumoutzakis, Y. (1985). *The development of imitation during the first six months of life.* (Uppsala Psychological Report No. 377). Uppsala, Sweden: Uppsala University Press.

Kucheman, D. (1981). Algebra. In K. M. Hart (Ed.), *Children's understanding of mathematics* (pp. 102–119). Oxford: Murray.

Kuhl, J. (1992). A theory of self-regulation: Action versus state orientation, self-discrimination, and some applications. Applied Psychology: *An International Review, 41,* 97–129.

Loizos, L. (1992). Structure and development of spatial and meta-spatial abilities from 10 to 18 years of age. *Psychology: The Journal of the Hellenic Psychological Society, 1,* 71–91.

Makris, N. (1995). Personal theory of mind and its relationship with cognitive abilities. Unpublished doctoral thesis. Department of Psychology, Aristotle University of Thessaloniki.

Markus, H. R. and Kityama, S. (1991). Culture and self: Implications for cognition, emotion, and motivation. *Psychological Review, 98,* 224–253.

Markus, H. and Wurf, E. (1987). The dynamic self-concept: A social psychological perspective. *Annual Review of Psychology, 38,* 299–337.

Marsh, H. W., Byrne, B. M., and Shavelson, R. J. (1992). "A multi-dimensional, hierarchical self-concept." In T. M. Brinthaupt and R. P. Linka (eds.), *The self: Definitional and methodological issues* (pp. 44–95). Albany: State University of New York Press.

Marsh, H. W., and Hattie, J. (1996). "Theoretical perspectives on the structure of self-concept." In B. A. Bracken (ed.), *Handbook of self-concept* (pp. 38–90). New York: Wiley.

Marton, F. (1999). The mind's minds. *Developmental Science, 2,* 410–411.

McAdams, D. P. (1995). What do we know when we know a person? *Journal of Personality, 63,* 365–396.

Mead, G. H. (1925). The genesis of the self and social control. *International Journal of Ethics, 35,* 251–273.

Meltzoff, A., and Moore, K. (1995). "A theory of the role of imitation in the mergence of self." In P. Rochat (ed.), *The self in early infancy* (pp. 73–93). New York: Elsevier

Miller, S. A. (1988). Parents' beliefs about children's cognitive development. *Child Development, 59,* 259–285.

Miller, S. A. (1995). Parents' attributions for their children. *Child Development, 66,* 1557–1584.

Mischel, W., and Ebbesen, E. B. (1970). Attention in delay of gratification. *Journal of Personality and Social Psychology, 16,* 329–337.

Mischel, W. Shoda, Y., and Peake, P. K. (1988). The nature of adolescent competencies predicted by preschool delay of gratification. *Personality and Social Psychology, 54,* 687–696.

Mithen, S. (1996). *The prehistory of the mind: The cognitive origins of art, religion, and science.* New York: Thames and Hudson.

Moretti, M. M., and Higgins, E. T. (1990). "The development of self-system vulnerabilities: Social and cognitive factors in Developmental Psychopathology." In R. J. Sternberg and J. Kolligian, Jr. (eds.), *Competence considered* (pp. 286–314). New Haven: Yale University Press.

Neisser, U. (ed.) (1994). *The remembering self.* Cambridge: Cambridge University Press.

Nicholls, J. G. (1990). "What is ability and why are we mindful of it? A developmental perspective." In R. J. Sternberg and J. Kolligian, Jr. (eds.), *Competence considered* (pp. 11–40). New Haven: Yale University Press.

Oosterwegel, A., and Oppenheimer, L. (1993). *The self-system: Developmental changes between and within self-concepts.* Hillsdale, NJ: Erlbaum.

Pascual-Leone, J. (1970). A mathematical model for the transition rule in Piaget's developmental stages. *Acta Psychologica, 32,* 301–345.

Pascual-Leone, J. (1988). "Organismic processes for neo-Piagetian theories: A dialectical causal account of cognitive development." In A. Demetriou (ed.), *The neo-Piagetian theories of cognitive development: Toward an integration* (pp. 25–64). Amsterdam: North-Holland.

Pascual-Leone, J. (1989). "An organismic process model of Witkin's field dependence-independence." In T. Globerson, and T. Zelniker (eds.) *Cognitive style and cognitive development* (pp. 36–70). Norwood, NJ: Ablex.

Pascual-Leone, J. (1998). SSSs or functionalist models of processing? A commentary on Kargopoulos and Demetriou's paper. *New Ideas in Psychology, 16,* 89–96.

Pascual-Leone, J., and Goodman, D. (1979). Intelligence and experience: A neo-Piagetian approach. *Instructional Science, 8,* 301–367.

Perner, J. (1991). *Understanding the representational mind.* Cambridge, MA: MIT Press.

Phillips, D. A., and Zimmerman, M. (1990). "The developmental course of perceived competence and incompetence among competent children." In R. J. Sternberg and J. Kolligian, Jr. (eds.), *Competence considered* (pp. 41–66). New Haven: Yale University Press.

Piaget, J. (1950). *The psychology of intelligence.* London: Routledge and Kegan Paul.

Piaget, J. (1974). *The grasp of consciousness: Action and concept in the young child.* Cambridge, MA: Harvard University Press.

Piaget, J., and Inhelder, B. (1967). *The child's construction of space.* London: Routledge and Kegan Paul.

Platsidou, M. (1993). *The information processing system: Structure, development, and interactions with specialized structural skills.* Unpublished doctoral thesis. Department of Psychology, Aristotle University of Thessaloniki.

Platsidou, M., Demetriou, A., and Zhang, X. K. (1997). Structural and developmental dimensions of human information processing: Longitudinal and cross-cultural evidence. *Psiholoska Obzorja, 6,* 23–69.

Rogers, L. J. (1997). *Minds of their own: Thinking and awareness in animals.* Boulder, CO: Westview Press.

Rothbart, M. K. and Bates, J. E. (1998). "Temperament." In N. Eisenberg (vol. ed.) and W. Damon (series ed.), *Handbook of child psychology: Vol. 3. Social, emotional, and personality development* (5th ed., pp. 105–176). New York: Wiley.

Shavelson, R. J., and Marsh, H. W. (1986). "On the structure of self-concept." In R. Schwarzer (ed.), *Anxiety and cognition* (pp. 305–330). Hillsdale, NJ: Erlbaum.

Shayer, M., Demetriou, A., and Pervez, M. (1988). The structure and scaling of concrete operational thought: Three studies in four countries. *Genetic, Social, and General Psychology Monographs, 114,* 307–376.

Shepard, R. N., and Cooper, L. A. (1982). *Mental images and their transformation.* Cambridge, MA: MIT Press.

Smith, L. (1998). Modal knowledge and maps of the mind. *New Ideas in Psychology, 16,* 115–124.

Spanoudis, G., Demetriou, A., Platsidou, M., Kiosseoglou, G., and Sirmali, K. (1996). A longitudinal study of speed and control of processing from childhood to adolescence. *Psychology: The Journal of the Greek Psychological Society, 3* (1), 29–70.

Sternberg, R. J. (1988). Mental self-government: A theory of intellectual styles and their development. *Human Development, 31,* 197–224.

Sternberg, R. J. (1990). "Prototypes of competence and incompetence." In R. J. Sternberg and J. Kolligian, Jr. (eds.), *Competence considered* (pp. 117–145). New Haven: Yale University Press.

Sternberg, R. J. (1999). Some divergent thoughts on a convergent model. *Developmental Science, 2*, 411–412.

Sternberg, R. J., Conway, B. E., Ketron, J. L., and Bernstein, M. (1981). People's conceptions of intelligence. *Journal of Personality and Social Psychology, 41,* 37–55.

Stipek, D., and MacIver, D. (1989). Developmental change in children's assessment of intellectual competence. *Child Development, 60,* 521–538.

Stipek, D., Recchia, S., and McClintic, S. (1992). Self-Evaluation in young children. *Monographs of the society for research in child Development, 57* (Serial No., 226).

Stroop, J. R. (1935). Studies of interference in serial verbal reactions. *Journal of Experimental Psychology, 18,* 643–662.

Tanaka, J. S. (1987). "How big is big enough?": Sample size and goodness of fit in structural equation models with latent variables. *Child Development, 58,* 134–146.

Thomas, H., and Lohaus, H. (1993). Modeling growth and individual differences in spatial tasks. *Monographs of the Society for Research in Child Development, 58,* (Serial No. 237).

Trevarthen, C. (1979). "Communication and cooperation in early infancy: a description of primary intersubjectivity." In M. Bullowa (ed.), *Before speech* (pp. 321–347). New York: Cambridge University Press.

Triandis, H. C. (1989). The self and social behavior in differing cultural contexts. *Psychological Review, 96,* 506–520.

van Aken, M. A. G., and van Lieshout, K. F. M., and Haselager, G. J. T. (in press). Adolescents' competence and the mutuality of their self-descriptions and descriptions of them provided by others. *Journal of Youth and Adolescence.*

van Geert, P. (1994). *Dynamic systems of development: Change between complexity and chaos.* New York: Harvester Wheatsheaf.

van Lieshout, C. F. M. (1999). Self, mind, personality, and thinking styles: just expressions of a single cognitive system? *Developmental Science, 2,* 413–415.

van der Molen, M., and Ridderinkhof, R. K. (1998). "The growing and aging brain: Lifespan changes in brain and cognitive functioning." In A. Demetriou, W. Doise, K. F. M. van Lieshout (eds.), *Life-span developmental psychology* (pp. 35–100). London: Wiley.

Vosniadou. S. (1994). Capturing and modelling the process of conceptual change. *Learning and Instruction. The Journal of the European Association for Research on Learning and Instruction, 4,* 45–69.

Wellman, H. M. (1990). *The child's theory of mind.* Cambridge, MA: MIT Press.

Wesson, R. (1993). *Beyond natural selection.* Cambridge, MA: MIT Press.

Witkin, H. A., Goodenough, D. R., Karp, S. A. (1967). Stability of cognitive style from childhood to young adulthood. *Journal of Personality and Social Psychology, 7,* 291–300.

Zelniker, T. (1989). "Cognitive style and dimensions of information processing." In T. Globerson and T. Zelniker (eds.), *Cognitive style and cognitive development* (pp. 172–191). Norwood, NJ: Ablex.

Zhang, X. K. (1995). *The structure and development of the processing system and its relation to the complex cognitive abilities: A cross-cultural study in Greece and China.* Unpublished doctoral thesis. Department of Psychology, Aristotle University of Thessaloniki.

Index

motivation 4, 7
Mourousaki, S. 164

Neisser, U. 2
neo-Piagetian concepts 20
neuroticism 15, 24, 180, 204
Nicholls, J. G. 2, 21, 23, 26
numerical operations 6, 146–7
numerical task 148

observation: self/others 25
occupational choice 72–7, 227–8; activity
  styles 55, 56, 72–7; developmental
  changes 106–7; executive style 72;
  extraversion 16–17, 72; judicial style
  72–3; legislative style 72; personality
  73–4; self-image 201
Okamoto, Y. 5
oligarchic form 17
on-line experience, problem solving 85–90
Oosterwegel, A. 18, 27
openness to experience 15, 168, 174, 180,
  181, 190–1; age 24; legislative style 16;
  neuroticism 204
Oppenheimer, L. 18, 27
orientation in space 6
originality 204

Pachaury, A. 6, 8
Papadaki, M. 6
Papantoniou, A. 6
parenting styles 27, 212
parents: cognitive abilities xvii–xviii, 120,
  121–2; composition 122; looking glass
  model 142–3; personality 127–8, 131,
  132, 141–2; self-concept of child 29;
  self-system 34
parents' representation: accuracy 138–42;
  reflected appraisals 124; self-
  representation 123
Parisi, D. 200
partner choice 4
Pascual-Leone, J. 5, 8, 24, 215, 216
Pavlopoulos, V. 164
Peake, P. K. 205
performance: *see* cognitive performance
Perner, J. 11
person category 109, 138, 139, 141
personal characteristics 71, 81; cognitive

abilities 211; developmental changes
  104–6; mother's representation 140–2,
  234; self-attribution 225–6, 233; self-
  representation 70–7, 76, 234; social
  factors 211; *see also* personality
personal characteristics inventory 44–5,
  50–4
personal constant xvii, xix, 117–19, 199,
  201, 203
personality 1, 18–19, 188–92; Big Five
  factors xviii, 15, 23–4, 164; cognition
  5–6, 13; domain-specific systems 208;
  evolution 213–14; functioning styles
  16–17; general model 14; inhibitory
  control 205; lifestyle 29; mind 181,
  204, 208–9; mothers' representations
  140–2, 234; parental influence 127–8,
  212; reciprocal representations 143; self-
  awareness 206, 207–8; self-image 199;
  self-representation 193–6; self-system
  204–8; self-understanding 19–28, 206;
  social roles 24, 71; thinking styles 16,
  23–4, 58, 179, 181, 193–6, 204–5
personality inventory 165, 168, 172, 180
Phillips, D. A. 23, 99
Piaget, Jean xx, 34, 153, 215
Pipp, S. L. 20, 118
planning 56, 72
Platsidou, M. 4, 6, 36, 59, 145, 150, 156
Plunket, K. 200
Prevez, M. 6
problem solving 25–6, 56, 72, 85–90, 198
processing efficiency xviii, 5, 146–8, 208
processing speed 202–3, 235; numerical
  146–7; self-image 164, 210; self-
  representation 201–2; Stroop-like tasks
  146–8
processing systems 9, 168, 185; domain-
  specific systems 179; *g* factor of
  intelligence 217; hypercognitive system
  144; problem solving 198; second model
  156–7; self-image 160–1, 164;
  specialized capacity systems 144, 179;
  storage 202–3; structural modelling 155
professional responsibility 72, 85
proportional reasoning tasks 36
psychodynamic school 1
psychology: cognitive developmental 1–2,
  216; cognitivist 199–200; developmental